Europe in Transition

Europe in Transition, 1660-1815

ROBERT ZALLER

University of Miami

HARPER & ROW, PUBLISHERS, New York
Cambridge, Philadelphia, San Francisco,
London, Mexico City, São Paulo, Sydney

1817

Credits

Pages 31, 50, 63, 72, 90, 96, 105, 107, 122, 129, 141 courtesy of the New York Library Picture Collection; page 112 from *A Diderot Pictorial Encyclopedia of Trades and Industry,* plate 374; pages 48, 68, 69, 77, 80, 144, 145, 151 adapted from Gay/Webb; *Modern Europe*, by permission of Harper & Row, Publishers, Inc. Copyright © 1973 by Harper & Row, Publishers, Inc.

The cover is a contemporary French etching of Parisians moving cannons to Montmartre on July 15, 1789; courtesy of the Granger Collection.

Sponsoring Editor: Jean Hurtado
Project Editor: Lois Lombardo
Production Manager: Willie Lane
Photo Researcher: Mira Schachne
Cover Design: Betty Sokol
Compositor: ComCom Division of Haddon Craftsmen, Inc.
Printer and Binder: R. R. Donnelley & Sons Company
Art Studio: Fine Line, Inc.

Europe in Transition, 1660–1815

Library of Congress Cataloging in Publication Data
Zaller, Robert.
  Europe in transition, 1660–1815.

  Bibliography: p.
  Includes index.
  1. Europe—History—1648–1789.   2. Europe—History—
1789–1815.   I. Title.
D273.Z34   1984   940.2′5   83-18683
ISBN 0-06-047368-1

To Lili, *γιά τ'ὄνειρο*

Contents

Preface   **ix**
Introduction   **1**

one   THE STRUCTURE OF OLD REGIME
          SOCIETY   **5**
          Europe in 1660   **5**
          The Map of Europe   **6**
          The Old Regime   **9**
          The Monarchy   **12**
          The Aristocracy   **14**
          The Clergy   **19**
          The Great Divide   **21**
          The Third Estate   **23**
          The Peasantry   **23**
          The Towns   **29**

two   THE AGE OF LOUIS XIV   **35**
          The Administrative Revolution of Louis XIV   **35**
          War, Society, and the State   **40**
          The Wars of Louis XIV: The First Phase
               (1667–1688)   **41**
          A New King for England: William of Orange
               and the Glorious Revolution   **43**
          A World at War (1688–1713)   **45**

three   EXPANSION AND EMPIRE   **55**
            England: The Background to Empire   **56**
            The First British Empire   **60**
            The Emergence of Russia   **67**
            The Balance of Power   **78**

four   THE ENLIGHTENMENT   **85**
            The Scientific Revolution and Its Diffusion   **85**
            The Philosophes   **93**
            The Career of Voltaire   **96**
            The Social Contract   **97**
            The Enlightened Despots   **103**
            The Counter-Enlightenment   **109**
            The Spread of Literacy   **111**

five   THE FRENCH REVOLUTION
                AND NAPOLEON   **115**
            How the Revolution Came   **116**
            The Revolution of 1789   **120**
            Reform and Reaction (1789–1791)   **124**
            From Monarchy to Republic (1791–1793)   **127**
            The Radical Phase (1793–1794)   **128**
            The Thermidorian Reaction   **133**
            The Directory (1795–1799)   **135**
            The Unfinished Revolution   **136**
            The Napoleonic Aftermath   **138**
            From Republic to Empire (1799–1804)   **138**
            Napoleon at War (1799–1815)   **140**
            The Restoration and the Hundred Days   **147**
            The Congress of Vienna   **149**

Bibliography   **153**
Index   **159**

Preface

The challenge of writing about the Old Regime is that of dealing with any period that terminates in revolutionary upheaval. One is tempted either to view the period as a mere prelude to the revolution, or the revolution as a sudden departure from the period. *Europe in Transition* aims both to present the Old Regime as a unified system and, by means of structural analysis, to disclose the weaknesses and limitations that made it vulnerable to change. By this method, individual events can be related to a general pattern. The numerous wars of the period, for example, are not simply related as dynastic incidents but incorporated within a larger analysis of war as a value structure within Old Regime society (the concept of *gloire*), a regulated mode of interstate rivalry (the balance of power), and an aspect of economic and bureaucratic development. Similarly, the Scientific Revolution is viewed not as an isolated phenomenon, but related closely to the Enlightenment, the decay of traditional salvific religion, and the waning of divine right authority. The French Revolution can thereby be seen as the outcome of change within the Old Regime rather than as the abrupt collapse of an apparently stable and self-confident society. At the same time, the requirements of traditional narrative have not been scanted. The result, it is hoped, will enable the reader to see the Old Regime not merely as a prolonged countdown to the modern world, but as an era with a specific character of its own.

This book is the better for much wise advice. I would like to thank particularly Richard L. Greaves, who read it with tact, care, and unfailing good counsel. My thanks are also due to my editor, Jean Hurtado, who was deeply supportive throughout, Lois Lombardo, who supervised the final stages of production, and the entire staff of Harper & Row.

Robert Zaller

introduction

The economic historian Fernand Braudel has spoken of a "long sixteenth century," spanning the years from 1450 to 1650. During this time, the population of Europe doubled, and its expanding economy penetrated every corner of the globe, including a New World whose very existence had been previously unsuspected. The same period saw equally far-reaching changes in European man's conception of himself and of his relation to the cosmos. These changes are epitomized in the terms *Renaissance* and *Reformation.* These terms imply a separation between events that were largely interconnected, but in one sense the division is a useful one. The Renaissance, however profoundly it changed the general orientation of European culture, did not directly and immediately affect its social and political organization. The Reformation, on the other hand, created upheavals in church and state and provoked a century and a quarter of civil and international wars. The term *wars of religion* conventionally used to describe these conflicts is somewhat misleading, for secular issues—trade, empire, territorial aggrandizement—were inextricably interwoven with them. But it is nonetheless true that differences of religion were a critical factor in virtually every European war between 1525 and 1650.

The last and greatest of these conflicts was the Thirty Years' War (1618–1648), whose genesis lay in the tangled religious geography of post-Reformation Germany, half Catholic, half Lutheran, and in the relation of its many individual states to their nominal ruler, the Catholic emperor of Austria. But it also involved the long Dutch war of independence against Spain, begun in 1555, the rivalry of the Hapsburg dynasties of Spain and Austria with the Bourbon kings of France, and the aspirations of the northern monarchies of Denmark

1

and Sweden. It was this volatile compound that turned what had begun as a revolt of Protestant nobility in Austria's non-German province of Bohemia into a German civil war, and finally a war of all Europe played out on German soil.

When the war ended with the Treaty of Westphalia in 1648, an age ended with it. The dream of the Catholic Counter-Reformation that the religious and political unity of Christendom might be restored had been not only defeated but repudiated. The very success of Austrian forces in Germany in the early stages of the war had provoked intervention by Catholic as well as Protestant powers, both equally fearful of a new Hapsburg hegemony. The religious status quo had become part of its political status quo, and any serious alteration of the former entailed unacceptable consequences for the latter. In short, the religious division of Europe was now a condition of its political stability, much as its division into East and West is today; it had become part of the framework within which conflict might be waged, but not an object of conflict itself.

Another age ended with Westphalia too. The Thirty Years' War was the last major war in Europe to be fought primarily by mercenary armies. Such forces were not merely unreliable and prone to indiscipline. Part of their pay was calculated in the profits of rapine. Conquered cities were subjected to systematic looting and atrocity, in some cases so frequently that whole regions became gradually depopulated. Lacking regular supply, mercenaries lived directly off the land they occupied, thus despoiling those they "defended" no less than those they attacked. Since their only permanent interest was in fighting itself, they were able to nullify truces and even treaties by initiating hostilities among themselves. Thus the war went on in part because the armies that fought it were beyond civilian control. Some mercenary generals were clearly more powerful than the rulers who employed them, and some, like the famous Count Wallenstein, dreamed of establishing principalities for themselves. Mercenaries had long been a staple feature of European warfare, but the experience of the Thirty Years' War proved them so dangerous and unmanageable that rulers thereafter began to raise and maintain forces under their direct control. While few states could afford standing armies of any size, the advantage of such forces became so obvious that every power concerned to play a role on the European stage soon moved in that direction. In the extreme example of eighteenth-century Prussia, the military function was to subordinate every other function, not only of the state but of society as well. Thus, in its military dimension no less than its religious one, the Thirty Years' War provided the impetus toward an increasingly secularized and centralized system of individual states.

The outbreak of the Thirty Years' War coincided with the onset of a major economic depression in Europe, the herald in turn of a long-term period of stagnation and decline. Population growth had begun to level off in the Mediterranean area as early as the 1570s, partly as a result of excessive cultivation and soil exhaustion. The war decimated Germany, which according to some estimates lost as much as a third of its population. Even a relatively small-scale war such as that between Denmark and Sweden in 1658–1660 cost Denmark 20 percent of its population. The shrinkage of the labor market brought an abrupt halt to economic expansion, dependent as it was in this preindustrial age on human muscle. Price levels also reflected the general stagnation. After increasing fivefold between 1500 and 1600, they remained stable or even declined modestly until 1750.

Governments reacted to the long slump with a variety of measures, including tariff and industrial regulation, trade wars, tax levies, and currency manipulation. These policies, taken together, are generally referred to as mercantilism. This term, however, implies more conscious direction than was probably the case. Mercantilism should be viewed as an attempt to cope with economic crisis rather than as a systematic program of state-building or national unification. The revival of economic life after 1750 brought with it an almost immediate demand for less rather than more state intervention, and it was not until well into the nineteenth century, when political power had passed to the hands of a new social group, the bourgeoisie, that the state was perceived as having a useful role to play. Mercantilism should in this respect be regarded as a precursor of the modern economic order rather than as a direct link to it.

Strained by protracted war and economic decline, the political system of Europe underwent a period of acute crisis in the 1640s and 1650s. France, Spain, and England all suffered major upheavals, and lesser shocks were felt in the Netherlands, Sweden, Brandenburg-Prussia, and elsewhere. In France, a rebellion set off by high court judges appealing to popular liberties against an allegedly arbitrary royal government sparked a full-scale aristocratic uprising against the Crown. (A similar appeal by the judges 140 years later was to have markedly different consequences.) In Spain, a successful rebellion by Portugal in 1640 restored the independence of that country, united to the Spanish throne 60 years before, while serious insurrections broke out in Catalonia and the Italian dependencies of Sicily and Naples. But the most serious challenge to the established order occurred in England, where in 1640 a rebellion began against the autocratic rule of Charles I. By 1642, the country was engulfed in civil war, and in 1649, after a series of fruitless attempts to negotiate with Charles, he was formally tried for treason before a revolutionary court, convicted, and executed. No other single act more shocked seventeenth-century Europe, and none, indeed, was more threatening to its social order; some radicals demanded a democratic franchise and even the abolition of private property. England abolished both monarchy and aristocracy, and for the next 11 years was governed by an unstable oligarchy of merchants, landed gentry, and military men, whose dominant personality and at last quasi-regal head was Oliver Cromwell. Cromwell's death in 1658 precipitated a conservative reaction that led to the restoration of the monarchy under Charles II, but the Crown never regained its former authority.

The upheavals of the mid-seventeenth century suggested to many that the end of the world was imminent. In England, Parliament under Cromwell seriously entertained a proposal to abolish all laws in favor of the Mosaic code in anticipation of the last days, while a few years later, thousands of eastern European Jews, led by a self-proclaimed messiah, attempted to return to the Holy Land. But, despite the portents, the prophets were wrong. Europe was not yet ready for revolution, nor the world for its end.

one

The Structure of Old Regime Society

EUROPE IN 1660

After a century of troubles and a generation of open rebellion, Europe in 1660 abruptly settled down. The Peace of the Pyrenees between France and Spain (1659) and the treaties of Oliva and Copenhagen (1660) among the northern powers put an end to the last, lingering fires of the Thirty Years' War. Charles II returned to London in June, 1660, dramatically resolving England's long civil crisis. That same summer, Louis XIV rode triumphantly through Paris with his Spanish bride, Maria Theresa, and a few months later assumed actual control of the nation of which he had already been king in name for 18 years.

Yet if Europe was about to turn a corner, it was far from apparent. After the long, debilitating war on the Continent, men saw a shrunken society, its population stagnant, its commerce withered, its frontiers contracted, its religion divided, its governing institutions in disarray, and even, as in England, its basic social structure called into question. The great thrust outward that had sent explorers, conquerors, and colonizers to the ends of the world seemed to have spent itself. The American colonies and the Eastern trading companies were both a disappointment, and the Spanish treasure fleet that toiled home each year from the West Indies with a little less than the year before seemed a melancholy epitaph to the dreams of a New World. The Mediterranean, whose ports had launched the great era of expansion, had dwindled to the status of a provincial lake; not for centuries had it been so depressed. In the east, too, the frontiers of Europe were drawing in. The long-dormant Ottoman Empire was again on the march; by 1683 its troops would be outside the gates of Vienna.

Within a period of 20 years, England and France had experienced major social upheavals, while revolutions in Portugal, Andalusia, Catalonia, Naples, and Sicily marked the crisis of the Spanish Empire. Germany lay prostrate. Peasant insurrections had shaken Europe from Ireland to the Ukraine. Surveying the universal turbulence of his time, the English philosopher Thomas Hobbes envisioned a state of total anarchy in which

> there is no place for Industry, because the fruit thereof is uncertain; and consequently no Culture of the Earth, no Navigation, nor use of the commodities that may be imported by Sea; no commodious Building; no Instruments of moving, and removing such things as require much force; no Knowledge of the face of the Earth; no Account of Time; no Arts; no Letters; no Society; and which is worst of all, continual fear, and danger of violent death; And the life of man, solitary, poor, nasty, brutish, and short.

Some of Europe's decline was not reversed for centuries, and some of it, in relative terms, has never been reversed at all. The great days of the ports of the German Hanseatic League and the Italian city-states were over. Germany, with the exception of Prussia, was not to regain its political importance until the nineteenth century. The Italian states did not free themselves from foreign domination for 200 years. Spain, still a power of consequence in 1660, fell into a torpor from which it has only begun to emerge in our own time. Indeed, with the general decline of both Christian and Moslem states on both sides of the Mediterranean, the whole of southern Europe became chronically depressed. And though Europe as a whole was to emerge from the seventeenth-century depression, the Mediterranean did not, and to this day the states that surround it are among the poorest on the continent. This was a fact of historic import. From remotest antiquity, the Mediterranean had been the great highway of Europe. Henceforth, the balance of power in Europe was to lie with those states that faced the Atlantic Ocean.

THE MAP OF EUROPE

For 150 years, Europe had been dominated by the Hapsburg dynasty, but the Dutch rebellion, the decline of Spain, and the Treaty of Westphalia had undone that. In the decade after the Thirty Years' War, there was a vacuum of power on the continent, when no single ruler or nation stood out above the rest but all seemed preoccupied with internal disorder: a moment when, it seemed, the political system of Europe trembled on the verge of breakdown. It was at this moment that Louis XIV took control of France and embarked on his quest of glory, and perhaps not the least of his triumphs was the new stimulus he gave to the old business of dynastic politics.

If the Hapsburgs had shown the possibilities of the dynastic principle in welding political power from widely separated cultural and geographical units, the House of Bourbon was to demonstrate the advantage of a single compact state and a single people united by language, heritage, and history. For France was to dominate Europe for the next century and a half not only politically, as the Hapsburgs had done, but culturally, too, as they had not.

EUROPE IN 1660

Hapsburg possessions

Hohenzollern possessions

Bourbon possessions

Holy Roman Empire boundary

NORWAY (Kingdom of Denmark)

FINLAND (Kingdom of Sweden)

SWEDEN

RUSSIA

LIVONIA

BALTIC SEA

NORTH SEA

DENMARK

Königsberg

EAST PRUSSIA

SCOTLAND

IRELAND

UNITED PROVINCES

BRANDENBURG

POLAND

Amsterdam

Elbe R.

Berlin

Oder R.

Vistula R.

ENGLAND

London

SAXONY

SILESIA

ATLANTIC OCEAN

Antwerp

Rhine R.

BOHEMIA

HUNGARY

SPANISH NETHERLANDS

Strasbourg

Danube R.

Paris

Vienna

Loire R.

FRANCHE Comté

AUSTRIA

SWITZERLAND

TYROL

STYRIA

Geneva

SAVOY

Milan

VENETIA

OTTOMAN

Rhone R.

FRANCE

Genoa

Venice

LUCCA

PAPAL STATES

EMPIRE

TUSCANY

PORTUGAL

Lisbon

Madrid

CORSICA (Genoa)

Rome

KINGDOM

Naples

SPAIN

OF THE

SARDINIA

TWO

MEDITERRANEAN

SICILIES

SEA

CRETE (Venice)

0   200   400

Miles

7

The familiar hexagon of France had been built up slowly. Its frontier on the Alps had been established for 200 years, on the Saône for 215; it had reached the Pyrenees only in 1659. It was a nation of 20 million, and a glance at its neighbors will show why those 20 million bulked so large in the eyes of Europe. Spain had a population of 5 million (compared with 8 million a century before); England had 5 million more, Austria 6 or 7 million, far-off Russia perhaps 8. Germany alone among the nations of Europe had a population comparable to that of France, at least prior to the Thirty Years' War. Never a politically unified state, however, it was more of a geographical expression than ever after that war, a patchwork of 2000 separate sovereignties. The largest of these, the mark of Brandenburg, was to evolve into a major power in its own right in the eighteenth century; some 300 others were sizable enough to be represented in the Diet of the Holy Roman Empire: the remainder, concentrated chiefly in south Germany and the Rhineland, were the self-styled "knights of the Empire," mere private landowners who, in the prevailing chaos, had set themselves up with a castle, some peasants, and a few acres of woodland as sovereign entities. The states of Germany still owed nominal allegiance to the Holy Roman Emperor, an Austrian and a Hapsburg, but if this title meant little before the Thirty Years' War, it meant even less now, and the Hapsburgs increasingly turned their attention to the east.

There was one other major population group that did not appear on the political map of Europe at all. The 11 million people of Italy were still largely in the weakened grasp of Spain. Of the more or less independent states on the Italian peninsula, only five were worth counting: Tuscany, Genoa, and Savoy in the north, Venice in the east, and the central belt of Papal States, more important for their rulers than their resources. All these entities were mere shadows of their former selves, however, with the exception of Savoy, the little Rivieran duchy whose skillful rulers were able to set it up as a broker in European politics for 200 years.

Between the Holy Roman Empire in the west, Russia in the east, and the Ottoman Turks to the south was wedged a jagged quadrilateral nearly 1000 miles square that stretched from Danzig on the Baltic to Kharkov near the Black Sea. This was the Republic of Poland, which was nominally an elective monarchy and in fact neither a republic nor a monarchy but an anarchic oligarchy of great landowners who could agree on nothing but denying the country any effective government whatever. Thus, despite its great size and a population of more than 6 million, Poland did little more than take up space—a space increasingly coveted by its neighbors.

Scandinavia was occupied by two powers: Sweden, which comprised all of Finland and the northern half of Norway as well as its present-day territory, with a scattered population of 1.5 million, and Denmark, including lower Norway, which sat athwart the strategic Baltic gate. Far the weaker of the two at the beginning of the seventeenth century, Sweden was to emerge, though briefly, as a major power by the end of it.

Nothing signified the northward shift in Europe's center of gravity, however, so much as the rise of the Dutch Republic. Like the Venetians, whom they resembled and to a certain extent replaced on the European scene, the Dutch (or, as they called themselves formally, the United Provinces) were a merchant oligarchy. With a population of only 2.5 million, a government decentralized (at least in theory) almost to the point of nonexistence, and a flat terrain equally exposed to Catholic neighbors and the North Sea, the United Provinces seemed an unlikely bet for survival. Yet, while fighting a nearly 100-year war of independence and subsidizing foreign armies to boot, the Dutch came to dominate the economy of Europe as no power had ever done before. The Bank of Amsterdam was the greatest commercial institution in Europe—only the Bank of London in Victorian England was ever to wield a comparable influence. Dutch shipping carried half the world's trade, exclusive of China. Dutch cloth was the largest industry on the continent. Dutch agriculture was the most advanced; Dutch cows gave the best milk, Dutch fields the highest yield. Nor did this supremacy go unchallenged. Having finally cast off the Spanish yoke in the 1640s, the Dutch were compelled to prove themselves in wars against the English in the 1650s and the French in the 1660s. Not until 1715 were their borders at last secure, and from that very point their decline from greatness began. The growth of commercial shipping, especially in England and France, robbed the Dutch of much of their entrepôt trade; by 1739, twice as many ships docked in London as at Amsterdam. Louis XIV could not conquer the Dutch in almost half a century of warfare; the French revolutionary armies of 1795 succeeded in a matter of weeks.

THE OLD REGIME

The society of sixteenth, seventeenth, and eighteenth-century Europe is what we call, collectively, the Old Regime. Like all historical terms, it came into existence retroactively. Every age is, to itself, simply "modern." There could have been no Old Regime without a new one to follow it and thereby make it old, just as there could be no idea of a Middle Ages without later ages to follow them.

The event in European history that created the Old Regime was the French Revolution. When men looked back across the great divide of 1789, they decided that things had changed in some way that was both decisive and irrevocable. From the perspective of the Revolution, the world that had existed for the previous 200 or 300 years had no further existence in the present and no hope of revival in the future. It was, in short, the past. It was over. And being over, it was entitled to a name, a name that distinguished it from the new present. Hence, the Old Regime.

The problems raised by this terminology are obvious. In the first place, the French Revolution did not transform all things and places equally, nor all at once. Even in France, it became gradually apparent that the new society was not really so very different from the old. As early as 1856, the great historian Alexis de Tocqueville showed in *The Old Regime and the French Revolution* how French institutions had largely evolved into their modern form before 1789.

Second, the term *Old Regime* was never properly descriptive. If everyone agreed that the French Revolution was the end of it, no one was very clear about when it began or how it had distinguished itself from any preceding period. To liberals, it meant everything before 1789 that they did not like; to conservatives, it was everything they wished they had back.

This confusion is still with us today. The Old Regime is dated by some historians as early as 1500, by others as late as 1660. Such a difference in chronology suggests a considerable disagreement as to what, if anything, the Old Regime really was.

Yet the term is useful. For as the French Revolution recedes from us historically, its consequences still unfold, like an earthquake that produces effects long after the tremor has ceased. No one looking at Russia in 1850 would have credited the Revolution with any impact whatever on that distant land; a century later, no one could possibly have doubted it.

Moreover, the great revolution of 1789 was shortly accompanied by another one, more silent but in some ways even more significant. This was the Industrial Revolution. The first changed the way men thought, the second the way they lived. Between them they eradicated the institutions and even the physical traces of the old society, transforming what they could use and destroying what they could not. It may have been an exaggeration to speak of an Old Regime in 1789. It is not one now. To describe this world we have to speak of a society that differs at almost every key point from our own.

Ours is a class society. By class we mean a group of those who have the same source of income (wage earners in factories, salaried bureaucrats in offices, independent professionals charging fees, and so on), who possess a similar amount of income and wealth, and who share the same style of life. If the members of a given class are conscious of their common interests and act together to promote them, their formation as a social group is complete. This type of society, graded strictly according to the wealth of its members, came to maturity in Europe and America in the nineteenth century.

Parallel to the economic inequity of the class system, however, a counter-ideology of political equality and social brotherhood developed. These ideals, which circulated on a wide scale for the first time in the eighteenth century, were given decisive impetus by the French Revolution. They may now be said to have triumphed intellectually in the Western world. Popular sovereignty, equal opportunity, and equal access to education, justice, medical care, and so forth are recognized goals or principles in most countries. Thus, while present society (including the so-called socialist countries) is still organized on the class model, its dominant ideology implicitly repudiates that model. Our social reality is vertical, a greasy pole notched by wealth, whereas our value system is predominantly horizontal, a demand for equality on every plane. The result is the tension and unrest that characterize our society.

The Old Regime, by contrast, was an arrangement of estates and orders rather than classes. An *estate* is a social group defined not by possession of wealth but by possession of *status*—that is, by the degree of honor, dignity, and respect attached to it by society at large. Under the Old Regime, each estate occupied a fixed and definite place on the scale of status, according to which it received a specific set of privileges, obligations, functions, and symbols, a certain income, education, and style of life, and even a prescribed dress and diet, all of which served both as its share of society's rewards and to distinguish it in every possible particular from other estates. The notion of general equality, of rights and standards applicable on all levels of society (for example, one man, one vote), was utterly foreign to this system. Each individual had a narrow belt of others with whom he could mix as a comrade and equal, but toward everyone else his behavior was governed by inflexible rules of etiquette. To those above him he must show the proper, ritualized forms of deference and respect; from those below he must exact it.

Thus, the primary distinction in Old Regime society was not in being more or less rich but more or less honorable—or, to use the terms of the time, noble or base. Of course, riches and honor usually went together, as they do in most societies. It was the wealthy landowner who was held to be noble, not the impoverished peasant. But—and the distinction is crucial—the wealth of the nobleman was regarded as a function of his nobility, not the other way around. A man was rich because he was noble, not noble because he was rich. It was right and proper for him to be rich, just as it was appropriate for the base-born man to be poor. Society was unequal but just; indeed, its inequality *was* its justice. Every man got what he deserved, and every man deserved what he got.

This ideology was buttressed by a myth of cosmic proportions that has been called the Great Chain of Being. According to the myth, every created thing had its prescribed place on the universal ladder of existence, which led up to God himself. The angels were subordinate to Him as man was to the angels, as beasts were to men, and dead matter to living, on a descending scale of natural value. Moreover, each order of being had its own internal hierarchy as well. There were superior and subordinate ranks among the angels (the study of which, angelology, was still a serious scholarly pursuit in the seventeenth century), higher and lower animals, and nobler and baser men. The social order appointed to mankind was therefore a part of the order of the universe itself, and anyone who attempted to break it was committing a sin against the peace and harmony of the very cosmos, was defying God as well as man. When Louis XIV invoked the divine right of kings, he was invoking the principle of hierarchy, the natural subordination of all things by their grade and quality of being, and when the parish priest told his Sunday congregation to respect and obey their betters whom God had placed over them for their guidance, protection, and natural rule, he was doing the same.

The indoctrination of a proper respect for one's superiors was the primary goal of education for the great mass of population. In England, for example, children in the 10,000 parish churches of the realm were required to memorize and repeat the following lines from *The Book of Common Prayer:*

> My duty towards my neighbor is to love him as myself, and to do to all men as I would they should do unto me: to love, honor and succor my father and mother: to submit myself to all my governors, teachers, spiritual pastors and masters; to order myself lowly and reverently to all my betters . . . not to covet nor desire other men's goods: but to learn and labor truly to get my own living, and to do my duty in that state of life unto which it shall please God to call me.

The same theme of natural subordination runs through the political literature of the period. The previously quoted words were written in 1549; in 1672, the journalist Richard Steele wrote of the tenant farmer:

A just fear and respect he must have for his landlord, or the gentleman his neighbor, because God hath placed them above him and he hath learnt that by the father he ought to honor is meant all his superiors.

And in 1790, the statesman Edmund Burke could still write, with perhaps more confidence than the situation allowed:

We fear God; we look up with awe to kings; with affection to parliaments; with duty to magistrates; with reverence to priests; and with respect to nobility.

The official view of reality was never wholly accepted by the underlying population. The words of the old medieval lyric "When Adam delved and Eve span / Who was then the gentleman?" expressed a pithy dissent to the idea that God had ordained the social inequality of humankind. But there was little that could be done about the fact of it. If a man could be flogged or hanged for a few words in a tavern, if it was a mortal sin even to question God's dispensation on earth, there was little likelihood of effective opposition. But it was not overt repression that kept the masses in hand. Old Regime society was ruled not merely by force but by presumption as well. The aristocratic elite's belief in its own authority was so ingrained that it never doubted its right to rule. Not propaganda but a profound intellectual consensus imposed a censorship on all contrary ideas, just as that censorship then became an instrument for maintaining the consensus. The education of the poor might then appear not as a conspiracy to keep them benighted and illiterate but merely as sufficient to prepare them for the humble estate to which God had called them.

Old Regime society may then be imagined as a pyramid in which all power and privilege and most wealth rose to the top; as a state of affairs in which nine men sowed and the tenth man reaped. Let us examine the layers of this pyramid more closely.

THE MONARCHY

At the apex of the pyramid sat the kings. Kingship seemed the natural form of government to the people of seventeenth-century Europe. This conviction rested on two major assumptions: legitimacy and the concept of divine right.

Legitimacy originally concerned not the institution of monarchy but merely the rules of succession. In general, upon the death of a reigning monarch, the crown passed to the nearest of kin, though when there was no direct male heir, this could involve a bitter struggle for power and, often enough, civil war. However, the significance of this principle for us is the corollary that became attached to it over the years, that only a prince of the blood royal could rightfully rule. Louis XIII, Louis XIV, and Louis XV of France were all small children when they came to the throne. In each case, this meant a scramble for de facto power by prominent noblemen, an upsurge of local autonomy at the expense of the central government, weakness before foreign enemies, and the strong likelihood of civil disorders at home. It meant these things, moreover, not for a short period of adjustment but for the long years of a regency. But there was never any question that such burdens must be borne. A juvenile monarch was an act of God, like storm or drought. There was only one person in the kingdom at any one time with the mandate to rule conferred by the royal blood in his veins, and if that person happened to be only 5 years old, so it must be.

The Spanish carried the principle of legitimacy to the point of national suicide in the case of Charles II. When Charles ascended the throne in 1665, he was not merely a child of 4, but deformed and mentally retarded as well: the last heir of the inbred Hapsburg tree. It was unlikely that he would live to maturity and certain that he would produce no successor. The result of this would be the final extinction of Spain as a major power, and perhaps even its dismemberment as a state. Nor was this a purely Spanish problem. The failure of the Hapsburg line was sure to create a power struggle and perhaps a general European war. This is in fact what happened, and the war it led to was aptly called the War of the Spanish Succession. The only unreckoned factor was that the sickly Charles managed to drag his miserable life out to the year 1700. By that time, the long-awaited conflict had become so encumbered by other issues that when it broke out, it lasted 15 years and engulfed the entire continent. Thus, for 50 years, the history of Europe had in some sense hung on the heartbeat of an idiot.

The theory of divine right was most succinctly stated by its foremost practitioner, Louis XIV:

> He Who has given kings to men wanted them to be respected as His lieutenants, reserving for Himself alone the right to examine their conduct . . . There is no maxim whatever more clearly established by Christianity than this humble submission of subjects to those who are set over them.

This was the ultimate vision of Christian kingship: the king as supreme lord of those below him but a humble servant to the God above him, whose absolute power on earth was justified by his absolute submission to the will of heaven. Such an image of simultaneous power and abasement was one of great appeal to the people of the seventeenth century. It was also a formidable political weapon: for what the kings naturally stressed was the power it conferred on them rather than the submission it entailed. In actual practice, the theory of divine right boiled down to the assertion that the command of the ruler must be unquestioningly obeyed. The ruler might be a tyrant, his commands contrary to conscience, scripture, or even common sense, but this was not for the subject to judge. He must not presume to take upon himself an office that belonged to God alone. One French bishop went so far as to declare that not only were kings ordained by God but that they were gods themselves, and he defended an unpopular war by saying, "The King . . . has gone to war because to do this was just and reasonable; or rather . . . such a war is just because the King has undertaken it." At about the same time, an English minister asserted that not only must the subject obey evil commandments but even absurd or impossible ones, on pain of eternal damnation.

Such sweeping statements did not pass unchallenged. Modern political theory cut its teeth on opposition to the claims of divine right, and in England resistance was carried twice to the point of revolution before the seventeenth century was out. But in the interval between the decline of papal authority and the rise of popular sovereignty, divine right had its day. For more than 100 years, no other theory of government so successfully combined history, scripture, and the appeal to tradition, or enjoyed comparable prestige and acceptance. And while they had the advantage, the divine-right monarchs exploited it to the fullest. Not since the days of Rome had a secular ruler so dominated his society and shaped it to his will as did Louis XIV in France, Frederick the Great in Prussia, or Peter the Great in Russia.

If a king took divine right seriously, however, it laid a heavy burden on him. Louis XIV believed that God had given him exclusive responsibility for the welfare of 20 million souls. Fortunately, Louis never doubted that he was equal to the task. No man ever had a greater zest for governing. But governing—especially governing alone—could be hard, toilsome, and lonely. The kings of the Old Regime were by and large a sober and industrious lot. They built magnificent palaces but seldom enjoyed them. They worked long hours, sat through interminable council meetings, read endless dispatches and memoranda. They never retired. They worked up to the last day of their strength, holding a hundred threads of policy together. They might pursue a single objective for decades, and lose it at a blow. "Shall I be the one," cried William III of England when French troops crossed the Dutch border in 1701, "to lose without a battle what I have struggled for during more than 28 years?"

No Hollywood star ever lived in such a goldfish bowl as these kings. They were forever on display; they dined and dressed in public; they were not even alone in their own bedrooms. Their friendships and love affairs were subjected to relentless gossip, and some, finally, like Frederick the Great, apparently had no private lives at all. They were true equals only to one another, addressing each other as "brother" in the most exclusive fraternity in the world. They knew one another's tastes and habits, strengths and weaknesses. Yet few of them ever met. In the 72 years of his reign, Louis XIV set eyes on a fellow sovereign only once: He met Philip IV of Spain in 1660 on the occasion of marrying his daughter.

Yet if kingship was hard, it was also glorious, and if there were days when the kings must have longed to emulate the sixteenth-century emperor Charles V and retire to a monastery, there were others when they must have felt, in the words of the French bishop quoted before, like gods on earth. "I do not know what other pleasure we should not abandon for that [of governing]," wrote Louis XIV. "The calling of a king is great, noble, and delightful."

THE ARISTOCRACY

We have spoken of the king as the apex of a pyramid, but he might more justly be described as the tip of an iceberg, the visible symbol of an enormous structure of privilege and power. The sentimental image of the nation gathered trustfully under the protection of its father-king was a fiction that obscured the reality of an aristocratic society where the few exploited the many.

It is difficult to generalize about the nobility under the Old Regime because the extremes of wealth and prestige it contained and the disparity of interests it comprehended were so great that it looks to the perplexed observer more like a miniature society than a simple order. It included great magnates whose estates were as large as some countries and impoverished gentlemen like the *hobereaux* of southern France or the *hidalgos* of the Basque country who were scarcely better off than their peasant neighbors. The term "nobility" is often equated simply with "ruling class," which is true but not very accurate, for the fact that there were only 200 titled aristocrats in England at the end of the eighteenth century does not mean that England was governed by only 200 persons any more than the fact that there were 500,000 aristocrats in Spain at the same time means that Spain had half a million rulers. It is impossible even to give a simple definition of nobility when the term could equally describe a peer of the realm whose noble blood went back for centuries and a municipal clerk whose title was merely attached to the job he held.

Our difficulty stems again from trying to describe in the modern terminology of power what the people of the Old Regime saw primarily in terms of status and prestige. A recent English historian has argued that "the overall picture is not that of a caste of nobility graded by antiquity of lineage but of an upper class unified by money." This is a fair enough description of how the Old Regime nobility looks to us, but it does little to help us understand how it looked to itself or to those around it. We need to keep both perspectives in mind.

Contemporary observers clearly distinguished between a *nobilitas major* and a *nobilitas minor,* a greater and a lesser nobility. This corresponded partly to the formal grades of nobility—duke, marquis, earl or count, viscount, and baron, in descending order—but also to such factors as antiquity of title and degree of access to the king, who was, in one sense, simply the most highly titled aristocrat in the realm. In some countries, there were further formal subdivisions of status in addition to the regular grades of nobility. The Spanish aristocracy was divided into three ranks, of which the highest was the grandees, the ancient feudal nobility. Grandeeship was a distinction independent of any other title: a grandee might be a duke like Alba or a count like Lemos. All grandees were equal among themselves but superior to any noble of the other ranks, no matter what title he might hold. In France, the primary distinction was between inherited nobility—the nobility of the sword—and nobility acquired by office-holding, the nobility of the robe. The latter were held in much contempt by the former and were ridiculed at Versailles in the plays of Molière. Nonetheless, intermarriage between the two groups was so frequent that by the eighteenth century the older nobility and the upper magistrature were for all practical purposes merged. It was a classic liaison between new money and old status.

The disdain of the traditional nobility for this pseudoaristocracy of bureaucrats expressed something more than mere snobbery, however. The nobility of the sword, as their name implies, had originally been a warrior caste, and their whole claim to preeminence was based on the premise of a society that valued military prowess above all else. "This nation, wholly warlike, has identified glory with arms," wrote a seventeenth-century commentator, and the Archbishop of

Embrun, addressing a rebellious assembly of noblemen during the midcentury French civil war known as the Fronde, declared that the nobility could no longer tolerate being excluded from the conduct of affairs in a state that was "military by its very foundation." The trouble was that the nobility, whatever it had been in the days of chivalry, had been largely converted into a sedentary rural squirearchy, and the French army was no longer a feudal host but a corps of well-drilled professionals led by career officers. The nobility, in short, had in large part lost its traditional function, while still demanding the privilege and position derived from it. Noblemen alone had the right to bear arms in public, even in the presence of the king. They were exempt from taxation and billeting on the ground that they paid their service to the state in blood. They possessed the right of hunting, which included unlimited access to anyone else's property during pursuit, because such exercise kept them fit for war. The less the nobility could justify such privileges by actual deeds, the more they retreated behind a mystique of noble birth and blood, as if privilege were an inherent attribute of nobility as such, instead of being the reward for tangible service. But here was the rub. The more the old nobility stooped to marry the daughters of the nobility of the robe, the more they diluted the purity of blood on which their claim to privilege now rested. And if the prospect of a handsome dowry ultimately overrode all objections, the old nobility could not help but feel that they were eroding the very foundations on which they stood.

These suspicions were not confined to themselves alone. The nobility of the robe, while continuing to pay court to the old nobility—that is, to acknowledge the market value of its prestige—had far grander aims in mind. As their importance in the expanding state bureaucracy grew, they began to claim primacy in the social hierarchy for themselves. Theirs, they asserted, was the real service to the state, while the old nobility had nothing to offer but tales of former glory. They argued that the nature of society had changed and that they were now its most valuable, hence most honorable, members.

Some of the old nobility threw their lot in with the changing times. They moved to town, patronized the Enlightenment, and adopted libertarian poses. But most chose to make their last stand at Versailles, the great pleasure palace built by Louis XIV to commemorate the splendor of his reign. Versailles was not only the center of French government but also of a cult of adoration that revolved around the king. Presentation at court and access to Louis during the formal ceremonies of his rising, eating, and going to bed (the *lever, dîner,* and *coucher*) were the most exclusive honors in the kingdom. Eligibility to them was continually being restricted, until in 1760 it was ruled that to be received at Versailles, one had to show noble ancestry going back to at least 1400. Less than 1000 families in France met the test.

Within the court itself, precedent was elaborated into a fantastic art. To enter Versailles was to be forever trapped in a ritual ballet in which no detail was too small, no gesture too insignificant, no function too natural to escape the web of ceremony. It was a world in which the dukes of France could solemnly protest—as they did in June, 1744—that their wives had been deprived of the sole right to carry parasols in the Corpus Christi procession; a world preserved for us in the Duke de Luynes's 17 volumes on court etiquette and the 10,000 pages of the Duke de Saint-Simon's bitter gossip.

What the nobility worshipped at Versailles was not the king himself but the principle of blood in its highest possible incarnation. The king was the greatest aristocrat of all, and the more the nobility exalted him, the more they exalted themselves. It has often been said that Louis XIV lured the nobility to Versailles to neutralize them politically. This is true enough, but it does not explain why they connived so eagerly at their own ruin. They came to Versailles because, in a real sense, there was no place else for them to go. Here, undisturbed by reality, they could enjoy a fantasy of eminence and power they were no longer capable of in actual life. Versailles was the elephant's graveyard of the old French nobility.

The attack on the traditional nobility was not simply a French phenomenon, however, but Europe-wide. Almost everywhere, the old nobility they were either under intense pressure to enter state service, as in Prussia and Russia, or finding themselves replaced in positions of prestige and authority, as in Sweden and Austria. Only England, where the titular nobility was so small that the ruling elite was able to concentrate on limiting the monarchy rather than squabbling over questions of rank, and Spain, where society was so stagnant that nothing could threaten the power of the grandees, avoided this aristocratic civil war.

We must not, however, imagine anything like two well-defined factions locked in mortal combat. The conflict between the old and new nobility was more like that between the junior and senior partners of an old, established firm than between competing businesses, let alone rival systems. The new nobility were not out to destroy the privileges of the old but to inherit them. Although they protested against the barriers the old nobility had erected against them, they raised the same barriers against others in turn. Government offices had been officially sold in France since the early sixteenth century, but mere money could not buy them. The transition from a career in trade to one in the state bureaucracy could only be made by slow degrees. It took, as a rule, four generations to qualify for the highest offices, precisely equivalent to the "four quarters" of nobility it took to gain admission into the *École Militaire,* the famous officers' training school of the nobility of the sword. We cannot think simplistically of an effete old nobility being thrust aside by a "rising middle class" of vulgar, vigorous merchants. Money made in trade was not acceptable until it had been converted into the respectable currency of salaries, fees, and rents.

This will seem less strange to us if we reflect that, in a society where occupations were ranked not by utility but honor, income was also more or less honorable according to its source. To advance on the social scale, one had not only to spend money in an appropriate way but to earn it in an appropriate way. To aspire to the status of a gentleman on the income of a merchant was a contradiction in terms. Thus, the classic route to noble status was to "give up trade," buy into land or government service, and marry a rung or two up on the ladder.

New fortunes were often made in trade and new status won in government service. But the basic economic fact about Old Regime Europe was land, and the basic fact about the nobility was that they owned it.

The primary unit of noble wealth was the estate. The profits of the estate were partly measured in produce, of course—farming, ranching, mining, and logging. But the largest source of income came from various rents and fees, in cash or kind, levied on the tenant farmers who worked the estate as well as other peasants subject to seigneurial taxes. The nature of these exactions varied greatly from one country to another, from place to place within the same country, and indeed from tenant to tenant on the same estate. But however called, and under whatever custom, pretext, or device collected, the net result was everywhere the same: The European peasant under the Old Regime gave half or more of his labor to the nobility.

Among the landed nobility, the family title and estates were inherited by the eldest surviving son, a practice known as *primogeniture.* In addition, noble estates were generally limited by *entail,* which prohibited the selling of any estate except under very strict conditions: in England, for example, only by royal consent or the permission of one's fellow peers. These two provisions ensured the integrity of the title and protected the continuing rights of the family line, as represented by the next heir, against the incompetence or dissipation of any one of its members.

What, then, of the other children of nobility? Second sons usually went into the army, third sons into the church. The leading British generals in the American Revolutionary War—Clinton, Gage, and Howe—were all second sons or sons of second sons. Female children, unless the male line failed entirely, had only one career: marriage.

The sons of nobility sometimes still made good officers and dedicated churchmen. But these careers were essentially sinecures from which no serious effort was expected. The case of Prince Louis de Bourbon Condé, marshal of France and ecclesiastical pluralist, is instructive. Fleeing the field of battle, he asked an aide whether he had seen any fugitives. "No, my lord," was the reply, "you are the first." The same prince drew an annual income of 400,000 livres as titular abbot of four monasteries, although the only clerical function he ever performed was to build a marble tomb for his pet monkey, McCarthy.

The aristocratic ideal of life was one of refined idleness. This ideal was enshrined in Baldassare Castiglione's immensely popular *Book of the Courtier* (1527) and all the many manuals that followed it in the next two centuries on the art of being noble. It might have been perfectly acceptable for Henry VIII to tear chickens apart at dinner; it would have been unthinkable for Louis XIV to do so. The new ideal—what the English called a *gentleman* and the French an *honnête homme*—was a man poised and assured at all times, moderately educated but no scholar, moderately skillful but no expert: an exquisite amateur from whom no serious performance need ever be expected. Substantially unmodified, it remains the model of upper-class behavior in the West to the present day.

The emergence of this ideal coincided with the historical transformation of the nobleman from warrior to courtier. It provided the perfect rationale for an elite that had lost all real social function. A gentleman was a member of the ruling class who need not bother to rule. He was guaranteed a life of ease without obligation, status without effort, reward without service, all in return for good manners—or, for that matter, even without them. In the last analysis, whatever a nobleman did was noble, whether it lived up to his own professed standards or not. He justified himself fully by merely existing. This was never openly asserted, of course. It was not a theory, not even an attitude, but a climate of assumption, in which the privileges of nobility appeared not as privileges at all but as the natural consequence of being born noble, as a birthright.

In actual practice, of course, the situation of the nobility varied widely, from the terminal parasitism of the Spanish aristocracy, which had become wholly urbanized and lived on the profit of distant estates, and the unbridled arrogance of the Hungarian magnates, who burst out laughing in their Diet at the mere suggestion that they should legally limit the obligations of their serfs, to the almost servile condition of the nobility under Peter the Great or the industrious civil servants of the later Prussia. But insofar as we can speak of the idea of nobility as such, it had come increasingly to represent not one social group among others, with its own rights and responsibilities, but a condition of privilege and the way of life associated with the unfettered enjoyment of that privilege. During the reign of Maria Theresa of Austria, we hear of a masked ball for 7,000 guests; 18,000 candles were lit, and a full corps of physicians, surgeons, and even midwives stood by for any contingency. In winter, a favorite pastime of the Viennese nobility was a kind of toboggan race in which 30 gilded sledges, carved as dragons, serpents, peacocks, and griffins, sped "with amazing velocity" through streets laid with fresh snow trucked in from the country, winding up at the gates of the imperial palace. It was this that the ex-aristocrat Talleyrand had in mind when he made his famous remark, "No one who has not lived before 1789 has known the sweetness of life."

THE CLERGY

Of the three orders into which Catholic Europe was traditionally divided, the clergy were the first. Like so many of the categories bequeathed the Old Regime by feudal times, however, the title had become an empty husk, devoid of meaning. The church, whether Catholic or Protestant, had ceased to exist as an independent force in European society. Institutional religion had become an appendage of the state, a branch of government. After the pontificate of Urban VIII (1623–1644), the influence of Rome declined precipitously, and by the last quarter of the eighteenth century, the papacy was at its lowest ebb in seven centuries. The condition of the church was best exemplified in the career of the brilliant Gallican bishop Jacques Bénigne Bossuet (1627–1704), advocate of divine-right monarchy, defender of the faith as defined by Louis XIV, and scourge of heresy and dissidence. No servile flatterer, Boussuet did not hesitate to take Louis to task on his personal morality; no narrow fanatic, he sought to reconcile the new philosophy with traditional theology; no mere courtier, he tried to arbitrate the often bitter conflicts with Rome that marked Louis's reign. Nonetheless, Boussuet's name is indissolubly linked with Louis's, and the judgment is just. Neither would have been quite what he was without the other. Louis needed the intellectual respectability that only a theologian could confer on divine right, while Boussuet's fame and eminence, if not his talents, derived wholly from his association with the king. It was an unequal marriage, in which Bossuet was split between too many masters, his God, his pope, his king, while Louis obeyed himself alone. But it was the best he could do. The day had passed when the clergy could play a significant part in the life of their times except by serving the interests of a secular power.

In Restoration England, the reestablishment of Anglicanism once again united the monarchy and the church. Although the bishops did oppose James II in the crisis of 1688 (see page 44), they settled down for the most part cozily under his successors. The alliance between church and state in eighteenth-century England presented so monolithic a facade that the two were merged into a single descriptive term, the "Establishment." This meant peace and security for the church, but at a price of stodginess and conformity. The Anglican bishops of the eighteenth century preached a gospel of reason and accommodation that eroded away the sterner Calvinism of the old Anglican creed. At their best, the Anglicans tried to uphold a modest moral standard in an age of legitimized corruption; at their worst, their complacency implicitly condoned or even—in such notorious cases as that of Bishop Hoadly, a hack politician and hireling journalist in cloth—joined it.

In post-Westphalian Germany, the position of the Lutheran pastorate was even less free, and far less affluent. "A minister," remarked the German critic Herder, "is only entitled to exist now, under state control and by authority of the prince, as a moral teacher, a farmer, a list-maker, and an agent of the secret police." The moral and intellectual content of the sermon, once the very vehicle of the Protestant Revolution, had reached a nadir of triviality; a sermon on Matthew 10:30 ("But the very hairs of your head are numbered") was the occasion for a discourse on the growth, function, and proper Christian grooming of the hair.

A strong reaction to this denatured Christianity swept across Europe in the late seventeenth and eighteenth centuries. In Lutheran Germany, preached by Philipp Jakob Spener and Count Nikolaus Ludwig von Zinzendorf, it was called Pietism; in England, where John Wesley stumped for 50 years, Methodism; in the Catholic world, under the influence of Miguel de Molinos, Quietism. Despite manifest differences of style and creed, these movements had much in common. They emphasized the personal and mystical side of religion, the direct relation between man and God. They attacked the prevailing rationalism that had, in Wesley's words, "hooted witchcraft out of the world." Unlike the millenarian sects of the English Civil War, however, their religion had no overt political implication. It was turned inward, inculcating a submission before God and an indifference to the world that posed little threat to the social order.

Politically, then, the established clerical order was an appendage of the state. Socially, it faithfully mirrored the inequities of the Old Regime. The upper echelons of the church hierarchy were reserved for the sons of nobility, who siphoned off the profits of tithes and rents and left a mass of hardworking and underpaid parish priests to do the actual work of the church. With its often vast endowments and properties—the Catholic church in France owned 15 percent of all cultivated land, for example—the clerical order was in one sense simply a great holding company for the nobility. Even more serious, however, was the inner demoralization and loss of vocation, or at least pride, that increasingly afflicted the upper clergy as the eighteenth century wore on. Great prelates had always been rich and worldly, but they had never been openly apologetic about their calling. The church of the Old Regime had ceased to provide a moral alternative to the secular order. For that reason alone, it was doomed to share its fate.

THE GREAT DIVIDE

The ruling elite of the Old Regime embraced those who had both power and status and those with power on their way to status—that is to say, the established nobility and the wealthy merchants and squires who were in the process of becoming noble as quickly as the rules of the game would allow. Nobility in the ultimate sense thus meant full certification in the ruling elite.

The elite was served by a wide group of what we would now call professional people—doctors, lawyers, professors, and minor officials. Characteristically, such persons belonged to the elite not by the functions they performed but by the status they could afford. According to William Harrison's *Description of Britain* (1577):

> Whosoever studieth the laws of this realm, who so abideth in the university giving his mind to his books, or professional physic [medicine] and the liberal sciences . . . [and] can live without manual labor, and thereto is able and will bear the port, charge and countenance of a gentleman, he shall for money have a coat [of] arms bestowed upon him by the heralds . . . and thereunto being made so good cheap shall be called master, which is the title that men give to esquires and gentlemen, and be reputed for a gentleman ever after.

Harrison pokes fun at the status seekers who buy false credentials to become gentlemen "cheap," but this only emphasizes how eager men were to acquire them. We may well smile at this, unless we reflect on the transformation certain words have undergone between that era and this. Today a "gentleman" is anyone being waited on in a shoestore, an "esquire" is someone being solicited by a book club or insurance company, and "master" is the term for anyone not yet old enough to be called "mister." But in the England of the Old Regime, these terms were very precise marks of standing in the world, and were rationed accordingly. In England, where almost alone among the states of the Old Regime, the nobility did pay taxes, a simple mathematical scale has survived that ranks the status levels of the elite: the Poll Tax. In 1660, gentlemen were assessed at £5 per year, esquires £10, knights £20, and baronets (a class of life peers whose titles could not be passed on to their descendants) £30; above this line was the *nobilitas major* of barons at £40, viscounts £50, earls £60, and dukes £100. (By contrast, a common laborer would pay only sixpence, or 1/200 of the gentleman's tax.)

To "bear the port, charge and countenance of a gentleman," in Harrison's words, meant to be able to live up to a certain standard of elegance and display. It also meant absolute abstention from manual labor. This was the great social divide. If gentility was the bottom rung of nobility, the minimum definition of a gentleman was exemption from the common curse of earning a living.

But the real gulf between ruler and ruled under the Old Regime might be better expressed not in terms of how a man got his living but whether he could read and write. We do not know what percentage of the population of prerevolutionary Europe was literate. Wedding registries are our best clue. In the 1680s, a fifth of all the brides and bridegrooms in France were able to sign their names; by the 1780s the proportion had risen to over a third. Roughly the same percentages hold in England; we have no evidence at present for other countries. (It should be noted that significantly more men than women were literate; in the French village of Crulai in the 1680s, no bride was able to sign the register.)

But what can we really judge from a signature? How many of those couples who so painfully traced out the letters of their names could write anything else? How many of them could read a bill of sale, a satire by Voltaire, or the Holy Bible? If we are ever to understand life under the Old Regime, we must imagine the millions of men and women for whom the act of holding a pen before a sheet of paper was as foreign and fearful as raising a chisel up to a piece of uncut marble. These millions lived in a world that began and ended with the sound of the human voice. In a world run by writing, they could not even grasp, let alone defend, their interests. For everything beyond the reach of their own senses, they were as dependent on the testimony of others as an infant at its mother's breast. They might share the same planet and parish with gentlemen, but their lives were as different from that handful of men who could refer and record and speak to distant nations as members of different species. Like beggars with their belongings on their backs, they were forced to carry their lives and all they knew in their own minds.

Here are two statements, both made by Englishmen, a little over a decade apart:

> I have told you candidly my sentiments. I think they are not likely to alter yours. I do not know that they ought . . . I have little to recommend my opinions, but long observation and much impartiality. They come from one who has been no tool of power, no flatterer of greatness; and who in his last acts does not wish to belye the tenour of his life. They come from one, almost the whole of whose public exertion has been a struggle for the liberty of others, from one in whose breast no anger durable or vehement has ever been kindled, but by what he considered as tyranny . . .

> Wee hear in Formed that you got Shear in mee sheens [shearing machines] and if you Dont Pull them Down in a Forght Nights Time Wee will pull them Down for you Wee will you Damd infernold dog.

The first statement was made by Edmund Burke (1729–1797) in concluding his *Reflections on the Revolution in France;* the second is an anonymous note from a Gloucestershire weaver to a local clothier. The difference is not only that of a man at his leisure speaking for the problems of others and a man in despair barely able to speak for his own. It is the difference between those who rule the world and those who endure it.

THE THIRD ESTATE

The Third Estate was a catchall category for everyone who did not belong to the first estate of the clergy or the second of the nobility, a verbal dumping ground for nine-tenths of the population. It embraced so much—from textile workers to mountain shepherds, from prosperous bankers to absolute paupers—that it really described nothing.

Yet, however defective the term may have been from a sociological point of view, it told the truth politically. The Third Estate constituted the part of the population that was *ruled.*

Contemporaries were very clear on this point. Thomas Smith, an English lawyer of the sixteenth century, divided the kingdom of England into nobles, gentlemen, yeomen, and merchants, and "the fourth sort of men which do not rule." Among these he classed all "day labourers, poor husbandmen [farmers], yea merchants or retailers which have no free land, copyholders, and all artificers, [such] as tailors, shoemakers, carpenters, brickmakers, bricklayers, etc.": in other words, roughly the Third Estate. These, said Smith, "have no voice nor authority in our commonwealth and no account is made of them, but only to be ruled and not to rule other[s]."

How did these silent millions live? Reconstructing their lives and their world from often scanty and fragmentary evidence is one of the most important tasks of the modern historian. What follows can only be the briefest outline.

THE PEASANTRY

Eight out of ten people in prerevolutionary Europe lived in the "country," that is to say, in and around the countless thousands of villages that were the primary units of social, political, and religious organization in the Old Regime. The great cities—London, Paris, Vienna, Madrid, Moscow, Prague—rose above these Lilliputian communities like Alps above foothills. London, with over 500,000 inhabitants in the seventeenth century, contained 10 percent of the population of England. But the next four largest cities in the kingdom had only 25,000 to 30,000 inhabitants apiece, and 75 percent of the population lived in settlements of fewer than 500 persons. It is true that the English example is somewhat extreme. There was nothing in England like the autonomous life of the old Italian city-states or the "free cities" of the Empire like Strassburg. But the vast majority of Europe's population lived in communities of under 1000.

We must therefore imagine the scale of living of 100 million people who would be unlikely to see in all their lives as many people together at one time as we might casually pass on a city street today. "France," "Poland," "Russia" could have been little but the vaguest of abstractions to those whose few acres of homestead, tavern, and church happened to lie within the borders of the political entities that bore those names. This is not to suggest that the average rural hamlet was totally isolated. In the populous plains of the German Rhineland or Italian Lombardy, one might see the spires of ten churches from a single knoll. The great painters of the sixteenth and seventeenth centuries show us a landscape which, though hardly crowded and only partly domesticated, still comfortably reflects the human presence. And though each small community might be separate and sufficient unto itself, it was also a place on a map, a point in the network of roads and rivers, markets and fairs, parishes and provinces, and the whole web of economic, social, religious, and juridical relationships that constituted the society of which, with however limited an awareness, it was part.

The most immediate and important relationship in the life of the village was with its lord. Each village, with the land attached to it, formed part of one or more lordships, that is, of a feudal domain whose origins stretched back to the Middle Ages. At the same time, very few serfs remained under the Old Regime, at least in western Europe; most peasants owned their own land, though it might be no more than two or three acres and was rarely more than ten. Thus the average peasant was both a feudal tenant and an independent proprietor with respect to the same piece of land. This seeming paradox is explained by considering the slow evolution of the medieval system toward modern forms of ownership. Feudalism did not simply vanish; it was gradually modified into something else by concession and qualification. Over the centuries, the peasant had acquired most of the rights we associate with ownership—the right to sell, lease, exchange, give, and bequeath—while technically his land still remained part of a feudal proprietorship. In practice this meant that his exercise of these rights was still subject to the approval of the lord. No property could be transferred without the lord's consent and without payment of dues that often robbed the peasant of his profit. The lord was also entitled to substitute himself as purchaser at the same price.

Far more burdensome and extensive, however, were the payments and obligations to which the peasant was subject for the use and working of his land. Since local variations of the basic situation approach infinity, we shall confine ourselves to France as reasonably representative of the whole. The average French peasant owed his lord most or all of the following services: various *corvées* or compulsory work obligations such as road building and maintenance; a host of dues and fines for using the lord's corn mill or winepress or bakery (which was obligatory), and again on the corn or wine or bread he then sold; for all sales or transfers of land, as noted, and for seeking justice in the lord's court (there was generally no other); and for rent, in cash (the *cens*) or crops (the *champart*). If the peasant bred livestock, he owed the lord a part of the increase; if he slaughtered his animals for food, the lord could claim the tongue. The lord's rabbits and pigeons ravaged the peasant's crops, and the lord himself trampled them down in the hunt.

Time and custom had mitigated some of these obligations. The *corvée,* which in earlier centuries had sometimes involved two or three days' work a week, had been reduced to a few days a year, and was often commuted entirely for a small cash payment. Cash fines and rents, being largely fixed and traditional, had shrunk to relative insignificance with long-term inflation. On the other hand, levies in kind were as onerous as ever; the *champart* alone still amounted in the eighteenth century to between a tenth and a third of the peasant's crop. The nobility, moreover, faced with a drastic decline in the value of their cash income, squeezed their tenants hard to make up for it. Old rents and dues were resurrected, and heavy pressure was exerted to raise them. The open pastures and commons on which the peasants had traditionally grazed their cattle were annexed to noble estates, sometimes by decree, often by force. Nor did the peasant face this concerted pressure from the old local lord alone. The nobility of the robe and even noble *rentiers* from the town, in buying noble land, bought the feudal rights that went with it, and they pressed their privileges to the hilt. Indeed, these absentee landlords were often even more avaricious than the old nobility who, if not more compassionate, had at least a more realistic idea of what the traffic could bear.

After the feudal lord had finished, the peasant was faced with the claims of the state. The bewildering number and variety of state taxes were almost as onerous as the toll they took. Chief among them was the *taille*, a direct tax levied in some places on income and in some on property. Louis XIV introduced two new taxes, the "twentieth" and the poll tax, first imposed in 1695 during the worst famine of the century. These taxes were significant as the first designed to apply equally to all the king's subjects, noble as well as base, but they were vigorously opposed by the aristocracy and did not long survive Louis's reign.

The most hated word in the French tongue was *gabelle*. The *gabelle* was the tax on salt, a vital commodity used not only in the diet but as a fertilizer, preservative, and tanning agent. What made the *gabelle* particularly obnoxious was the way it was imposed. Salt could be bought only from licensed vendors, who reaped enormous profits on their monopoly. Moreover, since the purchase of a definite minimum was compulsory, and since these vendors would sell only small quantities at a time, persons living in remote districts had to trudge back and forth continuously to make up their quota. Nor was that all: Different grades of salt were sold, and a host of officials were employed to make sure that no one tried to cheat the state by making do with the cheaper grades alone. Finally, the *gabelle* was so inequitably applied that some provinces were entirely exempt from it, while in others whole towns were gradually depopulated by its severity. This naturally resulted in wholesale smuggling, which meant more officials and more corruption. Even dogs were trained at bootlegging, and if caught, they were solemnly sentenced to death under French law.

The *gabelle* was only one of many excise taxes, each with its own separate officialdom, levied on almost every imaginable product. Tax riots were so common that they gave parts of the country the look of endemic civil war. In the region of Boulogne in 1662, it took 38 companies of royal troops to put down disorders; scores were hanged, and 400 men were condemned to the galleys for life. In 1664, dragoons had to occupy Béarn to introduce the *gabelle*, and the insurrection lasted ten years. In the midst of war with the Dutch in 1675, an entire army had to be raised to put down the tax rebels of Brittany. The Duke de Chaulnes boasted that the trees of the province were bent with the weight of hanged peasants.

These risings were doomed to monotonous repression. No royal commissions investigated grievances; no government ministers, at least until late in the eighteenth century, proposed reform. The government's attitude was simple: All disorders were alike, and all alike to be crushed. Subjects in rebellion were rebels against God, less deserving of mercy than foreign armies. Only when the nobility took part in (and sometimes incited) peasant disturbances did they acquire political significance. Even in the great Breton revolt of 1675, the peasantry showed nothing that could be described as revolutionary consciousness; their demands went no further than a mitigation of existing dues and taxes. They looked not to making a new society but to restoring an old one, in which the king had been a gentle father and the lord:

> To commons and country lived a good friend
> And gave to the needy what God did him send.

This was the world not of history but of fable and legend. It was the only kind of better world the peasant could imagine: neither the real past nor the possible future, but a simple idealization of the present, with good harvests, light taxes, and a nobility willing to live and let live.

But the peasants were not limited in their vision simply by illiteracy. We have spoken, in generalizing, of "the average peasant" and "the peasantry." But the peasants were as divided among themselves by differences of status and wealth as any other social group. The interests of the rich peasant, who owned his land, plow, and team, produced for the market, and had a full larder, were no more identical with those of the sharecropper who scratched his living on a corner of someone else's soil and subsisted on buckwheat cakes, millet gruel, butter, and plain water, than are the interests of a corporate executive with those of an assembly-line worker, though both be considered members of the "middle class."

The prime determinant of a peasant's status was how much he owned of the tools he worked with: land, livestock, and implements. As a group, the French peasantry constituted 80 percent of the population, occupied nearly 100 percent of the land, and owned—subject to the limitations we have discussed—slightly less than half of it. There were few peasants in France without any land at all, but there were equally few—perhaps 10 percent—who owned enough to provide a secure living for their families. The great majority had only a few scattered strips, often of the poorest quality, and eked out an income doing odd jobs—as woodcutters, weavers, or field hands, or taking on any other casual labor that came their way. Still more depressed were the sharecroppers, who with little or no land of their own and no agricultural capital rented a small plot with stock, seeds, and tools, in return for which they surrendered half their crop. They lived in one-room earth-floored cottages that they shared with their animals, surrounded by dung heaps, stagnant puddles, and an incessant maze of flies—an army of sickly, stunted men and women brutalized by hopelessness and squalor into the semblance of another race. But even this was not the bottom. Below even the misery of sharecroppers were the landless men, day laborers who tramped from farm to farm in search of work, or (as they might easily become) roving bands of beggars and vagabonds, burning and looting the dwellings of anyone who possessed anything.

A village of 100 families exhibited the whole of this rural society in micro-cosm. At the top were one or two rich peasants, the "cocks of the parish," who owned full plow teams and supplemented their own holdings by renting land from the nobility, which they sublet in turn or worked with hired labor. These "cocks" often came to function as agents and overseers for locally powerful lords, forming the link by which their influence was exercised in the village. The entire commu-nity was dependent on them for work and credit, and their voice in the village council naturally carried most weight. Next came the eight or ten more or less independent smallholders, who in normal times could hold their own; an equal number of destitute men at the bottom; and a majority in between who lived most of their lives on the edge of survival.

For this majority, one bad harvest, a visitation by soldiers, or the death of a few sheep or a cow (owned by only half the peasantry) could begin an irrevers-ible tailspin of debt. In general bad times, millions fell into pauperdom, their small holdings sucked up by creditors, and corpses began to appear in the fields. In the great famine of 1694, men were reported drinking the blood of slaughtered oxen or trying to live by boiling roots and nettles. They would be found dead later, their mouths stuffed with grass. In famine's wake came plague, less a re-specter of social distinctions, and within a few months, a tenth of the people of France had perished. It was a disaster comparable in magnitude to what France endured in World War I.

Famine, unlike the mysterious plague, did not just happen. It was a com-plex social product. Bad harvests were, of course, a prime ingredient. But the crucial effect of bad harvests was not so much a shortage of grain—even in 1694, there was still enough to feed the kingdom—but a rise in prices. The ma-jority of peasants, as we have seen, did not produce or at any rate keep enough food even to feed their own families; they had to buy the rest, like any city dweller. When prices rose beyond a certain point, such people slowly began to starve.

Political as well as economic factors played a part in the famine of 1694. Six years earlier, Louis XIV had begun a war; the trade depression this brought on had already dried up much of the casual labor on which the average peasant depended. Then came the bad harvests, three in a row, each worse than the last. The army had first lien on crops and bought them at rock-bottom prices, driving up the cost of what remained still further. Corruption and speculation were rife, and panic spread in the countryside. There were food riots and assaults on the grain convoys. All of this had a single result: It pushed prices still higher. Between the summer of 1688 and the spring of 1694, they rose to five or six times the nor-mal level, and even more. The economy ceased to exist for large numbers of peo-ple, and these people died.

Louis expressed grief for his subjects and made, belatedly, some efforts to regulate prices and procure grain from the Baltic. But he saw no reason to inter-rupt his war, at least until the revenue from his devastated realm fell so sharply that he was unable to pay his troops. For this he drew a remarkable rebuke (pub-lished anonymously, of course) from an aristocractic author, the Abbé Fénelon:

Your people, Sire, whom you should love as your children, and who up to this time have been so devoted to you, are dying of hunger. The land is left almost untended, towns and countryside are deserted, trade of all kinds falls off and can no longer support the workers: all commerce is at a standstill . . . For the sake of getting and keeping vain conquests abroad, you have destroyed half the real strength of your own state. Rather than take money from your poor people, you ought to feed and cherish them . . . All France is now no more than one great hospital, desolate and unprovided . . . Little by little the fire of sedition catches everywhere. The people believe you have no pity for their sufferings, that you care only for your own power and glory. They say that if the king had a father's heart for his people, he would surely think his glory lay rather in giving them bread than in keeping hold of a few frontier posts . . .

The king's mistress, Madame de Maintenon, found the letter "well expressed" but irritable in tone. Louis's reign was to last another 20 years, and for 15 of them, France was at war.

We have dwelt on the French peasant not because his lot was worse than the European average but because it was rather better. If the French peasantry was still incompletely emancipated from feudalism, they had come a long way toward full independence. However precarious their situation might be, enough of them made a go of it to keep the legal and social gains they had won. But precisely the reverse process was taking place in eastern Europe. From the sixteenth century on, the lot of the peasantry in Austria, Prussia, Poland, and Russia steadily declined from indebtedness to peonage to servitude. The story was everywhere similar. First the peasant lost his land through debt, and with it the means of ever paying the debt off. This being the case, the lord commuted the debt from cash or crop payment to labor service. But to work, the peasant again needed land, tools, and food, which, advanced to him by the lord, perpetually replenished his debt and made him in effect a bondsman. The peasant's only recourse was flight, and so many peasants did flee that the state soon began to issue decrees binding them to the soil. Government registers were established, in which the name and residence of every adult male peasant was entered. At first these decrees were presented as temporary expedients, not involving any change in the peasant's legal status. But they soon became the basis of a formalized and permanent serfdom. As in the medieval West, the peasant could not migrate, marry, or practice a trade without the consent of his lord. His labor obligation was virtually unlimited. Peasants were sold from one lord to another, and in some places auctioned on the block. We hear of peasants being exchanged for gambling debts or even gambled for themselves. This astonishing degradation of the Eastern peasantry took place in a very short time. In Russia, for example, from the first decree issued by Ivan the Terrible in 1580, the entire process was complete within three generations.

The feudalization of eastern Europe can scarcely be overestimated as a factor in the subsequent history of the continent. The iron curtain of the Cold War was but a pale emanation of this original iron curtain that fell between East and West from the late sixteenth to early eighteenth centuries. Henceforth there were two Europes, one in which feudalism was a lingering anachronism to be swept away by the French Revolution and where a huge pool of free labor was available for the new industrial era, and another in which nine-tenths of the population was sunk in the most primitive misery until the end of the nineteenth century, commerce and town life dwarfish, and social and political development stagnant. But even this must be placed in world perspective. The condition of the Chinese and Japanese peasantry was as bad as or worse than that of the serfs of Prussia and Muscovy, and in the Ottoman Empire it was worst of all.

Under these conditions, it was often death that had the first harvest. In fertile and enlightened France, of every 100 persons born live, 25 died before their first birthday, 25 more before the age of 20, and another 25 before age 45. Only 10 would reach the age of 60, and a man of 80 was regarded with the same superstitious awe we accord a centenarian today. Contrary to popular belief, moreover, the age of marriage was rather late, between 26 and 28 for men and 23 and 25 for women, and illegitimacy was rare. In other words, more than half the population of prerevolutionary Europe did not survive to reproduce. The problem of the Old Regime was not how to control population but how to maintain it.

The only answer was to keep the birth rate as high as possible. The primary social responsibility of women was, simply, to breed, ladies of the aristocracy no less than wives of the peasantry. Forty babies were born per 1000 of population every year; almost one of every two women of childbearing age was pregnant at any given time. With malnutrition, miscarriage, and a 10 to 15 percent rate of maternal fatality, the average woman might luckily manage to breed five children, and—given a generation without undue calamity—two or three might reach maturity.

There was little room for sentiment. Widowers quickly remarried, and the loss of an infant to a hardworking peasant was less important than a bad harvest or the death of a horse. Only the strong and the brutal survived. In drink, violence, and orgy, the peasant lost himself periodically in life-gorging ferocity. Saints' days and other festivals were often a thinly veiled license to anarchy. The authorities tolerated such things, for fear of worse. In a world where the line between life and death was so easily crossed, celebration led often to sacrilege, riot to rebellion. Only by periodically permitting its symbolic destruction could a culture of oppression survive.

THE TOWNS

Here is a seventeenth-century description of Paris:

> No town is more muddy or more filthy. Its filth is black and stinking, with an unbearable stench that is offensive and noticeable for several leagues around.

Two hundred years later, the English poet Coleridge celebrated "the six-and-thirty stenches of Cologne," and a later commentator added that the other towns of Germany smelled no better. London ran with open sewers; its fields and suburbs were one vast dump; refuse and rubble piled shoulder-high against buildings; and its thoroughfares were described in 1748 as "a Hotch-Potch of half-moon and serpentine streets, close, dismal, long Lanes, stinking Alleys, dark, gloomy Courts and suffocating Yards." It was a labyrinth, unpaved, unnamed, unnumbered. Sheds and stalls blocked what space there was; overhanging stories threatened to collapse on the passerby; obscenities and ordure showered down on him; beggars and thieves jostled him; bullock carts spattered him; projecting steps and open cellars tripped him; mad dogs snapped and bit at him. Rats roamed freely; vermin crawled everywhere. Fire was a continual hazard. Many areas were completely unlit, despite municipal ordinances, and after 11 P.M., the entire city was plunged into darkness.

Yet the philosopher Montaigne could call Paris "the glory of France, one of the world's most handsome ornaments," and the census of 1801 boastfully described London as "the Metropolis of England, at once the Seat of Government and the greatest Emporium in the known world." These statements were true, too, because cheek by jowl with poverty and squalor one could find the utmost magnificence and wealth. Almost without warning, our pelted passerby might step from a dank alley onto a stately boulevard of polled trees, formal gardens, and splendid town houses whose long galleries and banqueting halls, paneled libraries, and elegant boudoirs seemed to form a single interconnected palace where the great and powerful held continual court. Sometimes rich and poor nakedly faced each other on the same street, but usually the rich fled the encounter as quickly as possible. Henry Fielding, the London magistrate and author of *Tom Jones,* remarked that once the fashionable part of town had included

> the whole parish of Covent Garden and a great part of St. Giles in the Fields; but here the enemy [i.e., the poor] broke in and the circle was presently contracted to Leicester Fields and Golden Square. Hence the People of Fashion again retreated before the foe to Hanover Square; whence they were once more driven to Grosvenor Square and even beyond it, and that with so much precipitation, that had they not been stopped by the walls of Hyde Park, it is more than probable they would by this time have arrived at Kensington.

By this eighteenth-century version of the flight to the suburbs, the present-day West End of London was built up. Thirty years later, the pace of migration was even more striking to a German visitor, who wrote in terms all too familiar to us of areas "where fertile fields and the most agreeable gardens are daily metamorphosed into house and streets."

Despite this retreat from the mob and its misery, the town-dwelling elite lived in serenity and self-assurance. This was all the more remarkable in view of the high level of crime and violence and the rudimentary nature of public order. Paris had a central police force from 1667, but London did not acquire one until 1829, despite a century of spectacular riots. The aplomb of the rich may in part be explained by the retinues of servants who acted as a private security guard, in part by the blunter sensibilities of the era. This was the day of public floggings and executions. Violence was a part of life, and the nobility brawled as much as anyone. But most important was the unshakable superiority of the rich, the

"If a Prince or Nobleman . . . fixes his residence in some pleasant spot . . . this place will become a city." A view of the Mall, London, 1751, from a contemporary engraving. St. James's Palace is seen on the left and the west towers of Westminster Abbey on the extreme right. Elsewhere in London, twenty people starved to death a week.

sense of themselves as the foundation of the universe, that is so naïvely summed up in the reformer Cantillon's description of the origin of the city:

> If a Prince or Nobleman . . . fixes his residence in some pleasant spot, and several other Noblemen come to live there to be within reach of seeing each other frequently and enjoying agreeable society, this place will become a City. Great houses will be built for the Nobleman in question, and an infinity of others for the Merchants, Artisans, and people of all sorts of professions whom the residence of these Noblemen will attract thither . . .

The economic predominance of the rich is thus converted into a pastoral myth, in which the nobleman creates the city very much as God created the world, and then assumes his place as lord of his creation.

In eighteenth-century London, there were between 3000 and 4500 aristocratic families resident part or all of the year, or from 1 to 2 percent of the population. To these we may add perhaps 1000 merchants of comparable or greater wealth, who may be very roughly compared to the 1500 or 2000 members of the nobility of the robe in Paris. These were the rich. Below them came an upper bourgeoisie of 10,000 to 15,000 "principal tradesmen" and 30,000 families who were vaguely described as "the middle sort," including clergymen, artists, and professional people as well as lesser merchants. These were the "men of property," a term that loosely embraced both the ruling elite and all those whose interests were at least generally consulted by it.

The remaining three-quarters of the population of London consisted of master craftsmen and small shopkeepers, skilled journeymen and apprentices, un-skilled and semiskilled laborers, and the destitute—a floating class of beggars and vagrants, the indigent aged and the orphaned young, casual domestics and unem-ployed immigrants, who numbered one-eighth of the city. The first of these groups managed to achieve a certain degree of security through unremitting toil, the second and third groups waged a bitter and constant struggle for survival, and the fourth was in the process of losing it. The introduction of cheap gin in the second quarter of the eighteenth century sent the death rate of the destitute soaring; Henry Fielding complained that it was "the principal sustenance . . . of more than a hundred thousand People in this Metropolis." A man too poor to eat could drink himself into a stupor for a single penny. But even a generation after the Gin Act of 1751 had substantially curbed the abuse, 1000 people a year were starving to death in London.

Most work in this preindustrial era was done in a multitude of small shops or on a piece-goods basis at home. The only large-scale organization of labor oc-curred in the building trades, mining, arms manufacture, and the merchant ma-rine. The working day often included half the night. Tailors worked from 6 in the morning till 7 or 8 at night, with an hour's break for dinner; a journeyman shipwright from 5 A.M. to 8 P.M.; a draper's assistant from 8 to 10 or 10:30. In 1776, the bookbinders of Paris struck to *win* a 14-hour day. Many trades were organized into guilds, legally incorporated bodies that enjoyed the local mono-poly of their specific occupation, but these guilds were more like social brother-hoods than modern unions and were only sporadically effective. As with the peas-ant and his lord, the worker was chronically in debt to his boss for advances of food and money. He was harassed at his work, cheated on his hours, short-changed in his pay. Often he had to accept goods for his wages: bolts of unsalable cloth, false measures of flour. Although less heavily taxed than the peasant, he was far more vulnerable to economic crisis. With no home of his own, no savings, and few possessions, with no reserves of food or animals to slaughter, he was all but helpless in times of famine and unemployment. The introduction of the fac-tory system thus meant not a series of new abuses but only the multiplication of ones long existing. The urban workmen of the Old Regime were already a pro-letariat without machines.

The worker was not passive in his distress, however. Street violence was continuous; riots were the norm. Almost anything could trigger them—an inci-dent at the tavern, a fracas at the theater, any sort of rumor—but the underlying grievances were always the same: wages and hours, rising prices, or any threat to employment. As early as 1675, the silk weavers of East London smashed 35 mechanical looms imported from Holland. In 1719, the weavers rose again to protest the importation of cheap calico fabrics from India and secured an act of Parliament against them. The riots of 1736, which included a bomb blast in the houses of Parliament, was occasioned by the use of immigrant Irish labor. Anti-Irish feeling also sparked the great Gordon riots of 1780, when London burned for six days. But here, finally, the revolutionary potential latent in these recurrent tides of popular rage burst into the open as the mob, abandoning the wretchedly exploited Catholic underclass that had been its first target, opened the prisons and attacked the Bank of England and the Royal Exchange.

In Paris, where even in normal times the average workman spent half his income on bread, the incidence of riots rose almost rhythmically with fluctuations in the bread price. Every major outbreak of the eighteenth century was connected with it, as the French historian C. A. Labrousse has shown, and in the spring of 1789, an ordinary bricklayer would have to have spent five-sixths of his wages on bread to maintain normal consumption. The bourgeois revolutionaries of 1789 found the rage of the Parisian masses a handy tool (the Bastille fell on the very day when the price of grain throughout France reached its cyclic peak). But they lived to regret having used it. The urban mob, if not much more sophisticated than the peasant one, had the advantage of regular practice, and displayed increasing cohesion in its tactics. Its entry into revolutionary politics was a fateful step. From that moment forward, "the people" became a force to be reckoned with. No other event so aptly symbolized the passing of the Old Regime. It was not only France that was to be revolutionized, but the nature of politics itself.

We have dwelt, perhaps inevitably, on Paris and London. They were two of the three greatest cities in the eighteenth-century world (the other was Tokyo), and they were both already in the grip of a profound transformation—the beginnings of modernity and of the modern situation we call, for lack of a better term, the urban crisis. But the medieval past still clung to many of the lesser towns of Europe, a past epitomized by the wall and the charter.

The wall was the most visible and distinctive emblem of the city, announcing its approach to the traveler from many miles away. Many town walls dated back to the late Roman period, and much urban history can be traced in the concentric rings of fortification that marked the stages of a town's growth (or decline). Walls were still functional in the early seventeenth century, as the survivors of sieges in the Thirty Years' War could attest, but by the end of the century many had fallen into disrepair, a process accelerated by rulers like Louis XIV who brooked no resistance to the central state. Still, for townsman and peasant alike, the wall was the symbol of the city. It defined the space between town and country in a clear and unmistakable way. There were no suburbs to speak of, and none of the urban sprawl that has homogenized the modern landscape; one was either in the city or outside. The wall also determined life within the city to a considerable extent. By circumscribing the town area, it created serious overcrowding as a larger and larger population squeezed into increasingly narrow and squalid streets. It made sanitation impossible and greatly increased the risk of epidemic. In a subtler sense, too, it engendered the intense parochialism and often ferocious civic pride that characterized the town dweller of the Old Regime.

Above all, however, the wall was a jurisdictional boundary: It marked the limit within which the special rights and privileges of the town were exercised. These rights were spelled out in the town charter. The most important one was the right of local self-government, usually through a council of magistrates. The council could collect taxes both for itself and for the central government (enabling it to escape the depredations of the tax farmers), hold court, hire employees, and raise militia. In addition, the charter often granted reduced rates or exemptions from various royal taxes and services, preferential access to wine, timber, and other commodities, riparian rights, and the like.

The most favored urban entities were the free cities of the Holy Roman

Empire. Such towns as Augsburg, Frankfurt, Nuremberg, Strassburg, and Ulm were virtually autonomous within the Empire. They coined their own money and exercised high justice. They had permanent seats in the Imperial Diet and dealt directly with the emperor. Some, like Strassburg, with its 3,000 eligible voters among a population of 25,000, had a high degree of popular representation, though actual political control usually devolved upon a handful of tight-knit old burgher families.

But the general aspect of town life in the last decades of the Old Regime was one of stagnation and decline. Despite a sharp demographic surge from about 1750 on, many towns were losing population. This was especially true in depressed and backward areas such as Spain, Italy, and much of Germany. Even the once-proud free cities were no longer what they had been. Strassburg was annexed by Louis XIV in 1681, and where Machiavelli had written with envy of the vigor and independence of the German cities in the sixteenth century, Frederick the Great could reply 200 years later that a word from the emperor sufficed to control them. The northern towns of the Hanseatic League, which had been a dead letter long before its official demise in 1669, had lost their grip on the Baltic trade, and were all, with the solitary exception of Hamburg, in an advanced state of decay. The ruinous fiscal policies of the later Hapsburg kings, together with a general economic decline, had all but destroyed commerce and manufacture in Spain, though it was able to achieve a partial recovery in the eighteenth century. Even sadder was the state of Venice. The first of the great medieval cities of Europe was in the last days of its 1000-year existence as an independent republic, and a comparison of the proud and imperial city depicted in the Renaissance by Bellini and Carpaccio with the melancholy languor of its last master, Francesco Guardi, summarizes its decline more eloquently than any words could. Europe at the end of an age seemed less ready for change than ever. A sleep of senescence had settled over the old, intractable institutions that had governed men for centuries. The texture of everyday life and experience—the ancient rhythm of sowing and harvest, the ancient dominion of master and man—had hardly changed since the days of the Crusades. But beneath this seemingly placid surface, Europe was on the brink of an epoch that within little more than 100 years would transform the entire globe in ways more startling than all the accumulated centuries of man.

two

The Age
of Louis XIV

THE ADMINISTRATIVE REVOLUTION OF LOUIS XIV

"L'État, c'est à moi," said Louis XIV: I am the state. "I am the first servant of the state," said Frederick the Great of Prussia, 100 years later. Between these two statements lay a subtle but profound transformation of the nature of kingship and government.

Louis was only stating the simple facts of the case. The monarchy itself was the only permanent institution of government in France. The king was served by various councils and councillors, but we would be led far astray if we tried to imagine anything like a modern bureaucracy, with its orderly chains of function and command. Rather, we must think of an informal group of men playing a kind of musical chairs with the various tasks of government. The same functionary might play the role of controller-general of finance in the morning and minister of agriculture in the afternoon; the official who supervised the upkeep of the royal palace also had charge of the administration of Paris, and kept an eye on the activities of the Huguenots. When the king traveled, the government went with him; the foreign ministry that accompanied Louis XIV to Vincennes early in his reign consisted simply of the old secretary, Henri-Auguste de Loménie de Brienne, in a sedan chair, followed by his son and two clerks in a coach and two aides on horseback carrying pen and ink.

The nucleus of central government was thus very small. During Louis XIV's 54 years of active rule, only 17 men served him as ministers, and never more than 5 at any time—"the Five Kings of France," as the embittered court diarist Saint-Simon called them. These men, together with a few dozen clerks, copyists, and legal officials, constituted the royal executive.

This simplicity of organization at the center contrasted with the vast honey-comb of offices that surrounded it. There were nearly 2000 officers in the Court of Chancery, and almost 1000 tax collectors for the *taille* (at least on paper) in the province of Normandy alone. One contemporary estimated that some 50,000 new offices had been created in France during the first half of the seventeenth century.

What caused this population explosion of bureaucrats was not an expansion of service or function, but the nature of officeholding itself. Officials acquired their posts not by running for them, nor by appointment, nor by a civil service exam; they bought them, cash on the line. If the office was a new one, the buyer paid the king directly; if one already in existence, he bought out the previous owner, the king receiving a percentage of the price. Once bought, the office belonged to the official just as any other piece of property might. He could sell it, lease it, and bequeath it to heirs. A government office was blue-chip stock, the soundest investment a rising young man could make. The resale value was always going up, and the profits of occupancy—in fees and graft—were limited only by the ingenuity of the officeholder.

This system will become clearer if we consider the medieval background from which it emerged. The king was still, at least in theory, the feudal landlord of the realm; that is, every landowner in France was directly or indirectly his vassal. This meant, literally, that the king owned France, though, as we have seen, something very much like modern ownership by free individuals had replaced the medieval theory in practice. But if the king owned the realm only in a vague and general sense, he certainly owned what pertained most directly to the exercise of his authority over it, namely, the government. When Louis XIV said, "I *am* the state," he might as well have said, "I *own* the state"; in a sense he was saying just that. As the king had once given fiefs of land to deserving noblemen, so now he conferred fiefs of office on his new nobility of the robe. What resulted, in short, was a second feudalism: bureaucratic feudalism. Nor was this a merely French or European phenomenon; it appears worldwide in this period, from the Ottoman Empire to China. The sale of office was apparently a universal way station on the road to modern government.

In few places, however, did it reach such development as in seven-teenth-century France. The mutual advantages of the system were obvious. The king acquired a steady annual income and created a new class directly beholden to himself. The officeholders acquired status, position, and profit. Only the ordinary Frenchman suffered, for it was he who had to pay the ever-proliferating schedule of fees that supported it. Viewed as a whole, the entire system was simply a vast scheme of indirect taxation.

In the long run, the system had serious drawbacks for the Crown. By multi-plying meaningless offices, it was creating a vested interest in misgovernment. The king's real authority, so clear at the top, was dissipated in a maze of clerk-ships. The gratitude of the new officeholding nobility, moreover, was short-lived. They soon became a powerful interest group in their own right, banding together into associations to defend themselves against accountability to king and public alike. The monarchy might effectively isolate the rebellious old feudal nobility at Versailles; it did so only to find a new and subtly more dangerous nobility ensconced at the heart of government.

The great stronghold of the nobility of the robe was the *parlements.* The parlements were the chief courts of the realm. There were roughly a dozen of them scattered among the major provincial capitals of France, but far and away the most important was the Parlement of Paris, whose jurisdiction extended over a third of the realm. Among its other functions, the Parlement of Paris officially registered all edicts of the Crown. Because, according to tradition, such edicts did not go into force until they were registered, the Parlement of Paris had taken to exercising a de facto veto over edicts it disapproved of by refusing to register them. This had occurred in the case of the Concordat of Bologna (1516), which established the autonomy of the Gallican church, and of the Edict of Nantes (1598), which granted toleration to France's Protestant minority, as well as on a number of lesser occasions; and in 1648, the Parlement's resistance to a suspension of interest payments on government bonds precipitated the Fronde, the most serious civil disturbance in France between the sixteenth century wars of religion and the French Revolution.

The Crown's difficulty in controlling its own officials was multiplied tenfold in governing the country at large. We have already seen something of the chaotic variety of customs and local dispensations in the application of a single tax, the *gabelle.* The same bizarre complexity applied to virtually everything else. Despite heroic efforts to reduce the laws of France to a single system in the sixteenth century, there were still hundreds of different legal codes in operation, in many cases several overlapping the same area, so that it was often impossible to say which law applied where. Each royal decree was thus like a pebble rolled off a mountain: There was no telling what boulders of local privilege it might have to circumvent, nor what its shape might be when it finally reached the bottom. The provincial parlements were kept forever busy "interpreting" the king's commands, and at the local level, where actual enforcement took place, there was no one to represent his authority. Village life was controlled by the lord; justice was dispensed in his court. Occasionally, a royal official might appear and cause a stir, but the effect was only temporary, and, being a local man himself, the official could not go too far. If necessary, a bribe would conclude his business. In the towns, new bureaus and jurisdictions proliferated ceaselessly with the reckless creation of offices, paralleling, duplicating, and conflicting with the old municipal administration without either replacing or improving it. This was not the extension of authority but merely its cancer, and the king's law had no profit by it.

In theory, the king was absolute master and proprietor of his realm. He was the only source of legitimate authority. The most trivial writ or warrant unfailingly carried his name. His very word was law; he was *lex loquens,* "law speaking." He alone could raise armies, conduct war, conclude peace. In practice, his power was limited, stymied, rebuffed at every turn. It died in the hands of clerks, courts, and local aldermen. It might almost be said that his power was absolute only when not in use; the moment it was invoked, it began to diminish.

This was not as paradoxical as it might seem. The king was the symbol of the unity and continuity of France. But "France" itself was still an abstraction.

The idea of the nation was to the reality of everyday life what the stars are to a sailor: something that orients his course and must be glanced at now and then. When the country lost itself in the multiplicity of its customs and interests or exhausted itself in civil war, a strong king could revive its ultimate sense of unity. But the people of France no more wanted the monarchy to come down to the ordinary details of their lives than sailors want the stars to fall into the sea.

Such was the nature of the French throne when Louis XIV announced to his council, two days after the death of his mentor Cardinal Mazarin in March, 1661, that he intended to govern France. Louis's apprenticeship had been a long one. He had been king for 18 years but never ruled. Skepticism was soon quashed, however. From the very beginning, Louis banished the old nobility from their accustomed positions of power. His new ministers were all men of bourgeois origin, who owed everything to the king and served his interests without question.

The most important of these new men was Jean-Baptiste Colbert. Colbert's talent and industry were the perfect complement to Louis XIV's ambitions. For 22 years he worked with a single goal: to make France the greatest economic power in Europe. To accomplish this, Louis permitted Colbert complete authority over trade, finance, and manufacturing, the navy and the colonies, the royal budget, the affairs of the clergy, the administration of the towns, and a dozen lesser concerns. One could briefly say that Colbert's mandate covered everything. Not even Mazarin or Cardinal Richelieu had ever exercised such power. But unlike his predecessors, Colbert was more the instrument than the author of royal policy.

Colbert seemed to take the commercial supremacy of the Dutch as a personal affront. Obsessed with production, he built hundreds of new foundries, ironworks, construction yards, arsenals. He offered every incentive to stimulate private capital: tariffs, embargoes, monopolies, technical advice, tax incentives, government subsidies. He lured textile craftsmen from the Netherlands, glassblowers from Venice, miners from Sweden, engineers from England.

Colbert's special project, however, was his state factories. He fussed over them like a man growing plants in a hothouse. Discipline was harsh and standards strict. Overseers pounced on every defect; at the third mistake, a worker would be put in irons for two hours with a sample of his work beside him. No swearing or idleness was permitted; only hymns might be sung, in a low voice which would not disturb one's neighbor. The whole atmosphere was that of a monastery whose worship was labor and whose god, production—at least in Colbert's blueprints. "We must resign ourselves to do the people good in spite of themselves," he wrote.

Colbert saw all of France as a huge workshop, its people laboring contentedly and efficiently under the watchful eye of a government whose function was to regulate, coordinate, and, of course, collect. When he took office, less than 40 percent of the taxes collected ever reached the treasury; six years later, two-thirds of the money collected came in, and the king's actual revenue was doubled. In 1664, there were only 60 merchant ships in the kingdom above 300 tons; at Colbert's death, more than 700. Not all of Colbert's works were successful. Some of his more grandiose schemes—such as a flotilla of joint-stock companies to dominate world commerce—came to naught. His attempt to regulate, standardize, and simplify France met opposition at every turn; he was constrained to work in a system that frustrated half his efforts. But he created the financial basis of Louis XIV's reign and laid the economic groundwork for a century and a half of French hegemony in Europe.

Much of Colbert's success, and most of Louis XIV's extension of royal authority, was made possible by the use of a remarkable new official: the *intendant*. The intendant was an agent commissioned directly by the king to carry out royal policy in a given province or locale. We hear of such agents in the time of Henry IV and Richelieu; one of the demands of the rebellious Parlement of 1648 was that they be curtailed.

Under Louis XIV, an intendant was assigned permanently to each province. He became the supreme local administrator, exercising police power, raising military forces, supervising all economic activity, assessing taxes, and presiding over the courts. We might simply call him the governor, except that the old provincial governor, invariably a powerful nobleman opposed to any encroachment of royal authority, was precisely the man he was designed to replace. But whereas the old governor was the apex of the local feudal hierarchy, whose interests he represented, the intendant was the driving point of central authority from Versailles. With his assistants or "subdelegates," whom he posted in the major towns of the province, the intendant was more like a Roman governor with his legates, and it has justly been said that not since the days of Rome had a government official wielded such power.

Of equal significance was the establishment of the first modern police force in Paris. At Louis XIV's accession, there were only 60 constables for the whole city, attached here and there to different districts, with no central coordination. For any serious disorder, the army had to be called out. In 1667, the king appointed a lieutenant of police for Paris. Despite his modest title, he soon became one of the most important men in the realm, working closely with the king and Colbert. His commission was very broad: to deal with all "illegal assemblies, tumults [and] seditions," to supervise the repair of the streets, the upkeep of hospitals, asylums and prisons, and the provisioning of the city, to direct relief in case of fire or flood, to inspect all warehouses, markets and fairs, hostelries, gaming halls, and brothels. Surgeons were obliged to report wounded men they treated to him; all arms were licensed through him. He was also the chief censor and possessed at least limited judicial authority.

By the end of the century, observers were struck by the order of Paris. With a force of 800 men, the lieutenant of police had made it the safest, best-lit, best-regulated city in Europe. The system was soon extended into the provinces. It was less effective there, being obliged to compete with older jurisdictions. Often the local officials bought the lieutenancy to neutralize its functions. But the lieutenants were still directly responsible to the intendant, who gradually bent them to his will. Resist as it might, a new order had come to the countryside. With many setbacks and exceptions, with much in its own methods that was self-defeating (especially the sale of offices), it slowly but inexorably tightened the web of central government around the old, anarchic France.

The genius of Louis XIV was not to create new powers for the monarchy but to exploit fully the ones that had always been there. The kings of the seventeenth century often called themselves fathers of their people; in fact they more frequently resembled harassed teachers trying to police a noisy schoolyard. They wished to give orders but were powerless to carry them out. Louis gave his orders and stood by them. His subjects might resist and rebel, but their position was purely defensive, and in the face of persistence they were finally bound to crumble. There was only one adult in the yard, one legitimate authority in the realm. The other kings of Europe admired Louis's results and copied his methods. What they could not copy was his energy, his longevity, and his will.

WAR, SOCIETY, AND THE STATE

All the mighty efforts of seventeenth-century states to extend their actual sovereignty, to suppress and enfeeble local institutions, to build roads, marshal resources, and squeeze ever-greater taxation out of an ever more reluctant population, had a single overriding end: to enable them to make war.

That war was the supreme activity of states was taken for granted in the seventeenth century, and its virtues were often extolled. "The people are very happy when they die for their kings," wrote the playwright Corneille. War was not merely the health of the state but the health of society as well. The level of seventeenth-century violence, from the brawls of the poor to the duels of the rich, was very much higher than our own, and the general view was that a nation too long at peace became slack and effete, like a body without exercise. Twenty years without war seemed to be about as much as the English could endure, to judge by the readiness with which the country plunged into war with Spain in 1624 over the objections of its monarch, James I, or the so-called War of Jenkins's Ear in 1739, which began when a demented seaman exhibited his withered ear to the House of Commons and claimed the Spanish had cut it off. Men were not insensitive to the horrors of war, especially the horrors committed by the other side, but they were a good deal more attuned to its virtues: pride, courage, resourcefulness, endurance.

Peace was not viewed as the clear alternative to war in the seventeenth century, as it is today. It was merely a negative condition, the absence of war, the truce or hiatus between wars. The English philosopher Thomas Hobbes held that relations between separately organized societies would invariably be warlike; the English jurist John Selden put the same notion in a nutshell: "War is lawful, because God is the only judge betwixt two that are supreme." This was the predominant view, and pacifism as such—the principled abstention from all violence—scarcely existed.

Not all wars were equally good, of course. Civil war was a great evil, and the wars of the Turks were not to be praised. But war itself needed no justification, however particular wars might. It was the normal mode of relations between states. Treaties and alliances were predicated on it, banking developed in response to it, the conduct of trade reflected it.

The concept of war as the highest expression of a nation's virtue reached its height in the idea of *gloire,* a French term literally but inadequately translated by "glory." Honor, reputation, fame—all these went into *gloire.* Perhaps the nearest modern equivalent would be "dignity," but the poverty of the comparison only reveals how obsolete the concept has become. To "lose one's dignity" is to suffer momentary personal embarrassment; to lose one's *gloire* would have been moral death.

Gloire, as this suggests, was personal as well as national. Great noblemen had it; it was both the essence and effulgence of their nobility. But the greatest *gloire* of all was, of course, the king's. The *gloire* of the king and the nation were reciprocal; like facing mirrors, the glory of one was dazzlingly reflected on the surface of the other. It was fatally easy for a king to identify his personal ambition with the nation's interest, but a conscientious ruler would strive to keep the distinction clear. Louis XIV wrote to his son, who was impatient to win a battle in Flanders: "I too hope that you will be able to acquire much *gloire,* but since you ought always to think of the good of the state, I do not doubt that you will conduct yourself with wisdom and prudence as you tell me that you always do."

Gloire was not only acquired on the battlefield. The grandeur and magnificence of Versailles were part of it, the pomp of state ritual, the patronage of learning and the arts. So was Colbert's desire for economic preeminence. For France to have the best and greatest *gloire,* she had to outshine her rivals in everything, from the renown of her dramatists to the productivity of her cows. But the ultimate test of a nation was in war. That glory crowned all the rest. It was what everything else was for.

THE WARS OF LOUIS XIV: THE FIRST PHASE (1667–1688)

Louis XIV was not an impetuous man. He waited six years for his first war, an invasion of the Spanish Netherlands, prefaced it with a battery of legal documents proving that the territory should rightfully have "devolved" upon his wife, Maria Theresa, at the death of her father, Philip IV, and sent out an army three times the size of his opponent's. The result, the so-called War of Devolution (1667–1668), was more a promenade than a military campaign. Flanders fell swiftly, and Louis made a sudden swoop on Franche-Comté, another Spanish province of which he claimed a third. With his military situation impregnable, and all of Europe thoroughly alarmed at this show of strength, Louis magnanimously surrendered all his conquests save a dozen towns in the Spanish Netherlands by the Treaty of Aix-la-Chapelle. In secret, however, Louis had signed a treaty with the Emperor Leopold I, envisioning a vast partition of the whole Spanish Empire upon the momentarily expected death of the feeble Charles II.

Louis's first foray into European power politics revealed what were to be the enduring traits of his diplomacy: Cautious preparation and a shrewd grasp of advantage balanced against a fondness for bold strokes and an instinct for publicity; the grand schemes for empire and dominion and the modest nature of his practical expectations. But to his contemporaries, the French king seemed bent on unbridled aggression. England and the Netherlands rapidly patched up their latest trade war, and, with Sweden, entered into the first Triple Alliance (1668) against Louis. This casual reversal of alliances—France and the Netherlands were theoretically allies against decrepit Spain—was nothing new in European politics, but Louis was infuriated by it. The Dutch claimed credit for forcing him to make peace; an irreverent cartoon depicted Louis's sun obscured by a great Dutch cheese. In turn, he fulminated against the republic of "maggots" that France had helped to create and which now presumed to direct its affairs.

The Dutch War (1672–1678) was the most nakedly aggressive of Louis's wars, and the most successful. By a series of swift diplomatic maneuvers, the Dutch were virtually isolated. The English navy was bought for the promise of a permanent subsidy by the Treaty of Dover (1670); Sweden and Denmark were bribed to close the Baltic. Colbert's patient bill collecting had paid its dividend. The French army was now the most powerful in Europe, the French treasury the richest. Whom France could not beat, she could buy; whom she could not buy, she could beat.

The year 1672 was the Dutch *Rampjaar,* the Year of Disaster. French armies poured into the Seven Provinces almost unopposed, and Louis entered Utrecht in triumph. Jan de Witt, the grand pensionary of Holland, opened the dikes to save Amsterdam and desperately sued for peace. Louis flung down his terms: The cession of all conquered territory, payment of a huge indemnity, and the virtual surrender of Dutch sovereignty. It was one of the great mistakes of his career. The Dutch had no choice but to fight a war of survival. A mob in Amsterdam lynched de Witt, and the country turned, as so often before in crisis, to the House of Orange. The 22-year-old William III was elected *Stadhouder,* or chief magistrate, a position unoccupied since the death of his father in 1650, and soon became the uncrowned king of the Dutch Republic. William hastily sought new allies, created a diversion on the Rhine, and was able to launch a counteroffensive. By the end of the year, Louis's lightning campaign had turned into a war of attrition.

The war dragged on for six years. Louis could not be dislodged from his strong position, but neither could he advance. He turned his attention to his checkerboard frontier with Germany, attacking Luxemburg, the Palatinate, and Franche-Comté once again. But the war had no significant aim, the army was tattered, the treasury drained, the country rebellious. The Dutch florin had outbid the French livre, and Louis found himself being slowly surrounded by an ominous coalition of enemies. The merchants of Amsterdam, for their part, were equally tired of the ruinous war. In a leisurely, seventeenth-century fashion, both sides agreed they had had enough.

Louis got good terms at the Treaty of Nijmegen (1678), though not as good as he could have had six years before. The Dutch, a powerful foe, escaped unscathed; Spain, a weaker one, was made to pay the price instead. Franche-Comté was annexed, and ten towns in Flanders and Germany were added to France. Louis had strengthened the "borders" of France; Nijmegen was in many ways a favorable adjustment of the untidy frontier left 30 years before by the Peace of Westphalia. Sebastian de Vauban, Louis's chief military engineer and the first technocrat of modern warfare, immediately proceeded to build up the new strongholds. Increasingly, frontiers were ceasing to be an area of amorphous and disputed sovereignty between nations and tending to become fixed and fortified lines. Louis frankly considered that the petty principalities, bishoprics, and free towns that stood between France and the German heartland were obsolete, debris to be cleared away.

Louis XIV might well be pleased with the results of his first two wars. France in 1678 was the most powerful state in the world. An army of a quarter of a million men was at his command. The Dutch, his chief commercial rivals, had been dealt punishing blows. The emperor's tenuous grip on the Rhine was all but dissolved. Once-proud England had been reduced to a client state. Spain was only waiting to fall. But in William of Orange, Louis had raised up his own greatest nemesis. That dour and cramped Dutchman, who might but for the events of 1672 have passed his life in obscurity, the forgotten son of a forgotten ruler, was to be for 30 years the heart and soul of European opposition to Louis XIV. But it was only a second stroke of fortune, a second revolution, that enabled him to oppose the Sun King of France with a power nearly equal to his own.

A NEW KING FOR ENGLAND: WILLIAM OF ORANGE
AND THE GLORIOUS REVOLUTION

When Charles Stuart returned from exile in 1660 to pick up the crown that had been struck off with his father's head, it was neither as conqueror nor as deliverer, but simply as the last alternative. The great civil war and the political experiments of the Republic and Protectorate had failed to resolve England's constitutional crisis. The so-called Convention Parliament, which had been hastily summoned to greet Charles, rested on the ancient catchphrase that "the government is and ought to be by king, lords, and commons," without specifying what the relative distribution among the parts was to be. Charles, in turn, agreed to a program of general political amnesty, religious toleration, a property settlement approved by Parliament, and recognition of all laws to which Charles I had given assent, even under duress: in short, a confirmation of the existing economic status quo and a return to the political stalemate of 1641.

There was much popular support for Charles II, and his first regularly elected Parliament was so royalist and reactionary in tone that he kept it sitting for 17 years lest he get a worse one. But this Cavalier Parliament of monarchists and Anglicans proved as intractable as the Long Parliament of radicals and Puritans had been. In a series of acts, collectively named the Clarendon Code after Charles's chief minister (who in fact opposed them), Parliament reversed the policy of religious toleration and imposed such stringent restrictions and penalties on the practice of all non-Anglican forms of worship that it created a permanent body of dissenters, the Nonconformists, who to this day comprise about 10 percent of the Protestant population of England. This accomplished, Parliament passed a series of discriminatory tariffs and navigation acts against Scotland and Ireland, another snub to the Scottish Charles, and plunged into war with the Dutch. "I find myself almost the only man in my kingdom who doth not desire war," Charles said pitifully. Having forced the war upon him, Parliament denied

Charles the means to fight it, blamed him for the inevitable defeat, and took its revenge by cashiering the unpopular Clarendon.

Charles's great dilemma was his complete financial dependence on Parliament. By deliberately pauperizing the Crown, Parliament could keep it feeble and subservient. Charles's revenue was less than half what the autocrat Cromwell's had been, and his fixed expenses were far greater. The all-absorbing concern of his reign was to find sources of income outside Parliament. His marriage to the infanta Catherine of Portugal brought a dowry of 2 million crusados, but that was soon exhausted. The sale of Dunkirk, acquired under the Protectorate, provided another temporary windfall. At last there was nothing to sell but English foreign policy itself—and Charles sold it. By the Treaty of Dover (1670), Charles committed himself to Louis XIV's war against the Dutch, and, by a secret clause, to the restoration of Catholicism in England. In return for this, he was to receive an annual subsidy of £225,000.

Charles, though himself a secret Catholic, had no intention of turning the country back to Rome. His only plan was to get as much money as possible out of Louis XIV. His participation in the Dutch War was nominal, and when he signed a separate peace with the Netherlands in 1674, the French were obliged to pay as much for his neutrality as they had for his alliance. The climax came in 1678, when the House of Commons gave Charles £1 million to go to war with France, and the French gave him even more not to. Charles pocketed both sums, and dissolved Parliament.

This policy had its price, however. For nearly a decade, anti-Catholic hysteria had been building, nurtured by the corruption and intrigue that shrouded the Stuart court. The secret provisions of the Treaty of Dover were widely guessed at, and Charles's personal Catholicism was common knowledge. In September, 1678, a former naval chaplain and convicted perjurer named Titus Oates came forward with accusations of a bizarre plot to assassinate Charles and crown his openly Catholic brother James, Duke of York, as king. Twenty-four persons, including 17 priests, were hanged in the ensuing panic, and three successive parliaments tried to ram through an Exclusion Bill to bar the Duke of York from the throne.

When Charles II died in 1685, he had sired 14 illegitimate children, but his brother James was his only lawful successor. No two men could have been less alike. Charles was lax, indulgent, pragmatic, a master of compromise and guile. James—James II as he was now—was rigid, devout, and as open as the face of the morning. He pursued his goal of bringing England back into the Catholic church with such reckless ardor that even the pope was alarmed. James suspended acts of Parliament, placed Catholics in high civil and military positions, and called Irish troops into the country to cow his own subjects. While Jesuit proselytizers freely roamed the country, seven Anglican bishops were brought to trial for refusing to read a proclamation of toleration, only to be triumphantly acquitted by a London jury. On that same day—June 30, 1688—a group of prominent political leaders wrote to William of Orange and offered him the throne of England.

William had ten years earlier married the eldest daughter of James, who was thus his father-in-law. He had little interest in the English crown as such, but a great deal in its value in the European chess game. A militantly Catholic England, bound to France, would make Louis XIV invincible. This James II appeared to be speedily delivering him, and should any difficulty arise, the French fleet stood ready to resolve it. It seemed that all the money Louis had poured into England since the Treaty of Dover would finally pay its dividend. On the other hand, an Anglo-Dutch dynasty would provide a firm counterweight to Louis XIV's ambitions all over Europe. The English situation held both the greatest danger and the greatest promise; whichever way it turned, all of Europe might well turn with it.

Louis XIV was indecisive. A Dutch invasion might precipitate a second civil war in England, and a Dutch army tied down trying to save Protestantism across the Channel was a much better proposition than a French army wasted trying to uproot it. Louis had plans for a new war in Germany; he was distracted by new rumors of the impending death of Charles II of Spain; and besides, it was already too late in the year for the Dutch fleet to sail.

William of Orange thought otherwise. He rallied diplomatic support on the continent and political support in England, and having first been driven back by a "Catholic" wind and then pushed forward by a "Protestant" one, landed unopposed on the southern coast in November, 1688. It was immediately clear that nine-tenths of the population was ready to welcome him as a deliverer. James stood deserted and alone, his most trusted advisers having betrayed him. In desperation, he threw the Great Seal of the kingdom into the Thames, hoping to create anarchy, and then attempted to flee the country. Even in this James was unsuccessful. He was caught by some fishermen and brought back to London. His son-in-law William, embarrassed, arranged a second "escape." This time there was no hitch. James II had come at last to Versailles, not with the gift of England, but as a penniless exile.

William's great gamble had tipped the balance—and incidentally changed the course of English history. In January, 1689, he and his wife became joint monarchs as William III and Mary II of England. It was just in time. No sooner had William landed in England than Louis XIV declared war on the United Provinces. Already, French armies were ravaging Germany. Europe had begun the trial of strength that was to last a generation.

A WORLD AT WAR (1688–1713)

The war that broke out in 1688, known as the War of the League of Augsburg and resumed after a brief hiatus on a wider scale and for grander stakes as the War of the Spanish Succession, has been described by historians as the first world war. More men fought in it, and died in it, than in any previous war in human history. Directly or indirectly, it involved the destinies of five continents. And although its principal objective was the containment of a great Western power, France, its final result was to confirm the westward drift of power in Europe more than ever before.

In the years after the Treaty of Nijmegen, Louis XIV showed that he could

win as much by peace as by war. French courts called chambers of reunion were
set up to unearth old claims in the frontier province of Alsace, whose people
plainly regarded themselves as German, although their legal status had been un-
clear since the time of the Thirty Years' War. From pseudolegal "reunion" to
outright seizure was a short step. In September, 1681, Louis annexed the free
city of Strassburg, while the churches of France sang Te Deums for three days.
The principalities of Zweibrücken (Swedish), Luxemburg (Spanish), and Orange
(Prince William's own hereditary province) were next. Spain, in a futile gesture,
declared war on France alone; the only result was a devastating French bombard-
ment of the Spanish Netherlands and the reduction of the free city of Genoa,
which had had the temerity to allow Spain to recruit troops on its soil. The hastily
patched-up truce of Ratisbon (1684) confirmed the French conquests for 20 years;
Louis did not doubt that there would be time in plenty to make them permanent.

The ease of Louis's triumphs was made possible by the most serious Turkish
threat to European security in 150 years. In 1683, given safe passage up the Danube by a rebellious Hungary, a Turkish army of 200,000 marched virtually unopposed up to the gates of Vienna and lay siege to the imperial capital and its 14,000
defenders. Emperor Leopold appealed to all Europe for help, and in Catholic
countries men and money were raised as for a crusade. Louis XIV replied to a
personal appeal from the pope that princes did not fight holy wars anymore, but
His Most Christian Majesty did make the gesture of raising the siege of Luxemburg while that of Vienna was going on. Finally, a relief force of 70,000 men under
King John Sobieski of Poland reached the beleaguered city, and, in the words
of a contemporary English account:

> After a Siege of Sixty days, accompanied with a Thousand Difficulties, Sick-
> nesses, Want of Provisions, and great Effusion of Blood, after a Million of Can-
> non and Musquet Shot, Bombs, Granadoes, and all sorts of Fireworks, which
> has changed the Face of the fairest and most flourishing City in the World,
> . . . Heaven favourably heard the Prayers and Tears of a Cast-down and Mourn-
> ful People, and retorted the Terror on a powerful Enemy, and drove him from
> the Walls of Vienna.

The victory of John Sobieski's vastly outnumbered army on the heights outside Vienna was justly celebrated as the event of the century. The war thus begun
went on for 16 years and drove the Turks permanently from the Danube valley.
Had France joined the Hapsburg coalition, it would certainly have accomplished
more, perhaps the permanent expulsion of the Ottoman Empire from Europe.
But Louis XIV was far more worried about the consequences of an Austrian victory than a Turkish one, and so achieved by inaction the most lasting result of
his reign: the preservation of Moslem power on the continent until the early twentieth century.

Over the years, the French king had developed a progressive fear of encir-
clement and invasion. The success of Hapsburg armies outside Belgrade seemed
a direct threat to the security of Paris. The accession of a prince to one of the
petty states of the Rhine who was not firmly in the French orbit immediately

raised the specter of a vast Germanic coalition against France. So it was that when French armies invaded the Rhenish Palatinate in September, 1688, to enforce the claims of Louis's sister-in-law to the province, Versailles issued a declaration blaming the war on the wicked schemes of the House of Hapsburg. As usual, Louis had had no choice but to resist the menace of armies 1000 miles from the nearest French frontier.

Louis and his war minister, Louvois, envisioned a rapid campaign. Neither the treasury nor the army was provided for a long war. The strategic object of the attack was to create a diversion to keep the badly beaten Turks on their feet, while simultaneously "rectifying" the French frontier a little deeper into Germany. From the Swiss border to the Spanish Netherlands, Louis had constructed the most formidable network of fortifications ever seen in Europe, but this was not enough security. Not only must the Palatinate be captured, it must be leveled, lest any future invader of France make use of it. Louvois drew the map of cities, castles, and villages marked for destruction: Mannheim, Tübingen, Heidelberg, Heilbronn, Worms, Eslingen, Oppenheim, Spier . . . The campaign of 1688–1689 was a winter of devastation that surpassed the worst ravages of the Thirty Years' War. Even the soldiers, sated with spoil, rebelled against the brutal and tedious work of demolition. But Louis was ever more insistent. Louvois wrote threatening letters to his generals: "His Majesty sees with pain that you have not taken the steps necessary to carry out his orders. . . . Let me tell you that there is nothing worse than half executing orders the King has given you. . . . His Majesty is angry. Everything must be burned."

The imaginary enemy who obliged Louis XIV to burn so many towns soon turned into a real one. Germany united as never before against him, and in September, 1689, William III, who had lost his principality of Orange but gained England, signed a treaty of alliance with Emperor Leopold of Austria. Within a year, Spain, Sweden, and Savoy had joined the alliance, along with the previously uncommitted princes of northern Germany. Even the Elector of Brandenburg, France's one reliable ally in the Dutch War, now joined the opposition. The original League of Augsburg (1686), a half-desperate, half-defiant nucleus of German princes, had now become a Europe-wide coalition.

The French, giving up Germany, fell back on their fortifications. Louis's engineer, Vauban, had built well, for seven years of fighting would fail to dislodge them. At Fleurus in Belgium (July, 1690), an allied invasion was broken up, and a few days later a naval success at Beachy Head enabled the French to create a flanking attack in Ireland with an army led by the deposed James II. But the Irish campaign failed at the Boyne River, and after some big but indecisive battles along the Rhine, the war settled down to the usual stalemate of siege, attrition, and secret diplomacy.

The Treaty of Ryswick (1697) reflected the lack of a clear military outcome. It was actually more in the nature of a private truce between William III and Louis XIV, with the emperor a grudging and unsatisfied cosignatory. Louis agreed to recognize William's crown, to return the principality of Orange, and to allow the Dutch to garrison fortresses in Flanders. William returned some conquests he had made in the New World (where the conflict was known as King

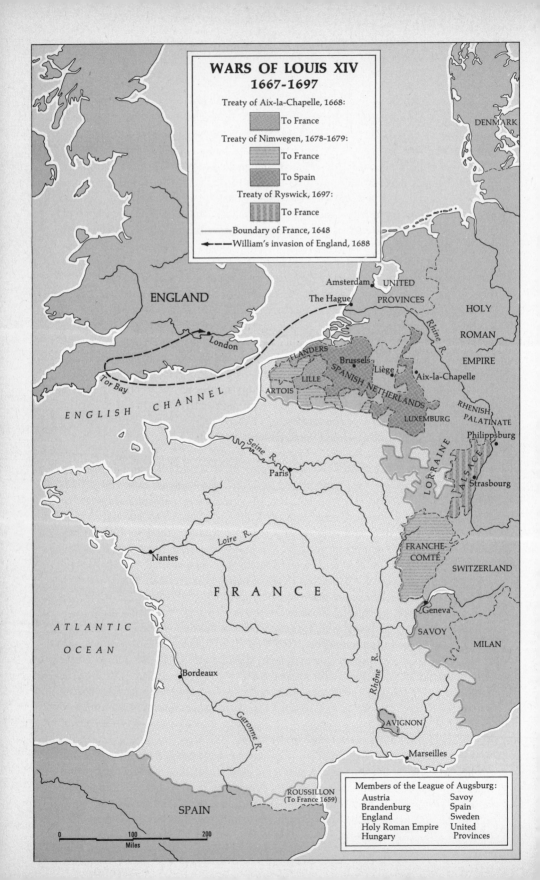

WARS OF LOUIS XIV
1667-1697

Treaty of Aix-la-Chapelle, 1668:

    To France

Treaty of Nimwegen, 1678-1679:

    To France

    To Spain

Treaty of Ryswick, 1697:

    To France

––––––– Boundary of France, 1648

– – – ▶ William's invasion of England, 1688

DENMARK

ENGLAND

Amsterdam · UNITED

The Hague · PROVINCES

HOLY

London · ROMAN

Tor Bay

EMPIRE

Rhine R.

FLANDERS

Brussels · Liège

SPANISH NETHERLANDS · Aix-la-Chapelle

ENGLISH CHANNEL

ARTOIS

LILLE

RHENISH PALATINATE

LUXEMBURG

Seine R.

Philippsburg

LORRAINE

ALSACE

Paris

Strasbourg

Loire R.

FRANCHE-COMTÉ

SWITZERLAND

Nantes

F R A N C E

ATLANTIC

OCEAN

Geneva

SAVOY

MILAN

Rhône R.

Bordeaux

Garonne R.

AVIGNON

Marseilles

ROUSSILLON
(To France 1659)

SPAIN

| 0 | 100 | 200 |
Miles

Members of the League of Augsburg:

Austria	Savoy
Brandenburg	Spain
England	Sweden
Holy Roman Empire	United
Hungary	Provinces

William's War) and rescinded his objections to French retention of Strassburg and Alsace. The emperor considered this a betrayal and signed the treaty only on the last permitted day. But it was Leopold who gained most from the peace. His armies, freed from service in the west, won a smashing victory over the Turks at Zenta and forced them to sue for peace (Treaty of Karlowitz, 1699). The broad conquests he had made in the east more than compensated the temporary set-backs on the Rhine. The imperial House of Hapsburg, whose influence in Germany had grown progressively weaker since the days of Charles V, had gained a new base of power in the Danube basin, which was to produce in time a fundamental realignment of European politics.

Thirty years had passed since the youthful monarchs, Louis and Leopold, had signed their secret treaty to partition the Spanish empire on the imminently expected death of Charles II. The two kings had fought mighty wars and come to the threshold of old age, and Charles was still living. A full account of all the intrigues and alliances, the claims and renunciations, the reams of legal and gene-alogical argument that had swirled about the issue of the Spanish throne would take volumes. It came down finally to two basic questions, however: Would Charles II's successor be a Hapsburg, a Bourbon, or some neutral third party? Would the Spanish empire remain intact or be partitioned to compensate the los-ing candidates?

For the first time in his life, Louis XIV strove sincerely to avoid a war. As Charles apparently lay dying in Madrid, he agreed with William III on a compro-mise candidate, Prince Joseph Ferdinand of Bavaria, but four months later Joseph died, a boy of 6, and Charles was still alive. Next, Louis, who had little hope that a French candidate could be approved in Madrid, agreed to recognize the Hapsburg claimant as heir to Spain, the Spanish Netherlands, and the Americas, asking only for southern Italy and the province of Lorraine in return. Leopold refused. He knew that the Spanish themselves were unalterably opposed to any partition and gambled on winning the entire inheritance.

On November 1, 1700, Charles II died. His will, made public immediately, astonished Europe. Charles had left Spain and the empire not to the Archduke Charles of Austria but to Philip of Anjou, the grandson of Louis XIV. The will did stipulate that the French and Spanish crowns were never under any circum-stances to be united, but Louis, in accepting it, firmly repudiated this clause, and Philip was third in line for the throne of France.

By this and other actions, Louis made clear to Europe that he now regarded Spain as a province of France. Italy was turned over to French administrators, French merchants took over the Spanish slave trade, and a military pact between France, Spain, and Portugal closed the ports of the Iberian peninsula to the Anglo-Dutch fleet, thus putting a stranglehold on the Mediterranean. Louis has often been criticized for these actions, which seemed directly aimed at provoking war. In fact, he was merely getting the jump on a war that had become inevitable when Leopold had refused to reach a settlement. Once the Spanish inheritance had become an all-or-nothing affair, it was certain that neither sovereign could acquiesce in such an enormous expansion of power on the part of the other.

Once again, therefore, Europe united to contain France. On September 7,

The Sun King: Louis XIV.

1701, England, Austria, and the Netherlands entered what would come to be known as the Grand Alliance. Most of the German states fell promptly into line. The terms of the alliance were not entirely to the emperor's liking, as William III continued to insist on a partition settlement. It was, indeed, the only realistic solution to the problem, but to get anyone to agree publicly to what everyone privately knew would require the bloodiest war in human history.

The Grand Alliance was William III's last work; six months later, in March, 1702, he was dead. Leopold I died in 1705, after a reign of nearly 50 years. A new generation carried on the war of their fathers. Only Louis XIV remained to the end, surviving his children, his statesmen, his generals, his adversaries, and his time.

The French, with their vastly extended frontier, had the advantage in the early years of the war. Making alliance with Bavaria, they moved into Germany from Italy and cut it in two. A serious revolt in Hungary, financed by Louis, gave Austria trouble on its eastern flank. Only at sea did the allies prosper, but the basic differences in their war aims, the unparalleled scope and complexity of the fighting, the reluctance of the English, and the timidity of the Dutch after William's death placed the entire alliance in jeopardy.

It was two great commanders who at last forced the war toward a conclusion. Prince Eugene of Savoy, the victor of Zenta, Italian by blood, French by birth and upbringing, had joined the Hapsburg cause after being denied a commission by Louis XIV. President of the Imperial War Council and chairman of the Privy Conference of Ministers, Eugene devoted himself to the House of Austria with the fervor of a religious convert. A far different man was the amiably unprincipled Duke of Marlborough. Born plain John Churchill, the son of obscure English gentry, he had betrayed the man who made him, James II, in the Revolution of 1688, skillfully climbed the ladder of favor under William, and emerged as the principal confidant of the new queen, Anne. What redeemed Marlborough was military genius. While his brother-in-law Sidney Godolphin held together a series of shaky coalition governments behind him, he took command of the Anglo-Dutch army and pressed the war home to France. No other commander before Napoleon ever dominated a whole military epoch as did Marlborough. At Blenheim in Bavaria (1704), he smashed the French campaign in Germany; at Ramillies (1706) and Oudenarde (1708), he drove Louis from Flanders and, with Prince Eugene, invaded France itself.

It was the darkest moment of Louis's reign. The winter of 1708–1709 brought another devastating famine, the inevitable result of the war. A bitter parody circulated at court: "Our father who art at Versailles, whose name is no longer hallowed, whose kingdom is no longer large, give us our daily bread. . . ." Louis sued for peace. But the allies made the same mistake that Louis himself had made with the Dutch in 1672: They laid down terms that made any defeat preferable to surrender. France was not only to give up every foot of soil won in the last 50 years but to join forces with the allies to drive Philip V from the Spanish throne. "Since I have to make war," Louis responded, "I would rather fight against my enemies than my children." A last army was raised, poorly armed and badly fed. "I am humble," wrote its commander, Marshal Villars, "when I see the back-breaking labor men perform without food." He would have been humbler still had he seen the tens of thousands of civilians who would starve to make his campaign possible. But at Malplaquet, on the very borderline of present-day France, he saved the war for Louis. Though Marlborough was left in possession of the field, technically victorious, he had lost so many men that he could go no farther.

Two years later, in 1711, Emperor Joseph I died and was succeeded by the archduke, Charles. Charles continued to seek the Spanish throne, and this effectively ended the war. The English and the Dutch would not fight to give him what they had tried for a decade to keep from the French: the direct union of one of Europe's two major powers with Spain. At Utrecht in 1713 they made peace with Louis, and the following year, left alone in the field, Charles VI followed suit at Rastadt.

The Peace of Utrecht, as the complex of treaties which ended the war is known to history, left Spain and the overseas empire to Philip V but ceded the Spanish Netherlands and Italy to Austria. The Dutch received so many commercial and military concessions in the new Austrian Netherlands, however, that they actually controlled the area. England took the small but strategic positions of Gibraltar and Minorca from Spain and Newfoundland and Nova Scotia from France. The French managed to keep Strassburg and Alsace; the allies, trying to turn the clock back 50 years in 1709, had to settle for 30 in 1713. It was a

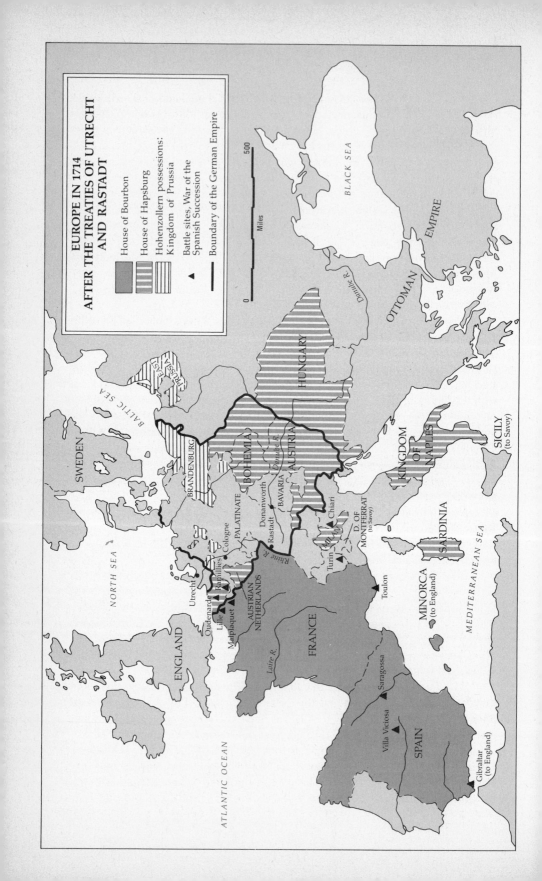

EUROPE IN 1714
AFTER THE TREATIES OF UTRECHT
AND RASTADT

House of Bourbon
House of Hapsburg
Hohenzollern possessions:
Kingdom of Prussia
Battle sites, War of the
Spanish Succession
Boundary of the German Empire

0   500
Miles

BLACK SEA

OTTOMAN
EMPIRE

DANUBE R.

BALTIC SEA

SWEDEN

PRUSSIA

BRANDENBURG

BOHEMIA

HUNGARY

AUSTRIA

PALATINATE

Cologne

Donauworth
Rastadt
BAVARIA
Danube R.

KINGDOM
OF
NAPLES

SICILY
(to Savoy)

NORTH SEA

ENGLAND

Utrecht
Oudenarde
Lille
Ramillies
Malplaquet
AUSTRIAN
NETHERLANDS

Rhine R.

MILAN
Turin
Chiari
D. OF
MONTFERRAT
(to Savoy)

SARDINIA

ATLANTIC OCEAN

FRANCE

Loire R.

Toulon

MINORCA
(to England)

MEDITERRANEAN SEA

SPAIN

Saragossa
Villa Viciosa

Gibraltar
(to England)

peace that pleased no one after a war fought for nothing. The allies lamented the better terms they could have had earlier. The Dutch felt betrayed by the English, and the Austrians felt betrayed by everyone. In England, which on balance fared best, the peace was so unpopular that the queen was forced to add 12 courtiers to the House of Lords to ram it through, and the great hero, Marlborough, was ignominiously sacked.

Yet the peace had important consequences. England had emerged as a great power; through war it had finally laid to rest the civil strife that had crippled it for a century, and it stood poised in 1713 on the brink of an era that was to transform it from a relatively minor state on the periphery of Europe to the mightiest empire in the history of the world. The great power of the sixteenth century, Spain, had at last been laid to rest at the beginning of the eighteenth, stripped of all that the powers of Europe wished to have of it. The House of Austria, weakened by its great gains in the long run, was more of a dynasty and less of a nation than ever before, its vulnerable frontiers scattered from the North Sea to the remote mountains of Transylvania. In an age whose future belonged to the compact and efficient, it was an unwieldy anachronism, a throwback to a bygone order of political organization; in inheriting the lands of Spain, Austria had also inherited its destiny.

As for France, it remained, despite defeat, the greatest power in Europe. If anything demoralized it, it was the immense longevity of Louis XIV. The year of Utrecht was the seventieth year he had worn the crown. Since the turn of the century, the country had looked forward to the succession, but Louis lived on, a little slower, a little stouter, but as vigorous as ever: The King's wife, Madame de Maintenon, was often heard to complain of his attentions. By 1712, he had survived both son and grandson, and his heir was a child of 2. In the summer of 1715, a black spot appeared on his leg. It grew larger: a fatal gangrene. The king had two weeks to prepare his final *coucher.* His servants, his ministers, his nephew, his wife, and his heir were all called in turn; to each he bade farewell. On September 1, 1715, Louis XIV died. He had lived longer than any French king before him; he had reigned longer than anyone else in history.

Few men have dominated their time as long and as thoroughly as Louis XIV. Many of his contemporaries surpassed him as men. He lacked the sheer genius of Newton, the moral intelligence of Fénelon, the soldierly heroism of Prince Eugene. Stripped of the persona of a king, he appears a very ordinary man indeed. But Louis was a king, and that is the whole fact about him. His very lack of imagination enabled him to play the role of a king as no one else before him could. One might liken him to a great actor determined to exploit a demanding role to the limit of its possibilities (except that Louis was not acting), and in a very real sense he exhausted the possibilities of kingship. After Louis XIV, what was there left to say?

Politically, too, the very achievements of Louis XIV were to make monarchy as he understood it obsolete. Louis's remarkable innovations in government and military organization, which make him a pioneer of the modern state, were made in the service of a traditional and even reactionary ideal. Louis centralized state power not to create a model of bureaucratic efficiency but to magnify the majesty and *gloire* of the French throne. If the modern state, in its dispersion of power and responsibility, has aptly been called the rule of Nobody, then the administration of Louis XIV is its exact antithesis. Everything in it was designed to culminate in the king. No council, agency, or minister had any function or existence apart from him. No initiative or decision could be taken without his knowledge and consent.

Louis himself was thus the strength and weakness of his own system, and if he had shown how much could be accomplished by royal absolutism, he had also shown its limitations. The English king had become a constitutional monarch by the Revolution of 1688, his powers sharply circumscribed by Parliament, but by that very token, government itself had become stronger, because it was now the permanent responsibility of a whole ruling class and not merely the private preserve of a single person. The Bank of England, backed by Parliament and the Treasury, became within a few years of its founding in 1694 the most important economic institution in Europe, capable of raising millions of pounds. By contrast, France was still in the primitive stage of tax farming, with a parasitic aristocracy that siphoned off the best resources of the kingdom. The French king was absolute, but his theoretically unlimited powers produced far less revenue and hence far less real freedom of action. The English were to prove in the eighteenth century what the Dutch had suggested in the seventeenth: that a politically stable oligarchy with a moderately representative base could be a far more effective instrument of government than an absolute monarchy built upon a fossilized system of privilege. Louis XIV was the culmination of the monarchic principle in the West; he was also the first harbinger of its decline.

three

Expansion and Empire

In 1699, Sebastian de Vauban, Louis XIV's great military engineer, wrote a memorandum to the king. The emperor of Austria, he suggested, was not France's great enemy, and the occupancy of the Spanish throne would not decide the destiny of Europe. France had already acquired as much territory in Europe as it could comfortably assimilate. The future belonged not to the power that could nibble off another Italian duchy or German archbishopric but to those who succeeded in the race to exploit the wealth of the New World. He urged the creation of large colonies in Canada and the Mississippi basin. Only by becoming a world power, Vauban argued, could France ultimately remain a European one.

Vauban was a true prophet. It was not the power of Austria nor even the genius of Marlborough that defeated France in the War of the Spanish Succession, but the seemingly endless reserves of wealth the English and Dutch could draw on to put army after army in the field; this wealth came from empire. Nor was it a coincidence that these two great powers had no territorial ambitions on the continent. The Dutch remained content with their little landspit on the North Sea that was barely a twentieth the size of France, and England, which for five centuries after the Norman Conquest had been futilely embroiled in European wars, had ceded its last continental possession in 1558 and, apart from Dunkirk and Gibraltar, never sought another. France, which shared with them the long Atlantic coastline, failed to profit by their example. Historically magnetized by the center of Europe, France came late to empire, and its two great attempts to dominate the continent—under Louis XIV at the beginning of the eighteenth century and under Napoleon at the beginning of the nineteenth—were both frustrated by a coalition of imperial powers, first England and the Dutch, then Britain and Russia.

In diplomatic terms, then, the entire period 1660–1815 might be looked upon as the containment of France by Europe, just as the period 1871–1945 was preoccupied with the containment of Germany. But if one withdraws a little from the map of the continent, as Vauban vainly urged Louis XIV to do, the most striking and ultimately significant thing about Europe in the eighteenth century is the immense expansion of its borders. Britain in the west girdled half the globe with its empire, while Russia, which had barely even figured before in European history, simultaneously embarked on its great conquest of central Asia and marched halfway into eastern Europe.

ENGLAND: THE BACKGROUND TO EMPIRE

The English Revolution of 1688 had returned Parliament once again triumphant to power, but it seemed to bring the country no closer to a resolution of the struggle between the royal executive and the House of Commons that had plagued it for the entire century. The Commons seized their victory to impose a set of conditions, the Bill of Rights, on their new monarch, William III. The executive practice of suspending acts of Parliament was declared illegal, as was the raising of money or the creation of commissions or courts of inquiry outside of Parliament. All these tactics had been applied by Charles II and James II in the previous ten years, and all of them had certainly been abused; yet to curb them permanently was to take away much of what Old Regime Europe understood as legitimate royal power. What was left to a king who could not levy his own taxes, could not create his own councils, and was constrained to obey laws he might abhor? There was still the army, of course, and Parliament thought of that next. No standing army might be maintained in the kingdom in time of peace without its consent, the Bill of Rights declared. Three subsequent acts completed what came to be known as the Revolutionary Settlement. The Toleration Act of 1689 granted the right of public worship to Protestant Nonconformists, though they were still debarred from holding public office; the Triennial Act of 1694 provided that parliaments be called at least every three years; and the Act of Settlement (1701) removed the judiciary from royal control and forbade Crown councillors to sit in the House of Commons. Henceforth the Commons was to be free of the corrupting influence of royal ministers and officeholders—or so at least it was thought.

This was a lot more than William of Orange had bargained for when he consented to become William III of England. To a councillor in the Netherlands he wrote, "I am persuaded that you and I have on our hands the most troublesome affairs in all Europe." Yet the problem for England in the turbulent generation after the Revolution of 1688 was not an enfeebled executive but a divided Parliament. During the latter part of Charles II's reign, two major factions had arisen over the question of excluding the future James II from the throne. The exclusionists, or Whigs, were the descendants of the radical gentry of the civil war. They believed in parliamentary supremacy, an aggressive foreign policy, and the expansion of trade. The antiexclusionists, or Tories, were in general more tra-ditional and conservative. They believed in kingship as the natural form of human government and were anxious to support the rather muddled compromise that had brought Charles II to the throne in 1660. They backed Charles in his last years as the only alternative to worse, but they drew the line at James II, and it was their reluctant and heavy-hearted decision to abandon the Crown in 1688 that doomed the Stuart monarchy.

The Revolution had ended this debate; Parliament had won. But the Whigs and Tories remained, warring no longer for principles but now for spoils. This was a natural outcome. Royal power had been indivisible, but parliamentary seats were up for grabs, and whoever controlled Parliament controlled the country. There were some 200,000 voters in England in 1688 out of a population of 5.5 million, very far short of what we would today recognize as a representative de-mocracy, but by the same token far too many to be easily dominated by one group or spoken for by one opinion. The result was that the Whigs and Tories, factions that had sprung up to debate an issue long since obsolete, hardened into perma-nent political parties—the first parties in modern political history and the direct ancestors of the two-party system today.

It must be borne in mind that the division between Whigs and Tories more often represented differences of opinion than differences of principle, more the careers of individual politicians than the destiny of the nation. Both parties, their adherents, and the electorate to which they appealed were all part of a coherent and unified ruling class based on land and trade. They had settled the one question that had seriously threatened their unity, the relations between king and Parlia-ment, and if the settlement was not equally to everyone's satisfaction—loyalty to divine right died hard in some Tory breasts—there was broad agreement to support it. Yet party strife, even if over secondary issues, could seriously hamper the functioning of government. Between 1689 and 1715, there were 12 general elections, more than in any other comparable period of parliamentary history, and each more bitterly fought than the last. Ministries toppled like matchsticks as the politicians sought combinations that could win the confidence of Parlia-ment. Moreover, the disunity of Parliament could only play into the hands of the king, who was still the constitutional head of government and regarded the politicians who conducted policy as his ministers. Parliament had won the strug-gle for sovereignty but had not succeeded in ruling. Before it could govern the nation, it must first learn to govern itself.

The solution to this problem was a politician of genius, Sir Robert Walpole, and a system of political management: patronage. Walpole, the son of a prosper-ous Norfolk squire whose estates went back to the twelfth century, rose slowly but steadily through the Whig hierarchy. There were more brilliant men in En-gland, but none better attuned to his age. Walpole understood how to make the system work. For 40 years he sat in the House of Commons, for 30 he held high office, and for 20—from 1722 to 1742—he was the effective ruler of the country, the first prime minister of England.

What made Walpole's success—and 50 years of Whig domina-tion—possible was the succession crisis of 1714. When William III died in 1702, his throne passed peacefully to Princess Anne, James II's daughter and the last surviving Stuart in England. But when Anne died childless in 1714, the choice lay between James Edward, the son born to James II in 1688, and George, Elector of Hanover, who had been designated Anne's successor by the Act of Settlement of 1701: in short, between the legitimate blood heir to the throne and the foreign ruler whose only claim was an act of Parliament. The Whigs, children of the Revolution, had supported Hanover from the beginning; the Tories, who had acquiesced in 1701, were divided when the moment of reckoning came. Some of them supported an ill-fated rebellion in Scotland on James Edward's behalf in 1715, and the whole party was branded with the stigma of treason. Thereafter, control of the government no longer meant control of Parliament but only of the Whig party, and within seven years Walpole, having achieved the latter, was within reach of the former.

Walpole's political philosophy was simple: He summed it all up in his own famous phrase, "Let sleeping dogs lie." The smooth operation of business and government was not to be impeded by ideology. The machine he constructed for this purpose is the dream of every politician; when asked which political figure from England's past they admired the most, both the Conservative Harold Macmillan* and the Laborite Harold Wilson† unhesitatingly replied, "Robert Walpole."

Walpole's success was based on the triad of Crown, Parliament, and patronage. The support of two kings—George I until 1727, then George II—was his anchor. He consulted their wishes, cultivated their prejudices, and flattered their mistresses; with them behind him he was, if not impregnable, at least exceedingly well entrenched; without them (for the Crown still had the last word on all honors and promotions), he could not possibly have survived. To both sovereigns, German-born and ill at ease with English institutions (George I spoke little of the language), Walpole was an oracle, the only reliable guide in a strange new world.

Walpole displayed equal mastery in Parliament. A superb debater and an expert on procedure, he had a sixth sense for the moods and whims of the House of Commons. But Walpole had more to offer than dexterity and eloquence. For the faithful, there was the ultimate reward of a government job. Before Walpole, patronage had been scattered throughout the various departments: The lord chancellor, the commander in chief, the commissioners of customs and excise, and others, all controlled jobs in their own bailiwicks. Walpole put these plums in his own pocket, and by dispensing them judiciously in return for good behavior and correct votes, he was able both to control the Commons and to build an administrative machine loyal to and dependent on him alone. The only hitch in the scheme was the provision in the Act of Settlement that no government officeholder could sit in the House of Commons. Literally interpreted, this meant that as soon as an MP was rewarded for voting the party line, he would cease to be able to vote; that is, literally interpreted, it would make the whole system impossible. Walpole got around this provision by simply ignoring it, just as he answered

*Prime Minister, 1957–1963.
†Prime Minister, 1964–1970, 1974–1976.

charges of bribery and corruption by blandly pleading guilty. If it took corruption to provide stable government and general prosperity, was corruption not a virtue; and if men could be better ruled by appealing to their greed than to their honor or highest beliefs, was greed then a vice?

Walpole's system was essentially an appeal to the English ruling class to stop rocking its own boat. It was skillful and flexible enough to survive for a century; England alone among the major powers of Europe withstood the era of the French Revolution with neither revolution nor collapse.

Walpole had created the political preconditions to empire; equally important were the economic ones. The Bank of England, founded in 1694 by a group of London merchants to help the government float an emergency loan of £1.5 million for the war against Louis XIV, soon became the cornerstone of the British economy. In principle, the Bank was similar to the semipublic banks that already existed in Sweden, the Netherlands, and some of the Italian cities. It would receive 8 percent interest from the government per year (William III had been borrowing abroad at almost twice as much) and pay its ordinary subscribers 4 percent. In political terms, it bound the new regime and the money lords of London together into an indissoluble alliance, and did more to ensure the success of the Revolution than anything else; as such, it was a stroke of genius comparable only to the way in which Henry VIII had bound men of property to the Protestant Reformation 150 years before by sharing with them the spoils of the Catholic church. In economic terms, it gave the government for the first time a regular, stable, and virtually unlimited source of credit. It also created the first systematic public debt, that is, the first public debt created with no real intention of ever paying it off. The entire governmental debt of England in 1688 was £644,000; only six years later, the government was proposing to borrow more than twice that amount at a single gulp. Although a provision for terminating the Bank and paying off the debt was written into the act of Parliament that chartered it, none of its sponsors seriously expected that this would ever be done. Twenty years later, at the end of the War of the Spanish Succession, the debt stood at £54 million. It may well be said that deficit financing made modern warfare possible, and with it the modern state. As Christopher Hill has wryly observed, "A national debt is the only collective possession of most modern peoples: The richer they are, the more deeply they are in debt."

The concentration of financial and political power implicit in the Bank was disturbing to many. Would not the government's ready access to money enable it to bypass Parliament and thereby defeat the whole purpose of the Revolution? The small Tory squires in the country, who bore the brunt of ordinary taxation, saw the whole scheme as a conspiracy between London bankers and the Treasury to get rich at their expense. They tried to start their own bank two years later, but the big money boycotted them, and they failed abysmally. It was already clear that this was a Whig world.

A more sophisticated threat to the Bank of England was the South Sea Company. Founded in hopes of cashing in on the riches that were expected to flow from the dismemberment of the Spanish empire, its directors—originally Tories, but now including highly placed Whigs—put forward a bold proposal.

They would take over the entire public debt at a lower rate of interest than the Bank, enabling the government to gradually pay off the principal with the difference. The debt and the Bank would thus be liquidated together, with the Company taking over its functions.

This appealed to many who not only resented the Bank's influence but were bewildered by the new finance and horrified at the size of the debt. The idea came from John Law, a Scottish promoter who had reorganized French governmental finances by combining the idea of a national bank with a monopolistic trading company. Law had raised capital by issuing paper money through the national bank with the government's credit behind it; the South Sea Company tried to accomplish the same thing by deliberately inflating its stock. A gullible public was sold on prospects of untold wealth from the New World, while the Company rammed its scheme through Parliament with massive bribes. King George I became honorary head of the Company, and South Sea stock soared to ten times its par value in June, 1720. Inevitably, the bubble burst, ruining thousands of investors; at the same moment, Law's experiment collapsed in France, thus creating the first two financial panics of modern capitalism.

The South Sea Bubble is an almost classic story of human cupidity and ignorance; yet it must be considered within the context of the great monetary revolution of which it was a part. Men who had always dealt in tens of thousands of pounds were suddenly dealing in tens of millions, while trying to teach the public how a nation could owe itself as much as it was worth without being bankrupt. By the mid-1720s, Great Britain (now including Scotland, joined to it by the Act of Union in 1707), was politically and financially the best-governed state in Europe, and on the verge of being the richest and most powerful as well.

THE FIRST BRITISH EMPIRE

The New World was two centuries old at the turn of the eighteenth century. To each man it meant his own dream: to the adventurer, gold; to the planter, profit; to the dissenter, freedom; to the politician, glory; to the missionary, salvation. The actual problems to be faced and gains to be expected were seldom assessed realistically. The risks were always high, and men would not undertake them unless their hopes were equally high. The result was often failure and sometimes disaster, and many a brave beginning guttered out for lack of systematic support from home. It could not have been otherwise: a random, haphazard, uncoordinated attempt to settle and exploit two vast continents that stretched from pole to pole by tiny nations in their wooden ships, always at cross-purposes to one another and likely as not at war. The remarkable thing was not how little it had accomplished but how much. By 1700, every major western European power had established a permanent enclave in the New World. The best land—that is, the most commercially profitable—had been staked out; there were few places left to go that would be likely to repay the investment. The colonies had been acquired largely by private enterprise, but they would have to be defended by state power, and to be worth defending they would have to be made to pay. Thus, colonies were increasingly viewed as adjuncts to the economy of the mother country in a closed system of trade. The age of adventure was over.

No single state in 1700 could claim a preponderance of power in the New World. The Spanish empire was the largest as well as the oldest. Historically, it had been the most profitable. But much of its wealth was now drained away in smuggling, and Spain was so feeble that the question was whether it would itself survive, let alone its empire. Portugal, too, had built a great empire in the sixteenth century, but most of it was gone, and with a home population of scarcely a million, it was unable to exploit what was left. The Dutch empire was afloat; their fleet drove the Portuguese from the Far East and preyed mercilessly on the colonial commerce of others. But they too had shot their bolt; the long wars with France had begun to take their toll. The future clearly belonged to the newcomers, England and France.

The British colonial enterprise had grown steadily if unspectacularly throughout the seventeenth century. It comprised a narrow strip of territory between the Appalachian mountains and the Atlantic seaboard running to near the mouth of the St. Lawrence River on the coast of North America, and a number of islands in the Caribbean, of which the most important were Jamaica (acquired 1655) and Barbados (acquired 1627). Economically, the colonies divided into three distinct areas. The Caribbean islands and the area from Virginia south on the American seaboard were plantation colonies: large estates, modeled on those of the Portuguese in Brazil, growing tropical crops (sugar, tobacco, coffee) that had become indispensable luxuries on the European market. The middle colonies of Maryland, Delaware, Pennsylvania, New Jersey, and New York produced staple grain crops and timber, but these Europe could produce for itself; most of them went into intercolonial trade with the Caribbean. The New England colonies were least valuable of all, and their ships competed—often illicitly—with the British fleet itself. Politically, too, they were the most intractable, having been settled by religious dissidents who developed stubbornly independent habits. The eighteenth-century statesman thought of colonies as passive economic resources, inhabited by servile populations; independence was the last quality he was trying to develop.

For these reasons, the tiny Caribbean islands bulked far larger in British colonial thinking than the territories of the North American mainland. Jamaica alone exported more than £600,000 of goods a year, three times as much as the middle and New England colonies combined, and it was probably even more valuable as a base for smuggling. Moreover, these islands had a population servile by definition, consisting almost entirely of Africans imported as slaves.

The slave trade far preceded the British empire, of course; it was as old as Columbus, if not older.* Between the fifteenth and nineteenth centuries, more than 10 million Africans were shipped to the Americas by every trading nation in Europe except Italy. For the first half of this period, slavery had been merely a lucrative sideline, but with the introduction of sugar and the plantation system in the West Indies after 1650 it developed rapidly. By 1700, it was big business, and by 1750, the fundamental institution on which the prosperity of western Eu-

---

*In 1441, ten Africans from the northern Guinea coast were shipped to Portugal as a gift to Prince Henry the Navigator. This is the earliest recorded transaction.

rope rested. The demand for sugar, hence for the labor that produced it, seemed inexhaustible. Jamaica alone absorbed more than 600,000 slaves, and between 1713 and 1792, the Caribbean islands exported £162 million worth of goods to Britain, almost all of it sugar. As early as 1729, its effects on the prosperity of the country were visible: "All this great increase in our treasure," noticed Joshua Gee, "proceeds chiefly from the labor of negroes in the plantations." Liverpool, a backward and insignificant port on the Irish Sea, became the slave center of Europe; at its height, it carried almost two-thirds of the English, and nearly half the entire European, slave trade. Immense fortunes were made; Whig merchants built magnificent estates in the country, and Tory squires built town houses in London and Bath. Some of this wealth trickled down, but the gulf between rich and poor widened, as it generally does in times of expansion. In 1709, the Bank of England was threatened by a mob; the age of urban riots had begun.

Slaving was a perfect example of what contemporary economic theorists called the "triangular trade." European ships brought their goods—often cheap textiles and gin—to African ports in exchange for slaves. As new cargo, the slaves were trans-shipped to the West Indies. Even allowing for a 15 or 20 percent mortality rate en route, the survivors would sell for five times their original purchase price. The same ships would then fill up with sugar to take home.

The transatlantic voyage was known as the "middle passage"—our century not being the first to call acts of horror by bland and noncommittal names. The trip was two months long. The slaves were segregated by sex and packed together below decks in chains, head to toe, helpless amid vermin and rats. In fair weather they were exercised on deck, under the lash; when the seas were rough, they were kept below with the portholes shut. The result is vividly described by a ship's doctor:

> Their apartments became so extremely hot as to be only sufferable for a very short time. . . . The floor of their rooms was so covered with the blood and mucus which had proceeded from them in consequence of the flux, that it resembled a slaughter-house. It is not in the power of the human imagination to picture to itself a situation more dreadful or disgusting.

The condition of the white seamen was not much better, except for rum and rape. The tensions of the voyage provoked insane acts of cruelty. The captain of one ship flogged a ten-month-old child with a cat-o'-nine-tails for refusing to eat, then plunged it into scalding water, tied it to a log, flogged it again to death, and forced its mother to throw it into the sea.

For those who survived, the average life expectancy on the plantations was seven years. Legally and morally, they did not exist at all. A planter who flogged a 14-year-old girl to death was actually tried for murder in Jamaica but was acquitted on the ground that "it was impossible a master could destroy his own property." Missionaries were curiously indifferent to this vast army of potential converts. The Society for Propagating the Gospel forbade its workers to catechize blacks; a slave caught going to church in Grenada was given 24 lashes.

The Age of Reason was thus also the Age of Slavery, and reason found its

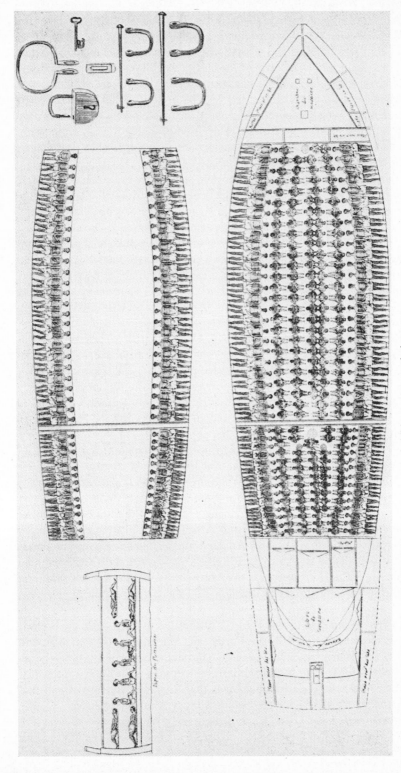

The hold of a slave ship. At least 10,000,000 men, women, and children were carried across the Atlantic in this manner on journeys that lasted an average of two months. Note the slavers' ingenuity in packing bodies in the fore and aft sections of the ship to utilize all possible space.

usual excuses for it. Some blamed the trade on the venality of African chieftains who sold their own people; others argued that since slavery had existed in Africa for centuries, it was nothing blacks were not accustomed to already. A simpler appeal was to the natural inferiority of the black race. Slaves were perpetual children; indulge their appetites and they promptly forgot their misery. Their nervous systems being less developed, they felt less pain than white men (although, strangely enough, more pleasure). They were incapable of understanding what liberty meant; how then could Europe be accused of taking it away from them? Their management by white men was a kindness; one slave ship was piously named the *Social Contract.*

The myth of the happy slave ran aground against the brute fact of rebellion. "Here's to the next insurrection of the negroes in the West Indies!" the critic Samuel Johnson sardonically toasted a literary gathering at Oxford. Jamaica was aflame in 1760; in 1791, half a million slaves under Toussaint L'Ouverture drove the French out of Haiti. Thomas Paine asked his fellow countrymen in 1775 how they could rebel against the British while still keeping slaves themselves. Thomas Clarkson and William Wilberforce began a campaign to abolish slavery in England, and in France, the Society of Friends of the Blacks struck a medal showing a chained, imploring slave with the caption "Am I not your brother?" The abolitionists rapidly triumphed in the early nineteenth century; England declared slavery illegal in 1807, the Netherlands in 1814, France in 1815. Their success was far less due to humanitarianism, however, than to the obsolescence of the old colonial system itself. Adam Smith had argued persuasively in *The Wealth of Nations* that free trade was far more profitable to England in the long run than a rigid protectionism that tied down capital, engendered pointless wars, and leaked away its profits in smuggling. The West Indian rebellions and the loss of the 13 colonies in America seemed to confirm his point.

The Act of 1807 declared the slave trade illegal, but not slavery itself, at least in the colonies, and this ensured that the traffic would continue. Even after the final abolition of slavery throughout the empire in 1833, a government commission reported that it was both larger and more efficiently conducted than ever before. The demand was no longer in the sugar islands of the Caribbean but the coffee and cotton plantations of Brazil and the southern United States. A candid observer wrote in 1857 that although England had technically washed its hands of slavery, it still shared in its profits as long as Lancashire mills were spinning American cotton. England supported the South in the American Civil War, and not until the abolition of slavery in Brazil in 1871 did the slave trade at last come to an end.

The French empire in the New World was similar to the British, but inferior in scope. It too was centered in the Caribbean: Martinique, Guadaloupe, and Santo Domingo (Haiti) rivaled Jamaica and Barbados, and Haiti ultimately became the richest single sugar island of all. But the French trade never approached the British in total volume; a rough guess is that England controlled about half the African slave market in the eighteenth century, France a quarter.

In North America, Cartier, Champlain, and La Salle had carved a path of exploration along the St. Lawrence River, the Great Lakes, and the Mississippi.

But their efforts were never backed, except under Colbert, by any consistent colonial policy. "New France" cut an impressive swath on the map, from Quebec in eastern Canada to the Gulf of Mexico. But it was thinly settled, and its trade was negligible; of the 75 companies chartered to develop it in the two centuries before 1789, none ever showed a profit. At a time when Philadelphia was already the second largest English-speaking city in the world, the entire population of French Canada was only 50,000. On the other hand, New France was garrisoned with a line of strong forts that represented, if nothing else, a barrier to the natural westward expansion of the 13 American colonies. Here, as in the West Indies, where more solid commercial interests were at stake, England and France were on a collision course to war.

The same story was repeated in the Far East. Portugal had arrived there first in the sixteenth century with traders and Jesuits, to be supplanted in the seventeenth by the Dutch, who opened a profitable spice trade in Java and the Moluccas and fought off all comers. England, unable to penetrate the Spice Islands, established itself on the coast of India, where it soon proved to have the best of the bargain. Indian silks, cottons, and dyes were in demand all over Europe, and the small trading posts at Madras, Calcutta, and Bombay—one day to be the three greatest cities of India—were second in importance only to the sugar capitals of the Caribbean. Colbert established the French East India Company in 1664, more than 60 years after its Dutch and English counterparts, and for 60 more thereafter it was little but a symbol. Under Fleury, however, the aged cardinal who was Louis XV's ablest minister, the French bid seriously for power in the Far East. Between 1728 and 1740, French exports from India increased tenfold. A powerful naval base was established on the island of Mauritius in the Indian Ocean.

Under the vigorous administration of Joseph Dupleix (1742–1754), French trade continued to expand while maintaining a profit margin of nearly 100 percent. But France's share of the Indian market still remained only half that of England's. Dupleix hoped to drive the English from the rich Carnatic (eastern) coast by allying himself with a claimant to the local Indian throne. This was a radical departure from the established European practice of nonintervention in Indian affairs; this was no savage America, but a populous and ancient civilization, and the small Western community existed there by the sufferance of native rulers. Dupleix's gamble paid off, however, and the French were rewarded not only by commercial but territorial concessions. As things were going, they seemed likely to establish a series of puppet states along the entire southeast coast of India, completely isolating the important British station at Madras.

England responded by seeking Indian allies of its own, and a war resulted. It was less that the war went badly than that it went on at all; commerce was hindered, casualties mounted, and relations between the two countries—which Paris at that moment was trying to cultivate—were strained. Dupleix was recalled, and peace restored. Once again, stronger forces and superior resolve had enabled the British to withstand an ambitious but underfunded French challenge to its overseas commercial empire.

There would be little in this tale of abortive intrigue to interest us were it not for the larger tragedy of India against which it was being played out. For several centuries, the Hindu masses of the subcontinent had been dominated by Moslem invaders from Persia and Afghanistan. The Moslems had set up a capital at Delhi, where a line of emperors, the Great Moguls, ruled from a throne of solid gold. But Moslem rule had become decadent by the beginning of the eighteenth century, and a number of Hindu princes had succeeded in establishing autonomous states. These princes fought with each other, with Delhi, and with rebels and pretenders within their own domains. New Moslem invaders swooped down across the northwestern frontier, hoping to exploit the prevailing anarchy. Reports of terrible slaughters reached the European trading stations from the interior. India seemed on the verge of political dissolution.

Dupleix was the first to sense the opportunity this presented. With a small core of European troops, it would be possible to train a native army and gain control of much of India. The next ruler of the subcontinent might be neither Moslem nor Hindu, but Christian and European. It is doubtful whether Dupleix's own thinking went that far. His original objective was merely to supplant the British. But the more he picked at the rotten underpinnings of Indian political life, the more astonished he was at how easily they gave way. From month to month his ambitions widened; conquest replaced commerce. Here his superiors called a halt to what seemed to them reckless political adventurism.

There was a solid commercial reason for undertaking conquest in India, however. The Indian trade was highly profitable. But whereas European demand for Indian products was high, Europe's goods had little appeal in India. Western traders had therefore to pay for what they bought in scarce bullion, which severely limited the commerce. Political control of part of the subcontinent would produce (in taxation, for example, or subsidies from local rulers) purchasing power in Indian currency itself.

The withdrawal of the French to a position of strict nonintervention left the field open to England. In 1756, a pretext for action came. The nabob of Bengal, alarmed at European activity in the south, stormed the British fort at Calcutta and locked the 146 surviving defenders in a single airless room. The next morning, most of them were dead. Robert Clive, a British East India Company official, avenged "the Black Hole of Calcutta" at the Battle of Plassey (June, 1757), greatly assisted by the prearranged defection of several of the nabob's commanders. The East India Company was the master of Bengal. It made a tool of the all but powerless Mogul emperor, extracting from him the right to collect taxes from a population larger than that of France.

By the mid-1760s, the British faced a critical turning point. Should they expand further in India? How should they administer what they already had? The East India Company was a private corporation under the jurisdiction of the Crown, yet it had effective political control over more people than the Crown itself. Its income from tax collecting already provided far more capital than it could ever use commercially. Company officials lorded it in London as millionaires; Clive himself, accused of profiteering in the House of Commons, sneered at the naiveté of the back-benchers: "By God, Mr. Chairman, at this moment I stand amazed at my own moderation!" How was England to regulate this state within a state?

The answer came piecemeal, in a series of parliamentary acts and government commissions that created a system of dual control. The Crown absorbed the basic political functions of governing India (defense, justice, legislation, and the like), leaving the details of administration and the conduct of trade to the company. It was a compromise that reflected the ingrained British reverence for property rights. The company reaped the profits while the government paid the bill.

The question of further conquest lagged for 30 years, the British consolidating rather than extending their territorial base. War with revolutionary France at last cast the die. The government dared not leave room for a French diversion in India. It moved systematically to bring the rest of the country under its control, either by direct administration through its Indian Civil Service or by puppet rulers living under the "protection" of British military missions. By 1818, after a quarter century of warfare and diplomacy, the *pax Britannica* covered virtually the whole of India.

Conquest transformed the British attitude toward India. The early eighteenth century had been eager for Asian goods, inquisitive about Asian culture. European traders mixed and married freely with Indians, learned their languages, adopted their customs. But with the establishment of British rule, there was no further necessity to please. Curiosity gave way to cynicism, cynicism to contempt. The separation of administration from commerce under the dual system isolated the Indian Civil Service from the people it governed. The missionaries who soon flocked to India were duly appalled by the savagery and heathenism of the population. By the early nineteenth century, the new rulers of India had ceased to regard their subjects as human beings. The Hindu, wrote Lord Hastings in 1813, "appears a being nearly limited to mere animal functions and even in them indifferent. Their [sic] proficiency and skill in the several lines of occupation to which they are restricted, are little more than the dexterity which any animal with similar conformation but with no higher intellect than a dog, an elephant, or a monkey, might be supposed to be capable of attaining."

Lord Hasting's racism marks the transition point between the haphazard, almost inadvertent conquest of India and its systematic exploitation: the transition between the old empire based on the New World of America and a new empire based on the Old World of Asia. In the 1780s, the orator Edmund Burke was warning that England had neither the military capacity nor the moral right to rule India; 50 years later, when India was the cornerstone of British prosperity, men like Benjamin Disraeli would argue that England had no moral right *not* to rule her, and bring her heathen millions the blessings of civilization.

THE EMERGENCE OF RUSSIA

Present-day Russia covers one-sixth of the land surface of the globe with approximately one-fifteenth of its population. Embracing hundreds of different peoples and languages, it is an empire within a state, held together not by race or culture but by geography and history.

The sheer flatness of Russia is its first and most enduring impression. From northeastern Siberia to the Carpathian Mountains of eastern Europe is a great

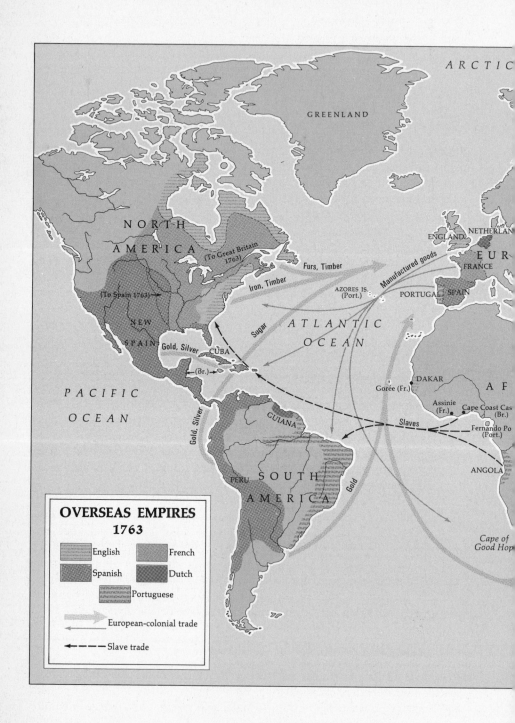

OVERSEAS EMPIRES
1763

English
Spanish
French
Dutch
Portuguese

European-colonial trade
Slave trade

GREENLAND

ARCTIC

NORTH
AMERICA

(To Great Britain 1763)

(To Spain 1763)→

NEW
SPAIN

Gold, Silver

CUBA

(Br.)

PACIFIC

OCEAN

Iron, Timber

Furs, Timber

Manufactured goods

Sugar

ATLANTIC

OCEAN

AZORES IS.
(Port.)

ENGLAND

NETHERLAN

EUR

FRANCE

PORTUGAL SPAIN

Gold, Silver

GUIANA

PERU

SOUTH

AMERICA

Gold

Gorée (Fr.)

DAKAR

Assinie
(Fr.)

Slaves

Cape Coast Cas
(Br.)

Fernando Po
(Port.)

AF

ANGOLA

Cape of
Good Hop

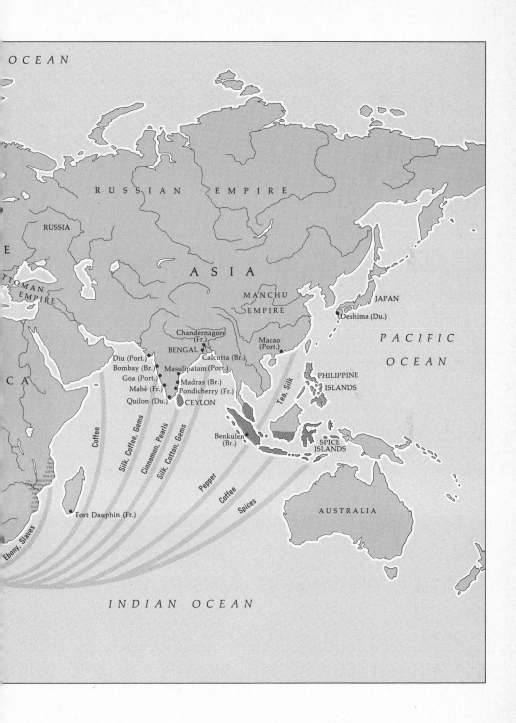

OCEAN

RUSSIAN EMPIRE

RUSSIA

ASIA

OTTOMAN
EMPIRE

MANCHU
EMPIRE

JAPAN

Deshima (Du.)

PACIFIC

OCEAN

Chandernagore
(Fr.)

Macao
(Port.)

BENGAL

Diu (Port.)

Calcutta (Br.)

Bombay (Br.)

Masulipatam (Port.)

PHILIPPINE
ISLANDS

Goa (Port.)

Madras (Br.)

Mahé (Fr.)

Pondicherry (Fr.)

Quilon (Du.)

CEYLON

CA

Coffee

Silk, Coffee, Gems

Cinnamon, Pearls

Benkulen
(Br.)

SPICE
ISLANDS

Silk, Cotton, Gems

Tea, Silk

Pepper

Coffee

Fort Dauphin (Fr.)

Spices

AUSTRALIA

Ebony, Slaves

INDIAN OCEAN

plain, 6000 miles from east to west and 4000 from north to south—the steppe. Along this vast expanse, crisscrossed by great rivers and belted by enormous bands of uniform, monotonous terrain, descending from the frozen tundra of the north through pine forest and grassland to the salt and sand deserts of the southern border, there is not a single significant impasse, not a single defensible frontier.

Along this natural highway invaders from the east have swept since time immemorial. The last and greatest of them were the Mongols, who in the twelfth and thirteenth centuries united the entire steppe in the largest empire in history. The western spur of this empire absorbed the proto-Russian state of Kiev, founded in the ninth century by a branch of the Slavic peoples who inhabited the steppe from the Ural Mountains to the Danube. Mongol rule was finally broken by the princes of Muscovy, an ambitious and unscrupulous family that had won privileged status from the Mongols by diligently collecting taxes for them and gradually succeeded in turning on their masters. By the end of the sixteenth century, they had reached beyond the Urals, and in the first half of the seventeenth, they strung a row of settlements across the Siberian wilderness, reaching Okhotsk on the Pacific in 1647, Anadyr in 1648.

Yet Muscovy had never won back the original Kievan Russia. In the fourteenth century, much of this region had been annexed by the loosely knit duchy of Lithuania, which in turn was absorbed by Poland. Thus, although by the mid-seventeenth century the writ of Muscovy extended 6000 miles east from Moscow itself, the Polish border was a mere 100 miles to the west. The great new Russian state had its back turned on Europe. Queen Elizabeth I of England tried to establish relations with it; her ambassador concluded his gloomy report in verse:

> Loe thus I make an ende: none other news to thee
> But that the country is too cold, the people beastly bee.

Russia's long isolation from the West had profound consequences on its development. Its rulers, who since 1472 had styled themselves *tsar,* "Caesar," had acquired a habit of command that Louis XIV might well have envied. Tsar Ivan IV (1533–1584), for example, forcibly resettled large sections of the population in the distant frontier provinces, burned a number of towns, degraded his nobility, and carried out a reign of terror with an elite corps of secret police, all without encountering any significant resistance whatever. The state was his private patrimony, and he was free to do as he wished with it. But the tsar was more than the supreme landlord of Russia. A peculiarly intense and idolatrous form of divine right had taken root in Russia. In Western Christendom, the division between the secular power of kings and the religious authority of the pope had always served as a brake on divine right theory. But Russia had followed the Greek Orthodoxy of the Byzantine Empire, where the church was subservient to the state. When Byzantium fell to the Turks in 1453, Russia remained as the last bastion of the true Orthodox faith. Theologians interpreted the calamity as a sign of Russia's special destiny. "Two Romes have fallen," wrote the Metropolitan Zosima, "the third Rome will be Moscow, and a fourth is not to be. . . ."

Russia itself was sacred; by the second half of the sixteenth century, people spoke habitually of "holy Russia." But in that case, the tsar, as ruler of the divinely anointed land, was a king of kings, the messiah of the future.

The society that evolved under this thesis bore little resemblance to those of the West. An all-powerful autocracy subjected the landholding aristocracy to state service, somewhat in the manner of medieval feudalism. Whereas the feudal king had reciprocal obligations to his vassals, however, the tsar had none, nor was there any theoretical limit to the amount of service he might require. The landowners, in turn, bore down on their peasants, whom they had reduced to absolute subjection by the mid-seventeenth century. The peasant was the unqualified possession of his lord, who could sell him like a horse or a meadow. His lot was thus worse than that of serfs elsewhere in eastern Europe, who were bound to the soil rather than the lord and could not be sold without their land. Russian serfdom was really indistinguishable from slavery.

From the top to the bottom of society, therefore, power was exercised in an absolute fashion. Toward those below, one had arbitrary privilege; before those above, neither claim nor appeal. Authority could only be questioned by authority. In this complete degradation of all political rights, the state was the prime mover. As it brought the landowners under its control, so, by edict and decree, it enabled them to control the peasantry. The only common denominator in Russian society was the whip. Princes and noblemen might be flogged and tortured by the tsar, just as their lowliest serfs were by them. The result, however, was not servility but desperate defiance. Those who had nothing to gain by their labor had nothing to lose by revolt. Each year peasants fled, destroying the crops, stealing farm animals, burning down the manor house, and killing the lord and his family. Many of them joined outlaw bands that numbered up to 100 men—formidable battalions in so sparsely populated a land—which preyed on caravans, pilgrims, travelers, and rich estates. By the 1660s, their ranks swelled by the tightening of serfdom, the persecution of religious dissenters, and hordes fleeing a major outbreak of the plague, the bandits ranged everywhere, an unconscious army waiting for its leader. He appeared in the person of Stenka Razin, a Cossack chieftain who led 200,000 men on a four-year rampage of pillage and destruction. Stenka wanted to tear down the oppressive machinery of the state, putting in its stead a pastoral democracy of small proprietors under a remote and benign tsar. Had he succeeded—and for a moment it appeared that he might—Russia would probably have been dismembered by Swedes, Turks, and Poles or, had it survived as an integral state, soon reverted to autocracy. Given the immense scope of the country, the scarcity of labor, the desperately primitive state of culture and technology, there seemed no feasible alternative to centralized control, no hope of reform but from the top. Stenka was captured in 1671, brought to Moscow in a cage, and beheaded. Tens of thousands of his followers were slaughtered with him.

This was the Russia that descended to Tsar Peter the Great in 1682. Peter was indeed great: almost 7 feet tall, with strength and appetites to match. His bouts of drunkenness and orgy were terrifying, his rages ungovernable. He reveled in the company of dwarfs, hunchbacks, cripples; the bizarre and deformed alone

Peter the Great. Wielding powers un-
dreamed of even by the divine-right rulers of
the West, Peter singlehandedly made Russia a great European power.

delighted him. His nobility he treated with cruelty and contempt. He had a wild, mocking irreverence toward all forms of authority, including his own: He signed himself with pseudonyms and nicknames, and traveled abroad incognito. He raised a street peddler to the rank of field marshal but joined his own army as a private and worked his way up through the ranks. He was truly at home only with soldiers, mechanics, technicians, men who worked with the touch of things; on his visit to the Netherlands in 1697–1698, an indulgent William of Orange permitted him to spend a week in the shipyards, where he worked as a common laborer. But if Peter often behaved like a prodigal colossus, he was also an insatiable student who seemed to be trying to assimilate the whole of Western technology in himself alone; if he flouted his own authority, it was only because it was so unchallenged.

The Muscovite kingdom had already begun to turn westward in the seventeenth century, wresting Kiev, Smolensk, and the eastern Ukraine from Poland. But it was Peter the Great who made Russia a European power.

Peter knew he could hack away at the Polish frontier, but he did not need more steppe; that would not bring him closer to Europe. What Peter wanted was a port on the Baltic Sea. The Baltic was dominated by Sweden at the end of the seventeenth century, but its new ruler, Charles XII, was a mere boy. Peter was not the only one to see his opportunity in this, and in 1700, Russia leagued together with Denmark, Poland, and Prussia to despoil the Swedish empire.

The allies had reckoned without their opponent, however. Charles XII, not yet out of his teens, proved to be a military genius of the first order. He knocked Denmark out of the war and then, wheeling on Peter, destroyed the new Russian army at Narva. Muscovy lay defenseless before him, but Charles, considering the Poles to be his chief threat, turned to deal with them.

Peter could have sued for peace, as Denmark had, but the tsar refused to admit defeat. He ordered every fourth church bell in Russia to be melted down for cannon, and slowly rebuilt his army. By 1703, he had secured the Gulf of Finland and begun, in the midst of war, to build his new port and capital, St. Petersburg. Three years later, the Poles collapsed, and Charles invaded Russia. Almost simultaneously, Peter faced a new Cossack uprising and an insurrection in the Ural Mountains, and, at the height of his troubles, he fell gravely ill as well. But Peter kept his nerve. He led Charles deeper and deeper into Russia, cut off his reinforcements and supplies, and surrounded him outside a small fortress in the southern Ukraine. The battle of Poltava (1709) annihilated the Swedish army. Charles fought his way with a few fugitives to Turkey, where, trapped thousands of miles from home, he could only watch helplessly as Peter overran the south Baltic coast.

Poltava not only assured the success of St. Petersburg, Peter's "window on the West"; it also put Russia on the map of Europe. Its significance was immediately realized in Vienna, where, the Russian ambassador reported, "It is commonly said that the tsar will be formidable to all Europe, that he will be a kind of northern Turk." From this time may be dated the fear of Russia that has played so important a role in the history of Europe. By 1711, Prussia was already sounding out its neighbors on the possibility of an anti-Russian alliance, and the British fleet soon appeared in the Baltic.

The Treaty of Nystadt (1721), which put an end to the Great Northern War with Sweden, confirmed Russia's new position. Russia obtained the so-called Baltic provinces of Ingria, Estonia, and Livonia and the southeastern Finnish borderland of Karelia. Included were the important warm-water ports of Reval and Riga and the fortress of Viborg, which dominated the entire Gulf of Finland. But more important than particular gains was the overall result of the war: Russia had permanently displaced Sweden as the leading power of northern Europe. Peter claimed that he had led Russia "into the light of the world" and celebrated his arrival by assuming the title of emperor.

Peter was as energetic at bringing the West to Russia as he had been at bringing Russia to the West. He reorganized government and finance on the latest Western models, replacing the old boyar duma (the council of the nobility) with a ten-man senate, in effect a supreme council of state, and reduced some 40-odd ministries to a streamlined 12, each with its resident foreign expert. He established the first greenhouses, laboratories, and technical schools in Russia, and founded the Russian Academy of Sciences. He had the first Russian translations of such Western classics as Aesop's *Fables* and Ovid's *Metamorphoses* made, ordered the study of all foreign languages, living and dead, and hired a German theatrical troupe to perform the French satires of Molière in the square of the Kremlin. He replaced the traditional Russian calendar with the Western one, to the horror of conservatives for whom the tsar had stolen time from God himself, and permitted intermarriage with Protestants and Catholics. He restyled the Cyrillic alphabet, introduced Arabic numerals, and brought out the first public newspaper in Russia, which he edited himself. Upon learning that the men of the West were clean-shaven, he sheared off the beards of his nobility; when a boyar demurred at eating a Western salad, he stuffed lettuce and vinegar down the man's throat until he bled from the nose.

In the end, Peter exhausted both Russia and himself. The building of St. Petersburg cost thousands of lives, and so did the Tsar's other public works. Peter was particularly obsessed with building canals. He dreamed of linking the Volga River with the Neva and the Don, the White Sea with the Baltic. These schemes required enormous capital and labor outlay, and almost none bore fruit, at least in Peter's lifetime. At unspeakable human sacrifice he laid a canal to Lake Ladoga, east of St. Petersburg, only to find it unnavigable. Russia lost population under Peter; the survivors were yoked to an ever more oppressive social system and taxed to the point of ruin (the one thing Peter was never able to borrow from the West was money). He himself died suddenly in February, 1725, worn out at the age of 52.

Peter's death brought a natural reaction. In the next 37 years, Russia had six rulers: three women, a boy of 12, an infant, and an imbecile. There were several palace coups, and some observers believed that Russia was heading toward a weak elective monarchy on the model of Poland. The nobility regained much of its old prerogative and by 1762 had emancipated itself from the rigid code of state service imposed on it by Peter. The status of the peasantry in the meantime became even worse. In 1741, serfs were omitted from the classes who were required to swear allegiance to the new sovereign; the criminal code of 1754 listed them only under the heading of property. Not only were they as salable as draft animals, they had become legally indistinguishable from them as well.

Political stability returned with the reign of the German-born Catherine the Great (1762–1796). As wife of the heir apparent, Peter, Catherine was well schooled in treachery; soon after Peter's accession, she organized his assassination. Never lacking in self-confidence, she saw in herself the perfect combination of womanly graces and masculine authority. "If I may venture to be frank," she wrote,

> I would say about myself that I was every inch a gentleman with a mind much more male than female; but together with this I was anything but masculine and combined, with the mind and temperament of a man, the attractions of a lovable woman.

Catherine's instinct for love—she had 21 attested affairs during her reign—was exceeded only by her instinct for power. Enthroned by a coup, without any pretense to legitimacy, she played skillfully on the prejudices and dissensions of the nobility. There was much talk of a constitution to limit the monarchy and other liberal notions from the West; Catherine declared herself in the forefront of reform and summoned a grand legislative commission in 1767 to rewrite the laws of Russia. Predictably, it bogged down in a vast mass of detail and ultimately accomplished nothing. The empress cultivated an "enlightened" and progressive image in keeping with the fashion of the times. She was a great patron of learning and invited the free discussion of daring social issues; Voltaire was delighted with her. But in practice, Catherine was bluntly reactionary. She dallied with the idea of emancipating the serfs, and even freed a few, but at the end of her reign there were more serfs in Russia than ever before. During the great rebellion of Emilian Pugachev, who crowned himself tsar in Kazan, the empress pointedly underlined the nature of her authority by signing herself "Catherine, a landlord of Kazan."

Pugachev's rebellion (1773–1774), the largest single uprising in the history of tsarist Russia, was the decisive domestic event of Catherine's reign. Like so many of his predecessors, Pugachev was a Cossack, the fiercely independent horsemen of southern Russia who were to prove, ironically, the last defenders of the Old Regime after the Bolshevik Revolution; like them, he raised the ancient, simple cry: land and freedom. Defeated at last in a series of pitched battles with disciplined government troops, Pugachev was taken in a cage, just as Stenka Razin had been a century before, and quartered in Red Square. Catherine made it an offense to speak his very name.

Pugachev's rebellion again revealed the dependence of the nobility on absolute despotism. The more their power over the serfs grew, the more they needed the power of a strong state to protect them from the inevitable backlash of peasant violence. In the latter part of Catherine's reign, this doubly reinforcing system of autocracy—of nobility over peasants and tsar over all—received its final consolidation. The Charter of the Nobility (1785) completely freed the Russian gentry from any service or obligation toward the central state, including taxation. Instead, the nobility of each province were organized as a corporate estate, charged with the responsibility of local government. This accomplished nothing but to concentrate their attention on their own privileges and interests. Catherine was simply giving them busywork. They were of little practical use to the state, which preferred its professional bureaucrats, and in any case Catherine had no intention of letting the provinces slip out of her control. Their sole function was to *own*. Russian feudalism had reached its zenith, just four years before the nobility of France were forced to renounce their privileges at the gunpoint of revolution. Thus did Russia row backwards into the future.

Western visitors to Russia were appalled by social conditions; Western statesmen were even more alarmed by Russian expansion. Three Russo-Turkish wars (1735–1739, 1768–1774, 1787–1792) gave Russia the north shore of the Black Sea, including Sevastopol and Odessa, and the advance might have been even swifter had not the defeat of an ally negated gains in the first war and Pugachev's rebellion forced a hasty peace in the second. Catherine, indeed, dreamed of conquering all of European Turkey and reuniting the "second and third Romes" of Constantinople and Moscow. In the West, Russian troops had reached as far as Berlin, which they occupied in 1760 during the Seven Years' War.

The most serious problem, however, was Poland. Poland had slowly declined since the fifteenth century and was now in an advanced state of disintegration. The Polish nobility had carried the principle of aristocratic anarchy to its ultimate conclusion. Their elective king was little more than a figurehead, and their national assembly, the Sejm, was crippled by a rule known as the *liberum veto,* by which a single negative vote not only defeated the measure at hand but dissolved the assembly and nullified all legislation passed prior to the veto. Actually, Polish political life boiled down to the endemic rivalry of a few great families, and these formal institutions expressed little more than their agreement to disagree. Poland was a state without a government, and against the organized monarchies of the eighteenth century, it was helpless. From Peter the Great's time it had become a Russian satellite, and this alone had prevented its actual dismemberment.

Russia's invasion of Turkey in 1768 turned the problem into a crisis. Catherine's armies made lightning gains, captured Bucharest, and threatened the Danube. Austria and Prussia, the other two major powers of eastern Europe, were thoroughly alarmed. If Russia could establish the same suzerainty over Turkey that it already had over Poland, the last buffer zone against tsarist expansion would be removed. The Austrians and Prussians demanded territory from Poland as compensation for Russian gains in Turkey. By the First Partition Treaty of 1772, Prussia lopped off Pomerania, Austria cut away Galicia, and Catherine, compensating herself for the compensations, absorbed 36,000 square miles of eastern Poland.

Having lost a third of its territory and half its population, Poland at last shook itself awake. Under Stanislas Poniatowski, a discarded lover whom Catherine had placed on the throne to serve as a puppet, the progressive nobility tried desperately to create a viable nation. It was too late. A new constitution, promulgated in 1791, merely provoked the Russians to intervene. Prussia hastened to join them, and Poland was partitioned again (1793). It was now reduced to a narrow strip around Warsaw, Cracow, and Vilna, and this remnant—too weak to serve as a buffer state, too tempting not to divide—was occupied by Russian troops pending a final partition. The end came in October, 1795. Prussia took Warsaw, Austria Cracow, and Russia what remained up to the line of the Bug and Niemen rivers. The second largest state in Europe had ceased to exist.

Russia had gained 6 million inhabitants and nearly a quarter of a million square miles from the partitions of Poland. Most of this region, the so-called White Russia, had been part of the original Kiev state. Thus, after more than 500 years, ancient Russia had been fully reunited with the Moscow of the tsars. Catherine herself, German-born and cosmopolitan, had little use for such historic parallels. The empress was willing to rule anybody. Nonetheless, Russia was now the only Slavic state in Europe, the only spokesman for millions of Slavs behind foreign borders.

In the exact century (1696–1796) between Peter the Great's assumption of personal power and Catherine the Great's death, Russia had not only fully joined the European state system but had emerged as the greatest power east of the Rhine. In 1660, Russia had less than half the population of France; by 1800, it had half again more—nearly 40 million people. In 1682, there were barely a dozen industrial workshops in the country—"factory" would claim too much for them; by 1800, between 2000 and 3000. In 1700, at Narva, a ragtag Russian army had been wiped out by a Swedish force one-fifth its size; by 1760, the Russian infantry was among the most respected in Europe; by 1800, Russia's standing army was 800,000 strong. The Russian upper classes, which had so obstinately resisted Westernization under Peter the Great, now spoke French among themselves,

ARCTIC OCEAN

ATLANTIC OCEAN

NORWAY

SWEDEN

FINLAND

BALTIC SEA

St. Petersburg

Riga

NOVGOROD

W. Dvina R.

N. Dvina R.

URAL MOUNTAINS

SIBERIA

Danzig

P R U S S I A

Moscow

HOLY

ROMAN

EMPIRE

POLAND

Warsaw

R U S S I A

Volga R.

Ural R.

Danube R.

Vistula R.

Kiev

AUSTRIA

HUNGARY

(Boundary of Poland before
the 1st partition 1772)

Don R.

Astrakhan

ITALY

CRIMEA

BLACK SEA

CAUCASUS MTS.

CASPIAN SEA

OTTOMAN EMPIRE

Constantinople

MEDITERRANEAN SEA

THE GROWTH OF RUSSIA

Russia in 1682

Acquired, 1682–1762

Acquired, 1762–1796

0   500
Miles

THE PARTITIONS OF POLAND

BALTIC SEA

LITHUANIA

(To Russia)

(To
Prussia)

(To Prussia)

(To Prussia)

(To Russia)

(To Austria)

PODELIA

(To Russia)

(To Austria)

1st partition,
1772

2nd partition,
1793

3rd partition,
1795

0   200
Miles

aped the latest Paris styles, and took the waters at fashionable German spas. Yet the vast mass of the Russian population continued to live in a timeless misery, more than half of it without even the legal status of human beings. Politically, economically, culturally, Russia had become a part of Europe; socially, it was farther away than ever.

THE BALANCE OF POWER

The partition of Poland was a perfect example of the idea of a balance of power that had become the guiding principle of diplomatic relations in the eighteenth century. The idea was quite familiar from the days when Europe had consciously united to check the excessive power of Louis XIV, and one of the treaties signed at Utrecht in 1713 explicitly declared as an objective the maintenance of peace in Europe through a balance of power. A British pamphleteer wrote in 1720, "There is not, I believe, any doctrine in the law of nations, of more certain truth ... than this of the balance of power." "What gravity or attraction is to the system of the universe," wrote another about 40 years later, "the balance of power is to Europe."

Put in its simplest form, the balance of power presupposed an alignment of individual states in an interlocking system designed to maintain a relative equilibrium of strength throughout all its parts. Should any state disturb this equilibrium by seeking to augment its power at the expense of its neighbors, a sufficient counterweight would soon be thrown into the scale to reduce it to its proper proportion. Aggression, concluded the philosopher Jean-Jacques Rousseau, was therefore futile, because over a certain length of time, resistance to any state of disequilibrium would become equal to the effort to create it and put the aggressor back in his original place.

At one time, balancing Europe had seemed a relatively simple affair. There were only two major power blocs, the Bourbon and the Hapsburg, and the history of Europe from the early sixteenth to the early eighteenth century could plausibly be seen as the maintenance of equilibrium between them. Newly emerging states automatically gravitated to one bloc or the other. The Dutch, for example, though a breakaway state of the Hapsburg empire, continued to play the same role in international affairs (a makeweight against Bourbon France) when independent as they had while under the control of Spain. But matters were now more complicated. Spain had lapsed from great-power status, while two nations on the periphery of Europe, Great Britain and Russia, had suddenly risen to it, to be shortly joined by a third, Prussia. This meant a confused scramble for readjustment in which, in addition to the traditional rivalry between Bourbon France and Hapsburg Austria, several new alignments appeared. Britain opposed France, Prussia opposed Austria, and both Prussia and Austria strove to check Russia. Could a general equilibrium be maintained among such disparate elements? A Prussian, Friedrich von Gentz, saw the solution in abandoning the ideal of a fixed and static balance for a fluid and open one in which the diplomats of Europe would maintain a state of dynamic counterpoise by continual adjustments in the scale. But even this more sophisticated conception of the balance of power (which presupposed equally sophisticated diplomats to carry it out) overlooked two significant factors.

The balance within Europe could be altered by conquest overseas; how, for example, was one to adjust for the British acquisition of India? On the other hand, states could strengthen themselves internally without ever stepping across their own borders. The German critic J. H. von Justi argued that efficiency of government, not extent of territory, was the real measure of a state's power. It was obvious that some states were more "modern" than others. The commercial supremacy of the Dutch had not been based on the length of their coastline; the British empire had been won not by millions of soldiers but by millions of pounds. If this were admitted, however, did it not imply a right by other powers to intervene against any state whose internal growth seemed likely to threaten the balance of power? This was what had happened to Poland. But if the principle of balance also meant the right of intervention, how was it to be distinguished from the aggression it was meant to contain?

The prime example of internal growth in the eighteenth century was Prussia. The origin of the Prussian state was in the electoral Mark of Brandenburg, a landlocked territory lying between the Elbe and Oder rivers, with its center in the small town of Berlin. By the mid-seventeenth century, through a combination of conquest and inheritance, the ruling Hohenzollern dynasty had acquired a string of territories stretching from the Rhine to the Niemen. It was by no means clear, however, that this new state would thrive. Its lands were scattered throughout the sea of principalities that was post-Westphalian Germany, and one of them, the Duchy of Prussia (from which the whole eventually took its name), was surrounded by hostile Poland. Its population was half Lutheran, half Catholic; its peasantry, half serf and half free. What unified it was the will of a series of remarkable rulers and the creation of a single all-encompassing institution, the Prussian army.

The maintenance of a standing army was the luxury of the rich and powerful in the seventeenth century, but the "Great Elector" Frederick William (1640–1688), having seen the devastation wrought in Germany (and his own dominions as well) by mercenary armies during the Thirty Years' War, was determined to have one, no matter how small. In 1648, he had only 8000 troops, but they were enough to gain him the eastern Pomeranian coast at Westphalia. The next Prussian ruler, Frederick III (who became King Frederick I in 1701 as a reward for joining the coalition against France), had five times that many, and his successor, King Frederick William I (1713–1740), doubled that number again. This was still not a very large army by contemporary standards; Louis XIV had at one time nearly 400,000 men under arms. But it was the best-trained and most up-to-date force in Europe. It was also the most pampered. Frederick William loved his soldiers far too much to expose them to combat. Typical of the king's obsession with the military was the formation of a regiment of giants, the Grenadiers, all over 6 feet tall and many closer to 7. (Frederick William stood 5 feet 5.) Royal agents scoured Europe for Gargantuas, literally kidnapping them off the streets. The king ordered his tallest male subjects to breed with the tallest females, an experiment that, predictably, failed: The children were of average height. Europe snickered at this royal drill sergeant and his obsessions. But no one laughed at the army he had created.

The Prussian army was far more than a military force, however. In a real

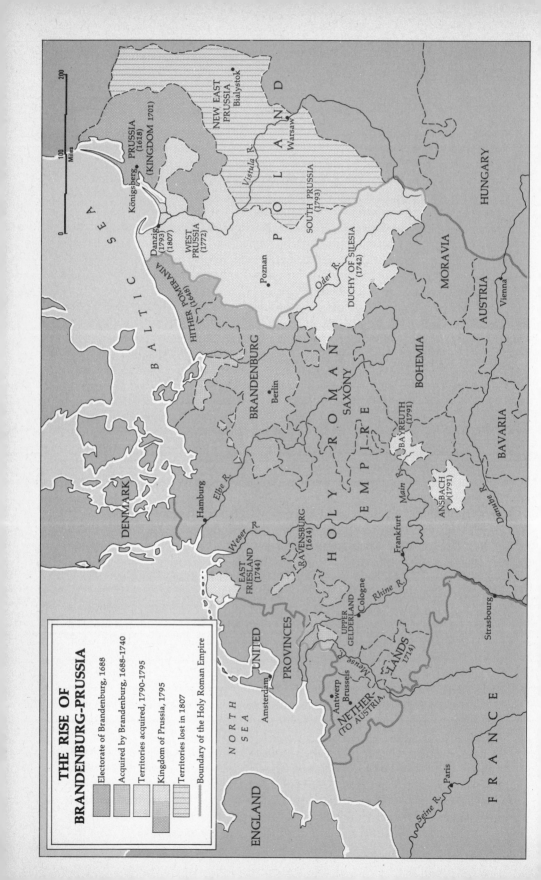

THE RISE OF BRANDENBURG-PRUSSIA

Electorate of Brandenburg, 1688
Acquired by Brandenburg, 1688-1740
Territories acquired, 1790-1795
Kingdom of Prussia, 1795
Territories lost in 1807
Boundary of the Holy Roman Empire

NORTH SEA

BALTIC SEA

ENGLAND

DENMARK

UNITED PROVINCES

Amsterdam

Antwerp
Brussels
NETHER-
LANDS (TO AUSTRIA)

UPPER GELDERLAND

Cologne
Rhine R.

EAST FRIESLAND (1744)

RAVENSBURG (1614)

Hamburg

Elbe R.

Weser R.

Main R.

Frankfurt

Meuse R.

Strasbourg

Paris
Seine R.

FRANCE

HOLY ROMAN EMPIRE

BRANDENBURG

Berlin

SAXONY

BAYREUTH (1791)

ANSBACH (1791)

Danube R.

BAVARIA

BOHEMIA

MORAVIA

AUSTRIA

Vienna

HUNGARY

DUCHY OF SILESIA (1742)

Oder R.

Poznan

HITHER POMERANIA (1648)

Danzig (1793)
(1807)

WEST PRUSSIA (1772)

Königsberg

PRUSSIA (1618)
(KINGDOM 1701)

Vistula R.

SOUTH PRUSSIA (1793)

Warsaw

P O L A N D

NEW EAST PRUSSIA

Bialystok

Miles
0   100   200

sense, it was the source of the nation itself. Prussia was not a state that had generated an army; it was an army that generated a state. The entire state apparatus, from the General Directory in Berlin (established in 1723 to coordinate major government functions) to the lowliest tax collector, quartermaster, or recruiting agent in the provinces, evolved from and revolved around the provisioning of the army. There was no separation of civil and military administration, either in theory or in practice. Every aspect of national life—economic, social, political, and educational—was subordinated to the army, developed or inhibited to serve its needs, justified only in relation to it. Frederick the Great said that his father had made a Sparta out of Prussia, and certainly no other modern society has lived so completely by the military ideal. By deliberate policy, the troops were not kept segregated in barracks but billeted among the population. One could not go anywhere without meeting soldiers, and their standards of discipline, drill, and obedience were constantly impressed on the entire nation. If it was true to say that the army was Prussia's only frontier, it might equally be said that Prussia was an army's parade grounds. The kingdom of the Hohenzollerns was the prototypic garrison state.

The death of two kings brought war to Europe in 1740. Frederick II, soon to be Frederick the Great, succeeded to the throne of Prussia, and the 23-year-old Maria Theresa became empress of Austria. Her father, Charles VI, had spent the better part of his reign trying to get the princes of Europe to agree to a document that would recognize her right to succeed him, the Pragmatic Sanction. Their promises were worthless. Charles Albert, the Elector of Bavaria, immediately claimed the throne. But Bavaria was regarded as a mere stand-in for France, whose ally it had long been. Once again, as with Spain, the weakness of a major power was about to provoke a general war.

It was Frederick of Prussia, however, who began it. Prussia had long coveted the rich and populous Austrian province of Silesia. In December, 1740, Frederick swept down on it, encountering little resistance.

Maria Theresa had little to offer. The Hapsburgs had been able to create an empire but not a state. Austria was a collection of large, loosely blocked slabs of territory, a heterogeny of peoples and customs: Belgian, Italian, German, Czech, Croatian, Hungarian. External loyalty to the Hapsburg crown had been purchased only by granting virtual self-rule to Hungary and Bohemia. Even less committed to Austria were Belgium and Italy, Austrian possessions for barely a generation.

Maria Theresa could give her subjects only one reason to fight for Austria: herself. She appeared dramatically before the Hungarian Diet with her infant son and appealed for help as an outraged queen and mother. In addition, she promised even greater autonomy within the empire to Hungary. The Diet responded with a levy of 100,000 troops.

The focus of battle soon shifted from Austria, however. Britain and France entered the war, the first for, the second against Maria Theresa, which is to say, simply against each other. Fighting ranged from the Great Lakes of North America to the Indian Ocean. The War of the Austrian Succession, as the general conflict is known, turned finally into another chapter in the great imperial war of the century. In the end, French successes on the European continent were nullified by English gains at sea, and the Treaty of Aix-la-Chapelle (1748) restored both parties to exactly their original position, reducing the entire war to an exercise in futility that the elder statesmen of England and France, Walpole and Fleury, had warned of vainly from the start. The only lasting change was the Prussian conquest of Silesia, and Frederick the Great, having achieved his objective, had left the war six years before.

Aix-la-Chapelle was merely a truce. The next few years saw a great deal of diplomatic maneuvering. Austria and France came together; Britain and Prussia paired off; and Russia, formally entering the European concert for the first time, joined the Austrians and the French. The alignment of Maria Theresa's war was now reversed; all former friends were now enemies, all former enemies friends.

The most startling change in this reversal of alliances was the Austro-French entente. The rivalry of Bourbon and Hapsburg had been the fixed star of European politics for two and a half centuries. Their rapprochement was the work of Count Wenzel von Kaunitz, the ablest Austrian diplomat of the century. Kaunitz's chief objective was the recovery of Silesia from Frederick the Great. Austria's former allies, Britain and the Netherlands, had forced it to give up Silesia and fight instead for the Austrian Netherlands (Belgium), a policy that was in their interests but not in Austria's. France, on the other hand, wanted Belgium very badly. The solution was simple. In return for a subvention of 115,000 troops and 12 million florins against Prussia, Austria would cede the old Spanish Hapsburg province that she could neither properly exploit nor defend.

With the adherence of Russia to the Austro-French alliance on the last day of 1756, Prussia's position was desperate. Surrounded on all sides by powerful enemies, it had only distant Britain for support. For the next five years, Frederick fought an apparently hopeless war for survival. Each year he staved off the inevitable with a last-ditch victory—Rossbach, Leuthen, Zorndorf, Leignitz, Torgau. But each year he returned to the field with fewer and fewer men. The Prussian army was reduced from 150,000 strong in its first campaign to 90,000 in its last. For all his skill and courage, Frederick was in despair. "To tell the truth," he wrote a minister, "I believe all is lost. I will not survive the ruin of my country."

But his opponents, too, were exhausted, and with the accession of Tsar Peter III in January, 1762, the alliance fell apart. Capricious and unbalanced, Peter was within months to be assassinated in the coup that brought Catherine the Great to power. But in the interval, he not only abruptly withdrew his troops from the front line but offered them to Frederick. Disgusted, the French pulled out next, leaving Austria to sign a separate peace with Prussia at Hubertusberg in 1763. Austria did not recover Silesia; France did not obtain Belgium. Prussia remained intact. The bitterest and bloodiest war in half a century had left the map of Europe just as it was before.

But the Seven Years' War of 1756–1763 worked a very decisive change on the map of the world. While Prussia and its opponents were fighting to stalemate in the center of the continent, Britain and France had resumed their war of empire. To contemporaries, the two seemed evenly matched. But the British had accumulated a long-term advantage in colonial population and naval superiority, and they had the services of William Pitt, one of the most commanding figures in Britain's history. Uncouth, choleric, and a commoner into the bargain, Pitt had been snubbed and excluded from power for 20 years, but (like Winston Churchill in 1940), in the crisis of war, no one else would do. For four years (1757–1761) his authority was, the niceties of the British constitution notwithstanding, virtually complete. In those four years, Pitt doubled the British Empire. French resistance both in India and North America was crushed by 1760. The slave stations in West Africa and the sugar islands of Guadeloupe and Martinique were occupied, crippling French revenues. A desperate attempt to invade England in 1759 resulted in the destruction of the French fleet at Lagos and Quiberon Bay. To cap the debacle, England occupied one of the French home islands off Brittany, the first piece of continental French soil (save Dunkirk) invested by British troops in more than 300 years.

It cannot simply be said (as Pitt suggested) that France lost her empire on the fields of Germany; the French position overseas had been vulnerable to a sustained British attack for a long time. Certainly the war with Prussia drained France's resources and divided the country's attention. But even more, it was symptomatic of a diplomacy embedded in the past. To secure old battlegrounds in Flanders, the French were prepared not only to give short shrift to the war with Britain but, by dismantling Prussia, to give Austria a virtually free hand in Germany. Pitt in Britain and Kaunitz in Vienna were abreast of their time, but the men at Versailles still seemed to be living the dreams of Louis XIV.

In the event, the French were lucky. They failed to defeat Prussia and in the Peace of Paris (1763), which preceded that of Hubertusberg by five days, won back from the feeble successors of Pitt much of what had been lost overseas. Guadeloupe and Martinique were restored, their sugar having proved a glut on the British market, and France was permitted to reopen its commercial stations in India. The French were able to get partial revenge for the loss of Canada by assisting the American colonists to win independence two decades later, and in 1782 they nearly captured Jamaica, a threat that alarmed the British far more than the loss of the 13 American colonies. Yet with all this allowed, the Seven Years' War marked the decisive triumph of the British Empire over the French. The French might snipe at Britain thereafter, but they would never again compete.

The Franco-British struggle, the partitions of Poland, and the great eighteenth-century wars between France, Austria, and Prussia suggest that the balance of power, insofar as the term has any real meaning, was less a mechanism for preventing wars than a rationale for starting them. Few were the voices raised on behalf of peace as opposed to power. The great Dutch jurist Hugo Grotius had sketched the outline of a system of international law in the early seventeenth century, and 100 years later, the Abbé de Saint Pierre argued that the states of Europe could end their anarchy only by placing themselves under a supranational authority. A number of philosophers, from Gottfried Wilhelm von Leibniz to Jeremy Bentham to Immanuel Kant, made proposals along similar lines, as did the Quakers William Penn and John Bellers and the Italian statesman Cardinal Alberoni. Needless to say, the states paid scant attention. Their working attitude was summed up in the remark offered by Frederick the Great upon attacking Silesia in 1740 that it was the natural tendency of states to expand to the maximum of their capacity to make and absorb conquest. That was all the philosophy a state needed to have.

four

The Enlightenment

THE SCIENTIFIC REVOLUTION AND ITS DIFFUSION

What we take for granted as common knowledge—that water and air are not single but compound substances, that the sun is larger than the earth, that weight determines whether a body will sink or float—has been the property of the human race for a very short time. The discovery of these facts, and the development of the structures of explanation in which they were embedded, took place principally in the sixteenth and seventeenth centuries. The process as a whole came to be known as the Scientific Revolution. The technological consequences of this revolution were not fully manifested until the nineteenth century, but the intellectual, social, and political consequences began to flow almost immediately.

The Italian poet Dante Alighieri (1265–1321) presented the then-accepted Ptolemaic view of the world in his great epic, *The Divine Comedy.* Dante believed the solid earth to be the hard core of the universe. The earth was entirely covered by the water of the oceans, except in the northern hemisphere, where land had been pulled up above sea level by the attraction of the fixed stars. The center of the habitable world, and thus of the universe itself, was, appropriately, Jerusalem, where the central drama of the world's history, the redemption of man, had been enacted.

Above the earth lay the canopy of air, and beyond it was the region of fire, which, being the lightest of the four classical elements (earth, air, fire, and water), rose highest. The stars and planets were attached to a series of interlocking spheres, like jewels on an invisible necklace. These bodies were composed of a fifth element, the quintessence, which, unlike the other four, was an immaterial substance, perfect, weightless, and incorruptible. Having no weight, the stellar bodies moved neither up nor down, but only wheeled about in leisurely circles, thus accounting for the motion of the heavens. According to Dante, there were ten spheres in all, the nearest carrying the moon, the next six the sun and the five planets, and the eighth the fixed stars. The tenth sphere was the region of the Empyrean Heavens, where the blessed spirits dwelt. The ninth sphere was vacant—that is, it carried no visible bodies—but because ten was a perfect number, its existence was assumed. It was called the Prime Mover, and its function was to turn the other spheres around the motionless earth to produce the alternation of day and night.

This view of the cosmos had been current since ancient times, and but for one nagging detail it fit the observable phenomena of the heavens perfectly. The detail was that a number of stars seemed to exhibit a contrary or retrograde motion, turning irregularly backward along the paths they had already traversed instead of moving symmetrically forward. The Greek astronomer Ptolemy had explained this by hypothesizing that these stars were attached not only to their spheres but to smaller discs called epicycles that moved contrary to the main motion of the larger sphere, thus producing the appearance of countermotion. By the time of Nicholas Copernicus (1473–1543), the number of such stars had increased to 83, making a tangle not only of Ptolemy's theory but of celestial navigation as well. Copernicus revived the idea, first suggested by Aristarchus in the third century B.C. and considered but rejected by Ptolemy himself, that the problem of retrograde motion might be solved by considering that the earth itself moved.

Copernicus's new system put the sun at the center of the universe, with Mercury, Venus, the earth, the moon, Mars, Jupiter, Saturn, and an outer ring of fixed stars rotating about it, each on its respective sphere, each moving in a perfect circle. This system, which except for the transposition of some of the planets and the replacement of the earth by the sun as the fixed center of the cosmos remained within the old Ptolemaic framework, reduced the number of epicycles to a more manageable 34.

But the fixed earth had been the linchpin of Ptolemy's system. If the earth were not the center of the universe, why should the sun necessarily be? If it were not fixed and immobile, why should any other heavenly body remain in place? With no fixed center, moreover, the stars and planets had nothing around which to revolve, hence no reason to be attached to orbiting spheres. Might the stars not be wandering at random through a limitless space, or revolving, perhaps, around other suns like our own, part of other worlds with beings such as ourselves? If the earth were not the physical center of the universe, why was the human race necessarily its moral center? If the Divine Creator could make one world, why could he not, with his infinite power, make an infinite number? By what right, indeed, did man presume to set bounds to his Creator and limit the possibilities of his creation? Just such a vision of an infinite universe was proposed by the Italian philosopher Giordano Bruno (1548–1600) at the end of the sixteenth century. If few shared this vision, many were disturbed by it. John Donne's "An Anatomy of the World" (1611), while satirizing the new astronomy, betrayed a deep cultural anxiety as well:

And new philosophy calls all in doubt;
The element of fire is quite put out,
The sun is lost, and the earth, and no man's wit
Can well direct him where to look for it
And freely men confess, that this world's spent
When in the planets and the firmament
They seek so many new; then see that this
Is crumbled out again to his atomies
'Tis all in pieces, all coherence gone;
All just supply and all relation.

The French philosopher and mathematician René Descartes (1596–1650), himself a crucial figure in the development of the new science, suggested that all hitherto assumed knowledge should be subjected to systematic doubt and scrutiny, and only be readmitted insofar as it could pass the test of reason. The Italian physicist Galileo Galilei (1564–1642) attacked traditional authority even more directly, declaring that where the Bible and science were in conflict over matters of fact, science was to be accepted. Galileo turned his telescope, the invention of Dutch lens makers, on the moon and the planets. He discovered four of Jupiter's moons through the new device, the first addition to the inventory of heavenly bodies since antiquity. This suggested an at least indirect confirmation of Bruno's thesis: If there were unsuspected bodies so near at hand, who could tell what might lie beyond the realm of human vision? No less significant was Galileo's description of the mountainous surface of the earth's moon, which suggested a process of erosion incompatible with the assumption of an unchanging, immaterial substance. At the same time, the German astronomer Johannes Kepler (1571–1630) discovered that the planets described elliptical rather than circular orbits around the sun, thus destroying the notion of perfect spherical motion.

By the end of the first quarter of the seventeenth century, the Ptolemaic system lay in ruins. Not only new discoveries in the heavens, however, but new ones on earth challenged human confidence in the completeness and sufficiency of current knowledge. The exploration of Africa and the Western Hemisphere brought home the fact that the earth itself was far larger than Europeans had realized, and the report of advanced civilizations in the New World was scarcely less momentous to the people of the sixteenth century than the discovery of extraterrestrial intelligence would be for us.

The new science revealed not only the vast extent of the world outside the human realm but also of the world within. Andreas Vesalius's *On the Fabric of the Human Body,* which appeared in the same year that Copernicus published his theory (1543), laid the foundations of modern anatomy and physiology, while William Harvey gave the first account of the circulation of the blood in 1628, and Anton von Leeuwenhoek, using a microscope of his own design, was the first to observe the teeming world in a spoonful of water or a drop of blood. For lack of better instruments and hence more detailed data, the analysis of the microworld so tantalizingly glimpsed by Leeuwenhoek remained undeveloped until the nineteenth century. But the early biological pioneers helped to demystify the human body as the astronomers had the heavens, showing the material basis of all physical reality and giving rise to the hope expressed by Descartes that all natural phenomena might ultimately be comprehended under a single system of mechanical principles, and the entire universe be described as the condition of matter in motion.

The most impressive thing about the new science, however, was its remarkable ability to build on its own mistakes. Copernicus had wrongly believed in a cosmos rotating about a fixed sun. Galileo's theory depended on a false belief in circular inertial motion and circular planetary orbits, while Kepler, who discovered the true laws of planetary motion, spent much of his life vainly trying to reconcile his astronomy with an abstruse Platonic and Pythagorean number mysticism. What was valuable in each of these thinkers was retained; what was dross or error fell off. With mounting excitement, the thinkers of the seventeenth century realized that they had not so much a gain in their factual knowledge of one subject or another but—as they thought—a key to knowledge as such.

Until about the middle of the seventeenth century, the Scientific Revolution was essentially the work of isolated individuals. The churches and universities alike were hostile to the new ideas. Galileo left the University of Padua under fire and was persecuted by the Inquisition; Kepler was driven from the Protestant faculty at Tübingen. Both men sought sponsorship and safety with royal or aristocratic patrons: Galileo with the Medici dukes of Tuscany, Kepler at the imperial court in Prague. The career of Descartes summed up even better the predicament of the early seventeenth-century scientist. A product of Jesuit schooling, he left his native France for the more tolerant atmosphere of the Netherlands and wound up finally at the court of Queen Christina of Sweden where, obliged to rise at 5 o'clock every morning to discuss philosophy with the eccentric young queen, he contracted pneumonia and died. Descartes himself suppressed what he regarded to be his most important work, *Le Monde* (*The World*), upon hearing of Galileo's arrest; it was never published.

A tenuous chain of correspondence and personal acquaintance linked these scientific pioneers. The enterprising friar Marin Mersenne (1588–1648) established contact with most of the leading scientists of the day, many of whom he introduced to one another. Private gatherings were organized in Paris in the 1650s at which scientific papers were read, often sent in from abroad. An English visitor's catalogue reveals the excitement and intensity of debate at one such meeting, as well as the residual elements of alchemy and astrology still present in the new science:

> The Source of the Variety of Popular Opinions, The Explanation of the Opinions of Descartes, The Insufficiency of Movement and Figure to explain the Phenomena of Nature . . . Then of the Brain, of Nutrition, of the Use of the Liver and Spleen, of Memory, of Fire, of the Influence of the Stars, If the Fixed Stars are Suns, If the Earth is animated, of the Generation of Gold, If all our Knowledge

springs from the Senses, and several others, which I do not at this moment remember.

In 1662, the Royal Society of London for Improving Natural Knowledge was chartered, and four years later Colbert, ever alert to enhance the prestige of the French monarchy, founded the Academy of Sciences. In short order, similar academies sprang up in Berlin, Uppsala, St. Petersburg, Stockholm, and Copenhagen. They served as clearinghouses for new knowledge, centers of research and publication, forums for debate, magnets for talent. By the last decades of the seventeenth century, we can speak of a scientific world, international in scope, cosmopolitan in character. At a time when in England laws were being passed to exclude those outside the official state church from the universities, the professions, and government service, the Royal Society opened its doors to all except professed atheists. In a Europe walled in by religious hatred, economic barriers, and dynastic strife, science created a new community.

Yet, vital and buoyant as the new thought was, there was much uncertainty about the ultimate direction of the scientific enterprise. There was exhilaration that the stale old dogmas had been swept away, but confusion and dismay about what could replace them. "The more I think, the more I doubt," wrote François Sanchez in 1581; Blaise Pascal confided to his notebook, "The silence of infinite space appalls me." The archskeptic Descartes had triumphantly emerged with an infallible method for declaring knowledge, but not everyone was prepared to accept it, not even, at all times, Descartes himself.

Science was in fact an uncertain dialectic between two quite distinct approaches to knowledge, the deductive rationalism of Descartes, with its bare, geometrized universe, and the inductive empiricism of Francis Bacon, with its observation and experiment in the physical world. Many striking results had been obtained from both methods, many brilliant theories advanced, but there was no standard of truth, no coherent pattern into which all the random insights and chips of knowledge could be fit.

Sir Isaac Newton provided it. By Newton's early youth (he was born in 1642), the elements for a grand synthesis between Galileo's laws of falling bodies and Kepler's laws of planetary motion lay at hand in the work of a score of other men. Descartes and Galileo had worked out the principle of inertia; from William Gilbert to Kepler to Christian Huygens the notion of gravity had been progressively refined; and Robert Hooke had discovered that the force of attraction between two bodies varied inversely with the square of their distance. What Newton did, in his *Principia Mathematica* (1687), was to show that the entire physical world could be explained by assuming that all bodies were in a state of motion regulated by the universal constant of gravity. He did this, moreover, not by mere speculative assertion or a priori reasoning, in the manner of Descartes, but by mathematical proofs based on the most up-to-date empirical observations, and for the next two centuries, experiments repeatedly confirmed his work in detail. By building his argument systematically both on observation and mathematics (of which he invented an entirely new branch, calculus, to describe the complex relations between bodies in motion), Newton reconciled the traditional antago-

"God said, Let Newton be! and all was light." Sir Isaac Newton (1642–1727).

nism between the two methods and showed the functional interdependence of both. Pure mathematics could show what the world *ought* to be, but only observation and experiment could prove what it actually *was*.

Newton's system was not at first universally accepted. The followers of Descartes, including the German Gottfried von Leibniz, who had independently invented calculus at the same time as Newton, regarded the notion of bodies "attracting" each other across empty space as deplorably mystical and occult. Newton replied that he made no attempt to explain what gravity was, only what it did, and what it did was regulate the motion of matter in space in a manner that could be expressed by simple equations. A more serious objection was raised by his fellow countrymen George Berkeley and the Scotsman David Hume, who argued that knowledge was a mere projection of the mind onto the world, rather than the other way around, and that what men perceived as necessary connections between phenomena in nature were only logical connections in their own thinking.

But the skeptics failed to persuade. By the end of his life (1727), Newton's thought had conquered Europe, and he himself was revered by many as a demigod. The French publicist Bernard de Fontenelle wrote, "He was reverenced to so great a degree that death could not procure him more honor, and he saw his own apotheosis"; the English poet Alexander Pope enthused,

Nature and nature's laws lay hid in night;
God said, Let Newton be! and all was light.

Within the century capped by Newton, science had advanced from heresy to curiosity, from curiosity to fashion, from fashion to dogma. That it remained philosophically incomplete and methodologically inconsistent did not trouble its adherents; philosophy itself became suspect insofar as it failed to rationalize the triumphs of science. By 1759, the mathematician D'Alembert could write that "the true system of the world has been recognized, developed and perfected."

For the layman, science was popularized in a host of books beginning with Fontenelle's *Dialogues on the Plurality of Worlds* (1686). Designed to bring astronomy "within the grasp of the feminine intelligence," it made a charming fable of the subject for which the Inquisition had burned Giordano Bruno at the stake 86 years before. Fontenelle himself was one of the most important cultural conduits of the Scientific Revolution. A literary intellectual and scientific dabbler, he served as secretary of the Academy of Sciences from 1699 to 1741, and he did more than anyone else in France to bring science to the attention of not only the educated public but the state as well. Like Sir William Petty and Gregory King in England, Fontenelle advocated the systematic collection of data on trade, population, and wealth and the application of scientific techniques in general to the art of government—what the nineteenth century was to call political economy. There was indeed, in his opinion, no branch of human thought, from art to morals to religion, that would not benefit from an infusion of the "geometric spirit."

Fontenelle's dictum was already an accomplished fact. There was scarcely a field where scientism—the application of scientific methodology to traditional knowledge—had not at least been attempted. John Locke's immensely influential *Essay Concerning Human Understanding* (1690) turned the mind itself into an object of scrutiny, while Baruch Spinoza's *Ethics Demonstrated in the Geometrical Manner* (1677) taught it how to arrive at moral certainty by mathematical reasoning. But the most sensitive and critical area for scientism was religion. The scientists themselves professed to see no contradiction between their discoveries and the truths of revelation. Newton wrote far more theology than science, and was apparently as proud of his treatise on the Book of Daniel as of the *Principia*. The theologians, for their part, came to conquer science in the same spirit that medieval scholastics had assimilated Greek reason to Christian revelation. The Oratorian priest Nicolas Malebranche (1638–1715), embracing the dualistic rationalism of Descartes, declared God the ultimate unseen cause of all material action. Some of the more enthusiastic divines carried the whole thing rather far, like Dr. John Craig, who in his *Mathematical Principles of Christian Theology* asserted that the story of Christ could be represented by the formula $CZ + (n-1)f + (T^2/t^2)k$. Curiously enough, Newton promoted the book.

Not everyone shared this facile optimism about the compatibility of science and religion, however. Devout scientists like the great English chemist Robert Boyle preferred to treat the two subjects as completely autonomous realms, each true on its own terms. In the preface to his *Origin of Forms and Qualities* (1667), Boyle declared somewhat defensively that his purpose was "to discourse of Natural things as a naturalist, without invading the Province of Divines by intermeddling with the Supernatural mysteries." Biblical miracles could still be explained as the suspension by God of his ordinary laws. But the burden of proof, as it were, had shifted to the miraculous, and some found the evidence (at least by scientific standards) sadly wanting. The Jewish philosopher Spinoza offered rational explanations for Old Testament miracles in his *Tractatus Theologico-Politicus* (1670); for example, he suggested that the Red Sea might have been parted by a gale. The French priest Richard Simon went much further in his *Critical History of the New Testament* (1678) and subsequent books, subjecting the Bible to a searching philological scrutiny that laid bare hundreds of discrepancies and inaccuracies in the text. Spinoza was an outcast even among the Jews, but Simon, a pious and orthodox Christian, could not be so easily dismissed. To purge the Bible of manifest errors, he asserted, was not to weaken religion but to strengthen it. How could rational men be asked to apply a double standard of truth, one for the Bible and another for all the other books in the world?

The trouble was that "rational men" could hardly be expected to accept the biblical revelation on reasonable grounds alone. "How is it," asked the Baron de Lahontan, "that you wish me to believe in the truth of this Bible written so many centuries ago, translated into several languages by ignorant men who did not understand its true meaning, or by liars who have changed, enlarged or diminished the words that are found there today?" Bishop Bossuet was nearer to guessing the real impact that Simon's work would have when he ordered the *Critical History* to be publicly burned.

The next step was an attack not on the grammar of the Bible but its content. Spinoza had confessed himself unable to believe in a punitive and arbitrary God who was "as mad as men are"; Pierre Bayle's *Historical and Critical Dictionary* (1697) poked open fun at the heroes of pagan and Christian mythology. With Bayle we already breathe the spirit of the eighteenth century, witty, ironic, irreverent. His work was a mine of ammunition for skeptics; Voltaire was one of the many later writers who were in his debt. And with Bayle (raised a Huguenot, converted a Catholic, relapsed a Calvinist, and finally, perhaps, nothing at all), we hear for the first time the authentic cry of the Enlightenment: "The champions of reason and the champions of religion are fighting desperately for the possession of men's souls."

For those who, like Newton and Boyle, still wished to believe as far as reason would allow, "natural religion" or Deism provided a halfway house between orthodox Christianity and outright skepticism. The Deists' god was variously conceived as a kind of universal mind (Henry More and the Cambridge Platonists in England), as the principle of organization among the autonomous elements of creation (Leibniz), or as a cosmic artificer who had wound up the clock of Newton's universe and simply watched it run. But he no longer had anything to do with such matters as grace, salvation, and eternal life.

Such a God, cold, distant, and abstract, seemed scarcely different from no God at all, and, by the mid-eighteenth century, a few spirits were bold enough to say so openly. The French physician La Mettrie, in *Man a Machine* (1747), denied any purpose to creation or any special place for man in it. The universe was a single material substance: "Man is not molded from a costlier clay. Nature has used but one dough, and merely varied the leaven." Baron d'Holbach, whose *System of Nature* (1770) dismissed the whole question of the origin of the universe as irrelevant, introduced the philosopher David Hume to a dinner party consisting of "fifteen atheists, and three who have not quite made up their minds."

The significance of the atheists was less in their opinions than the manner in which they held them. According to Christian tradition, the atheist was a man desperate and damned, without the hope that even the worst sinner still had of ultimate redemption. But these men were positively cheerful in their unbelief. To Pascal's terror at the silence of infinite space, La Mettrie replied that "the weight of the universe . . . far from crushing a real atheist, does not even shake him." The atheists saw themselves not as sinners who had lost their faith but as free men who had shaken off superstition.

To be sure, such opinions were still regarded as scandalous and abominable in all but a few avant-garde circles (Holbach wrote under pseudonyms, and La Mettrie, who did not, was expelled from France). But whether openly proclaimed or still under the fig leaf of Deism, educated European society had become increasingly secular in its modes of thought. There was general skepticism about ghosts, magical signs, and portents, and a growing tendency to substitute rational explanations of phenomena for occult or miraculous ones. Supernatural evidence could no longer be introduced in court except in such backward regions as Scotland and Massachusetts; in 1672, Colbert instructed the magistrates of France to receive no further accusations of witchcraft and sorcery. It might have been possible in 1653 for a Parliament in revolutionary England to entertain a resolution to abolish the laws of the country in favor of the Mosaic code because the end of the world was presumed to be imminent; such a scene could hardly have been imagined 50 years later.

An age had dawned that was supremely confident of itself and of the power of reason to penetrate the ignorance and superstition with which former times had veiled the clarity and harmony of the world—an age that in full consciousness of that goal called itself the Enlightenment.

THE PHILOSOPHES

The work of the Enlightenment was carried on by a group of self-appointed missionaries who called themselves "philosophes." These men were not philosophers in the traditional sense of thinkers who devoted themselves to lofty and disinterested speculation about general laws and principles; they were activists for whom knowledge was something to be converted into reform. The bible of the movement, Denis Diderot's *Encyclopedia,* defined the philosophe as one who, "trampling on prejudice, tradition, universal consent, authority, in a word all that enslaves most minds, dares to think for itself . . . [and] to admit nothing except on the testimony of his experience and his reason."

Experience and reason: For the philosophe, as for the scientist, this was the formula for attaining knowledge. But whereas traditional philosophers like Descartes looked upon reason as an innate faculty of the mind prior to all experience, the philosophes regarded experience as primary. Following the English philosopher John Locke, they believed that the mind at birth was a *tabula rasa,* a blank slate on which experience wrote its script. But the mind never apprehended true reality. Even pure sensation came to it masked in prejudice, superstition, and myth—all the accumulated ignorance and error of the past. The task of reason, therefore, was twofold: to dissect, expose, and demolish these false constructions, and to create new units of perception and value. By continually submitting its hypotheses to the test of logical consistency and fidelity to experience, reason could, by progressive refinement, approach the truth; and what an individual could accomplish in this fashion, an entire society could as well. For the effect was clearly cumulative: Every person thereby liberated diminished the sum total of error that all others had to overcome.

The upshot of this argument was the doctrine of progress, an idea that changed an entire civilization's conception of itself. For more than 2000 years, Western civilization had thought of its world as the shrunken and degenerate remnant of a glorious past. The Greeks believed that they had fallen from a remote golden age into the "iron age" of their present; the Romans of the Empire looked back to the virtue of the Republic, the Middle Ages to the sanctity of the Apostles, and the Renaissance back again to Rome. But most important of all was the Judeo-Christian myth of man's fall from the Garden of Eden. The golden ages that Greek and Roman pagans looked back on were historical epochs not unlike their own, and therefore offered at least the hope of return. But in the Jewish story of Genesis, man's expulsion from paradise, the perfect world of first creation, was final. Humanity could not be redeemed in historical time; indeed, history, time itself, was the very punishment inflicted on man for his sins.

The notion of secular progress, the improvement of the human condition in this world through human effort alone, thus required a radical transformation in Western thinking. The Scientific Revolution provided the basis of this transformation, and the philosophes, generalizing on its premises and practices, extended it to society as a whole. If people could master the forces of the natural world—and such was the secret promise of science—why should they be unable to master their own human one? In general literary culture, the question of progress first became explicit in the debate between the so-called Ancients and Moderns at the end of the seventeenth century, with the Ancients upholding the traditional view that man was a decrepit shadow of his former self, and the Moderns asserting that the age of Louis XIV was the equal if not the superior of any previous period in human history. The ubiquitous Fontenelle had the last word on this subject too. In the perspective of hundreds of centuries to come, he declared, the fifth century before Christ or the seventeenth after would both be seen as points on a line of ascending progress. A hundred years later, the Marquis de Condorcet, under sentence of death during the French Revolution, could still say, like an early Christian martyr dying with his faith on his lips, that "nature has placed no bounds on the perfection of the human faculties, and the progress of this perfectibility is limited only by the duration of the globe on which nature has placed us."

The doctrine of progress inevitably placed great emphasis on education. If the mind at birth was a blank slate, then how much progress might be advanced by filling it with correct ideas (and how much retarded by continuing to subject it to false ones)? Jean-Jacques Rousseau's novel *Émile* (1762) was an eloquent plea for the rights of childhood and the importance of individual development, and shortly afterward the Swiss reformer Johann Pestalozzi (1746–1827) opened the first of the schools that are so aptly called "progressive." That faith in the power of education, which is still so much with us today, was first enunciated by men like Locke, who imagined the minds of children "as easily turned this way or that, as water itself," or Claude Adrien Helvétius, who declared in 1758, "Goodness and humanity are not the work of nature, but only of education."

The great cause of the philosophes was to achieve a climate in which education and progress could go forward unhindered. We would call such a climate intellectual freedom. But the Enlightenment had a much narrower and more pragmatic name for it: toleration.

Toleration was originally an outgrowth of the Reformation, when after a century of warfare a few minorities had won the right to worship as they chose. In short, toleration generally appeared as a concession to political or military force rather than as a recognition of any individual right of conscience. It followed that toleration could be withdrawn as soon as the power that had granted it felt strong enough to do so. This was precisely what had happened to the Huguenot minority in France. In 1685, Louis XIV, after a long campaign of intimidation, revoked the Edict of Nantes by which French Protestants had enjoyed toleration since the end of the sixteenth century; they did not regain it until 1787.

The philosophes joined the battle for religious toleration less out of concern for religion than to publicize the issue of toleration as such. A favorite device was to adopt the pose of the detached, worldly foreigner in examining the foibles and prejudices of one's own country, as the Baron de Montesquieu did in his *Persian Letters* or Voltaire in Utopian travelogues such as *Zadig* and *Micromégas*. The philosophes donned the robes of Chinese sages—Leibniz had just popularized Confucius in Europe, comparing him with Christ as a moral teacher—to show the relativity of all customs and hence the absurdity of fanaticism and dogma. Ironically, they were often repudiated by the very people they set out to defend. When Pierre Bayle, on behalf of the Huguenots, asserted the right of all men to freedom of worship, he scandalized their leaders, who were as little willing to grant toleration to others as Louis XIV was to them.

The philosophes were thus an informal coalition of culture critics and reformers, united by common ideals and, generally, a common background. Most of them came from the upper bourgeoisie, and most of them were professional literary men who wrote for the increasingly educated public of the eighteenth century. Most of them were also French. Though the Enlightenment took root from St. Petersburg to Philadelphia, its center was unquestionably Paris. Here the great figures of the movement held court in the salons of the liberal aristocracy, from whence their pronouncements were carried by newspaper, pamphlet, and periodical to literary cafés and debating societies all over Europe. As a conservative opponent, Joseph de Maistre, later remarked, "An opinion launched in Paris was like a battering ram launched by thirty million men." Yet perhaps the most distinctive thing about the philosophes was their disdain for any merely national identity. They were the first "good Europeans," world citizens who made themselves at home anywhere that reason was honored and came to its defense anywhere that it was attacked; they would probably have sought no more fitting a description than the one given them by the historian Peter Gay: the party of humanity.

THE CAREER OF VOLTAIRE

The most celebrated and perhaps the most representative of the philosophes was François Marie Arouet (1694–1778), who called himself Voltaire. The son of prosperous Parisian bourgeois, Voltaire was until the age of nearly 40 best known as a satiric dramatist whose thrusts had cost him two trips to the Bastille and a public caning by Chevalier de Rohan-Chabot. The turning point in his career was a three-year sojourn in England, where he imbibed Lockean psychology and Newtonian physics, returning to popularize both in France. His *Elements of the Philosophy of Newton* (1738) stands as one of the clearest and most direct links between the Scientific Revolution and the thought of the Enlightenment. The rather lightweight man of letters emerged from his immersion in Newton as the mature and confident author of the *Essay on Customs* and *The Age of Louis XIV.* Nor did Voltaire share the facile optimism of some of his contemporaries, despite his faith in the transforming power of reason. The great Lisbon earthquake of 1755, which killed 70,000 people, drew from him a fierce rebuke to Alexander Pope's maxim, "Whatever is, is right," and produced in the Dr. Pangloss of his novel *Candide* (1759) literature's most famous example of the limits of positive thinking.

In 1751, after a brief attempt to enlighten the court of Frederick the Great, Voltaire bought an estate at Ferney, just beyond the French border in Switzerland. Here, for the last third of his life, he was a kind of one-man republic, firing

Satirist, critic, and conscience of his age: Voltaire here depicted as a Roman sage in a contemporary print.

off as many as 30 letters a day and entertaining a steady stream of visitors from all over Europe who came to give or seek advice, suggest worthy causes, and pay homage to the commoner whose word was more potent than kings'.

From Ferney, too, Voltaire launched his great crusades against bigotry and intolerance. "Écrasez l'infame!" he cried—crush the infamy!—and, more than anyone else, he did. The works of his later years, culminating in the *Philosophical Dictionary* of 1764 (which received the familiar honor of a public burning by the authorities), are a series of eloquent briefs for human freedom, and he was the first to champion the work of Cesare Beccaria, the founder of modern prison reform and an early opponent of capital punishment.

THE SOCIAL CONTRACT

The political thought of the Enlightenment was predicated on the assumption of a *social contract.* The social contract was an agreement by which a group of individuals previously existing in a condition of pure autonomy (the "state of nature") voluntarily placed themselves under the laws and norms of a society. It was thus both a theory of the origin of civilization (how and why men agree to cooperate) and of the origin of government (the rules that specify how such cooperation is to be attained).

The idea of a contract of government by which ruler and ruled assume certain mutual rights and responsibilities was a very old one; it was the emphasis on the prior establishment of society itself that was novel in social contract theory. Before a group can make rules, individuals must first make the group; before particular rules can be agreed upon, there must first be agreement to abide by rules in general. This had previously been taken for granted by political theory; the institution of society and the institution of government were thus conceived of as a single act. The effect of social contract theory in separating them was to raise the question of whether a breach of agreement by the ruler did not release the ruled from their obligation to the agreement as well: in short, the right of rebellion.

Such a question was highly pertinent in the seventeenth century, when historically new societies were in the process of formation (for example, the New England colonies in America), and it became even more so when, in 1642, the people of England rebelled against their king. The revolutionaries justified themselves with various social contract theories, but the most famous one to emerge from the struggle came from a spokesman for the other side, Thomas Hobbes (1588–1679).

Hobbes certainly cannot be considered as even a precursor of the Enlightenment. He had a profoundly pessimistic view of human nature, and the idea of progress would have struck him as absurd. Yet he did share certain things in common with the philosophes who came after him. An agnostic, he constructed his theory of society on purely secular grounds; an admirer of Galileo, he was one of the first thinkers to attempt a rigorous application of scientific method to society at large.

For Hobbes, man, like everything else in the universe, is matter in motion.

Like all other creatures, he seeks pleasure and avoids pain. Unlike all others, however, he multiplies past pleasures by memory and projects them on the future in the form of desire. But since actual pleasures are transitory and few, while desire is limited only by the scope of the imagination, men compete violently for pleasure in the state of nature in what Hobbes called the "war of all against all." The result is a stunted life and early death, succinctly described by Hobbes as "solitary, poor, nasty, brutish and short."

Since men are naturally antisocial, regarding each other as enemies and competitors, if they enter society, it is simply to avoid the misery of life in the state of nature. Man thus enters society as rational animals might enter a zoo, to protect himself from his fellows by a voluntary incarceration among them. The bars of this zoo are laws, and the zookeeper is the sovereign who allots each man his cage and rations, that is, his property and wealth.

Of course, the sovereign is also an individual (or a group of individuals; it does not matter what form of government is chosen, as long as it is absolute), with human desires. Because others surrender to him all their separate freedoms in return for the hope of security, the sovereign is in the unique position of being able to gratify all his personal desires without let or hindrance. But this is the only possible basis for society. In effect, men voluntarily submit to one tyrant to escape being involuntarily subject to the tyranny of every man they meet.

There are two observations to be made about this version of the social contract. First, each man makes his own contract with the sovereign, since he alone can surrender his own freedom. This means that each individual has a direct relationship only with the sovereign. Any association with other members of society is merely fortuitous; the individual has no obligation to them, nor vice versa. Society is thus nothing more than a multiplication of two, and a society that consisted of a single master and slave would be just as complete as one with a population of millions. (An interesting application of this idea can be seen in the nineteenth-century argument that labor unions were a violation of the right of the worker to enter into an exclusive contract with his boss.)

The second point is that the social contract is strictly a one-way affair. The sovereign receives the individual's submission but guarantees nothing in return, for, in Hobbes's view, sovereignty is absolute and can admit no limitation. Yet there is one condition under which the contract may be broken: It is impossible to surrender the right of self-preservation; dead men obey no orders, no matter how absolute the command. The individual may thus resist any command that jeopardizes his life. On the other hand, this right of resistance in no way invalidates the order itself. If the individual is free to resist a sentence of death, the sovereign is equally free to order all his other subjects to assist him in carrying it out.

Hobbes's theory was most completely expressed in his *Leviathan* (1651). It won him few adherents; traditionalists were as appalled by his rejection of divine right as rebels were by his dismissal of civil liberties. The latter found their spokesman in John Locke, but the former were never able to reply adequately. With the possible exception of Bossuet, no serious European thinker after Hobbes attempted to base a theory of society on supernatural foundations. *Leviathan*, written as a defense of absolute monarchy, did more to undermine the premises on which that monarchy rested than any argument ever put forward by its opponents.

Like that of Hobbes, the thought of John Locke (1632–1704) was the product of a period of political strife that culminated in civil war: The Glorious Revolution of 1688. No two men, however, could have drawn more dissimilar conclusions from their experience. For Locke, man is innately peaceful and gregarious in the state of nature, enjoying his natural rights to life, liberty, and the fruit of his own labors. He enters society not from fear but from the desire to increase his wealth and happiness further by rational cooperation with his fellows. The social contract is thus the voluntary association of free, equal, and separate individuals into the free, equal, and united members of a group.

The mere agreement to associate is, in Locke, sufficient to bring society into being. The act of association itself generates sovereignty, that is, the capacity of the group to make such laws and institutions as it deems necessary. This capacity belongs equally to all members of the group since, in the first state of society, there is no ground for differentiating among them. In the Lockean commonwealth, then, the people are sovereign, and they remain so in whatever form of government they choose to adopt.

The difference between Locke's conception of society and that of Hobbes is readily apparent. For Locke, the formation of society is completely distinct from the formation of government. Society is primary, and government merely an instrument to serve its purposes. In Hobbes's view, a society prior to government is logically impossible, because the acknowledgment of authority is the sole basis of society.

These differences are best seen in the question of rebellion. For Hobbes, rebellion immediately dissolves society and casts man back into the state of nature. It is therefore the ultimate crime, for however oppressive society may be, the state of nature is always by definition worse. But in Locke (as well as in the work of his influential German contemporary, Samuel von Pufendorf), rebellion is a legitimate reaction to a ruler who abuses the natural rights of his subjects. It dissolves not society but only government, and the people, resuming their original sovereignty, simply make a new one to take its place. This was Locke's interpretation of the events of 1688. King James II, having violated his people's trust by seeking to impose the Catholic religion contrary to the laws of the realm, had been justly deposed, and a new monarchy established on terms that gave better security against oppression.

Locke had great influence in the eighteenth century, particularly on the founders of the United States. Nonetheless, serious objections to his views remained. By locating sovereignty in the entire body politic, he was locating it nowhere in particular, and thus begged the whole question of power. Every rebellion (including that of 1688) begins as a coup d'état, with a minority acting on behalf of a majority it has not previously consulted. Even if the majority acquiesces in the resulting seizure of power, this does not alter the fact that its sovereign rights have been trespassed.

The derivation of natural rights was another problem in Locke's theory.

Like that of Hobbes, Locke's concept of society was completely secular. But if natural rights were not given by divine revelation and yet existed before any society, where had they come from and how did men perceive them? Locke's answer was that natural rights were disclosed by reason. But at least one of Locke's rights, the right of property, had already been contested by radicals in the Puritan Revolution of 1642–1649, and it was to be even more emphatically rejected in the work of Jean-Jacques Rousseau.

Rousseau was born in Geneva in 1712. Unlike his philosophe contemporaries, he was poor and ill educated, a perennial social misfit. A runaway at 16, he repeated the same pattern all his life, betraying friends, breaking promises, even abandoning his own children. At odds with almost all the dominant trends of the Enlightenment, he spent the last third of his life denouncing it; yet he is now remembered as its greatest and most gifted member.

Rousseau's opposition to Locke's views on property and the foundation of society is made clear in his *Discourse on the Origin of Inequality* (1755):

> The first man who, having enclosed a piece of ground, bethought himself of saying *This is mine,* and found people simple enough to believe him, was the real founder of civil society. From how many crimes, wars and murders, from how many horrors and misfortunes might not someone have saved mankind, by pulling up the stakes and filling in the ditch, and crying out to his fellows, 'Beware of listening to this impostor; you are undone if you once forget that the fruits of the earth belong to us all, and the earth itself to nobody.'

Rousseau thus depicts the state of nature as an idyllic primitive communism, corrupted by the sin of possession. That original transgression, hedged by law and enshrined in custom, created the basic institution of all society: property. But whereas Locke (and later followers like Bernard Mandeville and Adam Smith) viewed competition for private gain as healthy and stimulating, Rousseau saw in it the fount of all human evils. The lure of profit made men rejoice in the misery of others, sons wish for the death of their fathers, and speculators grow rich on plague, famine, and war. "If you reply that society is so constituted that each man gains by serving others, I will reply that that would be very well did he not gain still more by harming them. There is no legitimate profit that is not surpassed by the profit we can make by illegitimate means, and the harm we do our neighbor is always more lucrative than the services we render him." Man, born free, had enslaved himself by his own free will, so that now society obliged men to be "enemies out of duty, and knaves from self-interest."

Rousseau's idealization of the state of nature encouraged the popular fiction of the "noble savage," often identified with the American Indian or other distant and exotic races. Rousseau did in fact lead a "back to nature" movement, particularly with his novels *La Nouvelle Héloïse* and *Émile,* but it was certainly not to the state of nature that he wished to return. For better or worse, the human race was now civilized, and the virtues of society (its knowledge, its arts) were so entwined with its vices that it was impossible to abandon the worst without also losing the best. The future, Rousseau insisted, lay in society, and man's task was to re-create by justice the lost Eden of our "first and ancient innocence."

The theoretical basis of this new society is set out in *The Social Contract* (1762). Hobbes must be rejected, because "to renounce liberty is to renounce being a man"; but Locke is equally unacceptable, because the profit motive is no more than the "war of all against all" waged under the banner of law. Rousseau will be satisfied with nothing less than a condition in which man retains all the freedom of the state of nature while enjoying all the benefits and security of a just society. This is possible only if each man surrenders himself absolutely, not to a single Hobbesian monarch but to the entire collectivity. Since each man, while giving up his own rights, receives simultaneously the surrender of everyone else's, his original rights are returned manifold; yet, since everyone makes the same exchange, all men remain exactly equal to one another.

The collective entity in which all individual rights have been vested is called by Rousseau the *general will.* At any given moment, the general will represents the best interests of the community as a whole. Thus, on every public question there are many solutions that benefit particular groups or individuals, but the general will is the only one that (by furthering the aims of the entire community) benefits all.

Each man, asserts Rousseau, has a double interest: his own and society's. The first is his profit, the second his duty. Though, naturally, people tend to recognize their private interests first, their true ultimate interest is the welfare of the community, and the act of sovereignty (rightly understood) consists in their coming to realize the common interest and acting upon it. Sovereignty, in other words, is the effectuation of the general will.

Ideally, the general will would be enacted with the unanimous consent of the entire community. In practice, however, it could not be expected that all citizens would be able to transcend their private interests, and to wait for unanimity on every question would, Rousseau confesses, reduce the social contract to "an empty formula." It is necessary at some point to oblige dissenters to comply with the general will, for their own good as well as the community's. If they cannot recognize where their real freedom lies, Rousseau says, they must "be forced to be free."

Unfortunately, Rousseau does not tell us just how the general will is to be recognized, nor just where discussion must cease and obedience begin. He properly insists that a simple majority cannot decide the general will, since a majority consisting of a sum of merely private and selfish interests is no more valid than any single man's interest. Nor, by the same logic, does an arbitrary majority, like two-thirds or three-quarters, make any more sense. It might well be that only one man recognized the general will, and all his fellow citizens were deluded. In that case, it would clearly be their duty to obey him (and his to compel their obedience). Again, Rousseau does not explain how that single enlightened individual could prevail, nor what limit should be placed on his power to force everyone else "to be free."

Rousseau was invited on two occasions to draw up actual constitutions, for Corsica in 1765 and Poland in 1771. Aside from a few eccentricities (such as a prohibition on all riding carriages in Corsica), they are surprisingly moderate documents. The best practical maxim for an established state, Rousseau advised, was to change nothing unless it was strictly necessary. He was even reluctant to abolish serfdom, and proposed that it be done by slow degrees only, to minimize social dislocation.

But if Rousseau was unwilling to follow his own premises to their logical conclusions, others were. The Abbé Morelly, about whom nothing is known but his name, published in 1755 a rigorously communistic system, the *Code of Nature,* in which all property and commerce were abolished. Morelly wrote, "If someone needs an article of clothing, he will take it from the man who makes it; that man will take the cloth from the one who manufactures it; and that man will take the raw materials from the storehouse where they will have been brought by those who gather them . . ." For such a system to work, it was obvious that production and consumption had to be strictly regulated. Each man could take no more than he needed for his daily use; sumptuary laws pounced on the least hint of luxury, and hoarding was the cardinal social offense. On the other hand, rational planning and the elimination of "vanity" and ostentation made possible a reduction of toil for all and a guaranteed retirement at age 40. (What senior citizens were expected to contribute to society is suggested by a clause in the Code that forbade anyone over 40 to live as a bachelor.)

In Morelly's utopia, equality was to be pursued even to the size and shape of the buildings. This passion for uniformity seemed to be as much motivated by moral as economic considerations. Freedom must be sacrificed for security, and a fundamental distrust of humankind itself pervades Morelly's final injunctions: "Any moral philosophy not built on the plan and system of the Code will be absolutely forbidden. . . . Each chapter of the laws will be separately engraved on columns or pyramids in the public square of each city. Their intentions will always be followed literally according to the exact meaning of the text without the slightest change or alteration ever being allowed."

In Morelly, the ideal of human equality, carried to its ultimate limits, was fossilized into an eternal and unvarying despotism. Liberty *or* equality was the great paradox of eighteenth-century thought; there seemed no way to have them both. Broadly speaking, the conservative wing of the Enlightenment was primarily concerned with the former, the radical wing with the latter. Perhaps the greatest achievement of the conservative Enlightenment was the Baron de Montesquieu's doctrine of the separation of powers, first enunciated in *The Spirit of the Laws* (1748). Montesquieu argued that the only way to prevent concentrations of autocratic power was by clearly dividing the executive, legislative, and judicial functions of government, so that each could act as a brake upon the other. This system of "checks and balances" was written not only into the American Constitution but also into more ephemeral documents such as the French Constitution of 1791, the Prussian Code of 1792, the Spanish Constitution of 1812, and the stillborn revolutionary constitutions of 1848.

But Montesquieu himself was a member of the privileged nobility of the robe who had bought a lucrative office and spoke essentially for a reactionary aristocracy. There is certainly not to be gleaned in his writings the least concern with social justice, unless it be justice for his own class. More radical critics, like Claude Adrien Helvétius, dismissed him as a mere lawyer. The final decades of the Enlightenment saw increasingly severe criticism of basic social institutions, especially property. Writers like Thomas Spence and William Ogilvie in England and Gabriel de Mably, Brissot de Warville, and Restif de la Bretonne in France demanded a far-reaching redistribution of wealth if not complete communization, and their radicalism tinged even moderate reformers like Turgot and Necker, ministers of Louis XVI.

The most remarkable of these writers was Simon-Henri Linguet, a lawyer disbarred for his violent attacks on property and the legal code. Society, said Linguet, was founded on a crime, the appropriation of property, and its laws were the rules instituted by the criminals to protect their loot. Thus, a vast enslaved majority toiled in desperate poverty while the wealth they produced was stolen from them every day by their oppressors. Revolution was inevitable: "Never has want been more universal, more devastating for the class which is condemned to it; never, perhaps, amid apparent prosperity has Europe been nearer to a complete upheaval . . ." But, unlike Karl Marx, whom he anticipates in so many ways, Linguet had no hope that the revolution would make human life better. In the end, he advocated nothing, awaiting the future with despair.

The radical pessimism of Rousseau reached its final term in Linguet, just as the faith and optimism of the philosophes found its ultimate embodiment in Condorcet. Ironically, they shared the same fate. Both the prophet of doom and the apostle of progress perished during the French Revolution in the Reign of Terror.

THE ENLIGHTENED DESPOTS

"The enlightened despots" is a term applied somewhat loosely to a number of rulers who were sympathetic to the goals and programs of the Enlightenment. The alliance between absolute monarchs and radical social critics was not as surprising as it might seem. The philosophes, as we have seen, had a great deal of confidence in mankind but very little in men, and particularly that mass of men who were subject to the political process but excluded from it, the people. Contempt for the people breathes on almost every page of Voltaire, and Rousseau in a famous passage speaks bitingly of the ignorant masses who "dare to speak of liberty without having any idea of what it is."

But if the philosophes had little use for democracy, they put no more stock in the nobility. How could one expect society to be changed by those who benefited most from keeping it as it was? In practical terms, the only hope seemed to lie in monarchy. Only the Crown could muzzle the aristocracy yet awe the people, as Louis XIV had. If kings could be persuaded to serve reason as assiduously as they pursued *gloire,* what might they not accomplish? Thus the freethinkers of the Enlightenment entered into alliance with the dynasts of divine right.

For their part, the kings saw the philosophes as valuable propagandists in their struggle with the aristocracy. Moreover, in an increasingly secular age, the old supernatural arguments for royal absolutism were rapidly losing their force. It seemed safer, in the Age of Reason, to be the servant of the people than the servant of God. The philosophes were ready to assist this delicate metamorphosis.

They believed power could be tamed and made useful by becoming rational. Both sides converged on this common aim: to strengthen the central state by modernizing it.

The reign of Gustavus III of Sweden (1771–1792) was a good example of enlightened despotism in practice. Gustavus came to a throne enfeebled by 50 years of aristocratic anarchy and misrule. The country appeared on the verge of breakdown, with French interests supporting the various factions of nobility and Russian ones behind an alliance of merchants and peasants who demanded an end to idle privilege and a share in government. Gustavus regained power with an audacious coup and imposed a new constitution that reemphasized the sovereignty of the Crown. But he also instituted liberal reforms and posed as a disinterested administrator who could fairly adjudicate the claims of all parties and classes. For about a decade, this combination of force and blandishment was successful. But a resurgence of aristocratic power in the 1780s undermined his position, forcing him more and more openly into alliance with the popular party. The outbreak of the French Revolution added radical opponents to his reactionary ones, and a conspiracy of both resulted in his assassination.

A somewhat similar situation arose in neighboring Denmark, where a brilliant young German physician, Johann Friedrich von Struensee, emerged as the power behind the throne of the feebleminded young Christian VII (1766–1808). Struensee elbowed aside the ruling aristocracy, revamped the administration, and pushed ahead with a bold program of reform, including civil service examinations for government office. But his arrogant use of royal power united all factions against him, and he suffered a traitor's death after less than two years of power (1772). Style rather than content was Struensee's error, however, and by the end of the century, most of his reforms had been implemented by others.

A considerably more successful example of ministerial despotism was the Marquis de Pombal, the virtual ruler of Portugal between 1750 and 1777. Pombal carried out a typical reform program, encouraging free trade, rationalizing the legal code, and breaking the aristocratic monopoly of state offices. But his principal target was the Church, which owned two-thirds of the country, and particularly the Jesuits, who ruled Paraguay almost as a fief of the order. Pombal expelled the Jesuits in 1759 and confiscated all their property. Such an action would have brought papal thunders down in the past, but so feeble had the eighteenth-century church become that it could only watch helplessly as its own Inquisition was used to drive the Jesuits out. France, Spain, and other Catholic countries quickly followed suit, and the Jesuit order was actually dissolved in 1773, not to be restored until 1814.

Even Spain had its enlightened despot in Charles III (1759–1788), who strove to revive agriculture, subordinate the church, and make the empire functional again. After his death, his reforms disappeared like water into sand, but Charles did give enlightened despotism its most enduring motto: "Everything for the people, nothing by the people." It was a promise that could always be at least half kept.

Enlightened despotism was thus a Europe-wide phenomenon, with the significant exception of France. But its two most important representatives were

Frederick the Great of Prussia (1740–1786) and Joseph II of Austria (1780–1790).

Frederick the Great occupied much the same position in the eighteenth century that Louis XIV had in the seventeenth: a heroic, dominating figure who raised all Europe against him and survived by sheer nerve alone. Frederick himself encouraged the parallel: He built a palace at Potsdam clearly modeled on Versailles and pursued Voltaire for years with invitations until the author of *The Age of Louis XIV* accepted.

Frederick spoke the rhetoric of the Enlightenment and even wrote some of it; he was an assiduous commentator on politics all his life. His position, though deriving more immediately from Pufendorf, may be described in essence as a modified Hobbesianism. The people had made an irrevocable grant of sovereignty to the king that he might, standing above society, make laws for all. This authority passed by prescriptive right through the blood royal according to the principle of legitimacy. Yet, although the king was neither accountable to the law nor subject to removal, he had an ethical obligation to rule in the best interests of his people. Power was justified by social utility; the authority of a master was necessary to fulfill the role of a servant.

Frederick continually stressed his own responsibility for the general welfare: "My chief obligation," he wrote, "is . . . to make [my people] as happy as human beings can be, or as happy as the means at my disposal permit"; "I am the first servant of the state." The Prussian Code of 1794, published after Freder-

"I am the first servant of the state." Frederick the Great of Prussia sought to justify the powers of a divine-right monarch with the secular ideology of service.

ick's death but essentially a product of his reign, echoes the same spirit: "The welfare of the state and its inhabitants is the object of society." But we must remember that the people whom Frederick wished to make happy were not the abstract egalitarian masses of modern society but the hierarchical orders of the Old Regime: the nobility and the army, merchants and craftsmen, peasants and serfs. Frederick's social policy was, if anything, retrogressive, since he favored his nobility far more than his father had. The officer corps of the Prussian army was their private preserve, as well as the upper ranks of the civil service. They remained exempt from taxation and from all government control on their estates. Whereas Frederick William I had steadily encroached on Junker authority in the provinces, Frederick left them virtually autonomous. Frederick William had broken up large concentrations of landholding; Frederick not only left them alone, but urged the nobility to adopt entail as a means of preserving their estates.

Equally revealing is Frederick's record toward the lowest and most oppressed order of his society. As a good son of the Enlightenment, Frederick was personally appalled by serfdom; as king of Prussia, he did nothing about it, even on his own estates. Certainly, there is a positive side to Frederick's accomplishment. He substantially increased the population and productivity of the Prussian state, and after the Seven Years' War he worked tirelessly to rebuild the ravaged countryside. But the great mass of his subjects benefited little from Frederician prosperity. Life remained as oppressive as ever in what the philosopher Lessing called the most "slavish" state in Europe.

For Frederick, however, there was no contradiction in all this. He had made of enlightened despotism a secular analogue to divine right, in which the ruler's mystical relationship to God was replaced by an equally mystical relation to the state, the result in both cases being an absolute mandate to maintain the status quo. Most rulers of the period were content to mix sacred and secular theory in whatever proportion seemed to work best at any given moment, now donning the robes of divine right, now the plain livery of the workaday despot. Frederick would have none of this. He repudiated any religious sanction for kingship, even forbidding his subjects to pray for him in church. His offer of refuge in 1749 to the atheist La Mettrie was meant to shock; he succeeded even better when he offered to resettle the Jesuits in Prussia after the dissolution of their order. Anyone expelled by the church was a friend of the king of Prussia. Frederick maintained the traditional Lutheran faith in his own kingdom, of course—there was nothing to be gained by alarming the ignorant—but he restricted the pastorate to the middle classes only, not wishing to contaminate his nobility with superstition.

More clearly than any other ruler of his time, Frederick realized the impact of secularism on the foundations of authority in Europe. The world had changed, and monarchy must change with it if it expected to survive. A brilliant reactionary, Frederick had grasped the most daring idea of the Enlightenment—that the Christian god was dead, and perhaps all gods were dead—and marched with it firmly back into the past.

Quite a different case was "the revolutionary emperor," Joseph II. Joseph was the infant son whom Empress Maria Theresa had held aloft before the Hun-

The reforming emperor, Joseph II of Austria. Casanova saw "conceit and suicide" in his face.

garian nobility when Frederick the Great invaded Silesia in 1741. The two were seldom in harmony after that. Maria Theresa was unsophisticated, devout, scandalized by the Enlightenment, and, in her own way, one of the most capable rulers the House of Hapsburg ever produced. Her long reign (1740–1780) saw the beginnings of modernization in Austria. Silesia, lost to Frederick the Great, was never recovered, but the empress and her able chancellor, Prince von Kaunitz, set about to consolidate what remained. Administration was centralized in Austria proper and Bohemia, creating a model for the whole empire. Old guild monopolies and tariff barriers were overthrown, establishing the largest free-trade zone in Europe. Church land was expropriated and church control of education broken, despite Maria Theresa's personal hostility to the new currents of thought.

These changes were substantial, but they did not begin to satisfy Joseph. He was perpetually exasperated by his mother's half measures and totally at odds with her values. In 1765, he became Holy Roman Emperor and coregent of Austria, but Maria Theresa never let him exercise real power. When in 1780 he succeeded to the Austrian throne, he had a 15-year backlog of frustrated projects and ambitions.

What Joseph wanted was to create from the most heterogeneous state in Europe, a state that embraced almost every language and culture on the continent, a single political and social order. This stemmed partly from the tendency toward bureaucratic absolutism that was so much a part of the age, partly from a very personal desire to use the state as a moral instrument for the betterment of humanity. Joseph was genuinely distressed at the suffering of the poor, genuinely appalled by bigotry and intolerance; the persistence of serfdom in Austria under his mother's reign he found "incredible and inexpressible." The ills of mankind could not wait: "Hasten everything," wrote Joseph to a minister, "that brings me nearer to the accomplishment of my plans for the happiness of my people."

In ten astonishing years, Joseph promulgated 6000 edicts designed to transform backward, reactionary, feudalistic Austria into a model of progress and enlightenment. Serfdom was abolished, censorship lifted, freedom of religion decreed. Jews were given full civil rights and permitted to intermarry with Christians. Marriage itself was declared a civil contract, to the horror and outrage of the church. Apostasy and witchcraft were stricken from the legal code. Capital punishment and judicial torture were abolished. (In liberal England, by contrast, the death penalty was still inflicted for more than 200 different crimes.) But the most striking aspect of the new code was its insistence on equality before the law. The same crime was to receive the same punishment, be the offender pauper or count, and Joseph shocked Vienna when he forced a young nobleman to sweep the streets in a chain gang. Privilege, tradition, special interests were all brushed aside in the spate of imperial reform. "I have made philosophy the legislator of my empire," said Joseph.

The backlash was inevitable. There was scarcely a class or population group within the empire that Joseph had not enraged or offended. The nobility was furious at the freeing of the serfs and the leveling of its legal and financial privileges, the church at the grants of toleration and the dissolution of its monasteries. In Belgium and Hungary, where Joseph trampled over the ancient "liberties" of the privileged orders, there was outright rebellion. Even the peasants who were so much the object of Joseph's solicitude were often antagonized. They resented the curtailment of church festivals, were bewildered by the mass of edicts, and frequently sympathized with the local priest or noble whom Joseph declared their oppressor.

In the face of this opposition, Joseph redoubled his efforts. Censorship was reimposed, and a vast army of spies appeared: Not the least of Joseph's legacies was to create the first police state in modern history. At the end, large parts of the country were held down by military force alone. Many years earlier, the famous Casanova, asked what he saw in the young Joseph's face, replied, "Conceit and suicide." The remark was tragically prophetic. Joseph died a broken man at 48, his life's work in ruins about him. His successors, Leopold II (1790–1792) and Francis I (1792–1835), were forced to restore much of the old system, and serfdom was not finally abolished in parts of the Hapsburg Empire until 1867.

The career of Joseph II revealed the self-defeating nature of enlightened despotism. Having systematically undermined the traditional props of monarchy—the church, the nobility, divine-right theory—the enlightened despots argued that they were above society and ruled, as it were, on air. The result was that they had created the conditions for a revolution to which they were the last remaining obstacle. When the French Revolution broke out in 1789, Joseph condemned it bitterly, even though the revolutionaries sought many of the same goals as he. To Joseph, power could come only from above. He failed to realize that no one, no matter how powerful and determined, could bring about fundamental social change without the support and consent of those to be changed. In this was his tragedy, and that of his century.

THE COUNTER-ENLIGHTENMENT

The glittering culture of the salons, the audacious rationalism of the Enlightenment, touched the life of ordinary people at only one point: religion. Religion was not simply, as Karl Marx remarked scornfully in the nineteenth century, the opiate of the masses; it was, in most cases, their only culture as well, the only fun and human consolation they had. And they were losing it.

Religion was everywhere on the defensive in the Age of Enlightenment. The bishops of the established churches, Catholic, Lutheran, and Anglican, were aristocrats who rubbed shoulders with the philosophes and shared their repugnance at the old barbaric dogmas of revealed religion. Theologians like Samuel Clarke and Joseph Butler in England tried to find a new basis for morality in the innate order of the Newtonian universe rather than the Ten Commandments, and sympathetic philosophers like the German Leibniz argued that when God revealed the design of the world, all apparent evil would be so clearly seen as necessary to realize the good "that even the innocent would not wish not to have suffered."

This was cold comfort for millions who toiled and struggled, and what they could not get from their betters they began to make for themselves. Grass-roots religion—a phenomenon previously associated only with periods of great social upheaval such as the Reformation or the Puritan Revolution—spread out from late-seventeenth-century Germany all across Protestant Europe and even to the New World. As Pietism in Germany, Methodism in England, and the Great Awakening in America, it had the same general goal: to put heart back into religion, to stress the individual's destiny, and his responsibility for his own salvation.

The roots of Pietism lay in the tradition of German medieval mysticism, revived in the early seventeenth century by Jakob Böhme (1575–1624) and given popular expression by the evangelist Philipp Jakob Spener (1635–1705). The faculty of the Saxon University of Wittenberg discovered 250 "errors" in Spener's preachments, but by the end of the century Pietism had become the dominant spiritual movement in Protestant Germany. It found academic sponsorship in the Prussian University of Halle, and an aristocratic patron in Count Nikolus Ludwig von Zinzendorf (1700–1760), who sheltered the Moravian Brethren, an important Pietist sect, on his estate. It was a Moravian Pietist who counseled the spiritually troubled young English clergyman John Wesley (1703–1791), whose deep sense of personal unworthiness and guilt found little echo in the complacent Anglican church of the first Hanoverians. The turning point in Wesley's life was what he described as an experience of divine grace on an evening in May, 1738: "I felt my heart strangely warmed," he wrote. "I felt I did trust in Christ, Christ alone, for salvation, and an assurance was given me that . . . saved me from the law of sin and death." Convinced that only by opening the heart to such infusions of grace could man be saved, Wesley, aided by his brother Charles and the charismatic preacher George Whitefield, took his message to every corner of the British Isles. Excluded from the churches, harassed by the authorities, and often threatened by mobs, Wesley preached in mine pits and in open fields. By his own calculation, he delivered some 40,000 sermons, an average of 15 a week for 50 years. His followers, called Methodists, dedicated themselves to the virtues of thrift, toil, discipline, and abstinence; they were also, however, deeply conservative, often obscurantist, and hostile to Catholics and Jews.

The supreme artistic expression of the new piety was the music of Johann Sebastian Bach (1685–1750), the greatest composer of the Baroque period. In such works as his setting of Luther's hymn "A Mighty Fortress Is Our God," Bach restored the old revolutionary fervor of German Protestantism. In the *St. Matthew Passion,* he gave the suffering of Christ a human dimension that is worlds removed from the innocents of Leibniz who applaud their own pain.

The Catholic counterparts of Pietism also went by different names—Quietism in Spain, Jansenism in Flanders, France, and Italy. But all stressed personal piety against outward works, the individual conscience against clerical dictate. However, while Pietism was politically passive, the Catholic revival inevitably posed the question of authority. By its very nature it was a challenge to the papacy, whose claims to authority rose in direct proportion to the fall of its actual influence; this in turn involved the rulers of Catholic states. In France, where the church was already subservient to the state, Louis XIV and Louis XV strongly opposed the reformers; in Austria, where it was still relatively autonomous, they found toleration and favor under both Maria Theresa and Joseph II.

The most important of these movements was Jansenism, named after the Flemish bishop Cornelius Jansen (1585–1638), who worked out a doctrine very close to that of John Calvin, including predestination and the denial of free will. Such ideas seemed scarcely compatible with the Counter-Reformation church, but the Jansenists insisted they were loyal Catholics. They took powerful root at the monastery of Port-Royal near Versailles, attracting some of the leading French intellectuals of the seventeenth century, including the great philosopher and mathematician Blaise Pascal. In 1713, Pope Clement XI finally denounced Jansenism in the Bull *Unigenitus,* and Port-Royal was closed. But instead of being destroyed, Jansenism emerged more vigorous than ever, not as the doctrine of a spiritual elite, but as a rallying cry against papal supremacy and royal absolutism alike. By the 1730s, an estimated two-thirds of Paris was Jansenist. Esoteric theology had become mass-movement politics; what had begun as a rebuke to the moral laxity of the clergy had become a protest against the heartlessness and indifference of the great social hierarchies of church and state.

Among the middle and upper classes, reaction to the rationalism of the Enlightenment took the form of devotion to a new literary genre, the novel. The readers of Samuel Richardson's *Pamela* and *Clarissa* or Pierre de Marivaux's *Marianne* were the ancestors of the public today that reads novels for "a good cry," though the unabashed sentimentality of these early specimens would more likely make a modern audience laugh than weep. Horace Walpole's *The Castle of Otranto* (1764) introduced the Gothic novel of horror and suspense, while Goethe's immensely popular *Sorrows of Young Werther* (1774) provided the prototype of the Byronic young man of Romantic literature nursing the deliciously incurable pangs of lost love. The deliberate cultivation of emotion and sensitivity, the passion for ancient ruins and distant places, the preoccupation with the dark and occult that we think of as characteristically Romantic were all substantially foreshadowed in the midst of the Age of Reason. While the philosophes were stressing the universal in humanity, the German critic Johann Gottfried von Herder (1744–1803) argued that the individual nation with its unique language and culture was the basic unit of history. The Scot David Hume (1711–1776) and the German Immanuel Kant (1724–1804) cast doubt on reason itself, arguing that the mind imposed its own structures on a fundamentally unknowable reality. Their writings laid the basis for nineteenth-century Idealist philosophy and the Romantic movement, with its emphasis on the artist's subjective perception of the world.

We must not, however, think of the Enlightenment in terms of rationalism and the reaction against it. Rather let us conceive of it as a great current whose very strength created countercurrents that are inseparably linked to it. The romantic Goethe of *Wether* became the mature classicist of *Elective Affinities,* a novel in which feeling is subjected to almost clinical dissection, and the Kant who declared that the world could never be known was also the man who cried, "Dare to know!" But most paradoxical of all was Rousseau, the apostle of feeling and rigid utopian theorist, whom half his critics take for the greatest figure of the Enlightenment and half its greatest opponent, and who at the end of his life could explain his own contradictions only by saying that he resembled no one else in the world, and so could not be judged. If the eighteenth century was indeed an Age of Reason, it was also a time that still knew, as Pascal had put it a century before, that "the heart has its reasons, which reason knows nothing of."

THE SPREAD OF LITERACY

The culture of the eighteenth century reflected not only the emergence of new ideas but a new audience. In the 100 years before the Revolution, 18 more men and 13 more women in every 100 became literate in France, and comparable gains were made in England, Austria, Denmark, and parts of Germany. Not all these new readers were equally sophisticated, of course, and deliberate efforts were still made to keep the lower orders from acquiring this dangerous skill: "I allow of no writing for the poor," said the educational reformer Hannah More in 1801. But the poor were learning to read nonetheless. What they read were manuals of piety and devotional tracts, almanacs and astrological charts, bawdy satires, and tales of the miraculous. In the towns, there were innumerable pamphlets, broadsides, and flysheets on sale for a penny. They were crudely printed and badly written, but their influence was enormous; as the Austrian writer Johann Pezzl noted, "Books educate scholars; pamphlets educate people."

Newspapers began in Italy in the sixteenth century with biannual pamphlets that circulated at fairs; by the seventeenth century, weekly and monthly "intelligencers" and "corrantoes" began to attract a wide audience, and as early as 1629, the English dramatist Ben Jonson satirized the public thirst for news. Then as now, the state took a dim view of the free flow of information, and licensing fees and censorship inhibited the development of the newspaper. But in 1702, the first daily paper appeared in London; a century later, some 400 papers were being published in the British Isles, while Goethe in Germany complained that "we have newspapers for every hour of the day." Monthly magazines were equally successful, attaining circulations of up to 15,000. Most of these were aimed at a more leisured clientele, as the titles of such English publications as *The Spectator* and *Gentleman's Magazine* indicate. Daniel Defoe was the first to serialize a novel when he ran monthly installments of his enormously popular *Robinson Crusoe* in his own *Review*. Ostensibly an adventure of shipwreck and survival, *Crusoe* was really a compendium of middle-class virtues of thrift and hard work, and it has been aptly called the first great novel of the urban temperament. This phenomenon of literature aimed at various levels of education, taste, and values was new. It worried Goethe, who remarked, "Formerly there was one taste, now there are many. But tell me, where are those tastes tasted?"

The new mass-circulation literature helped define and articulate the values and aspirations of the laboring and merchant classes and hence make them more sharply aware of their social identity and interests. It also broke the aristocratic monopoly on "culture." For the first time, writers were able to support themselves without noble patronage. Their wider audience was reflected not only in the subjects they chose but also the way they depicted them. Writing for the court of Louis XIV, the playwright Jean-Baptiste Molière would treat social climbing with appropriate contempt in *The Bourgeois Gentleman;* a century later, Pierre de Beaumarchais scored an immense popular success with a sympathetic treatment of the same theme in *The Marriage of Figaro*.

The plastic arts also began to enter the public arena. Before the seventeenth century, there had been no museums, galleries, or exhibitions. Aside from church

The composing room of a print shop. The diffusion of literacy in the eighteenth century, reflected in the popularity of newspapers and novels as well as Diderot's great *Encyclopedia* (from which this engraving is taken), had revolutionary social consequences.

decoration and outdoor sculpture such as the fountains in Rome, art was the private luxury of rich connoisseurs and royal collectors. A very few painters, like Pieter Brueghel and Adrien Brouwer, depicted life in the street and the field, but most confined themselves to the allegorical scenes from Greek and Roman mythology preferred by their patrons. With the Englishman William Hogarth (1697–1764), fine art entered the marketplace. Hogarth turned his paintings into inexpensive prints and sold them by subscription and lottery. He adopted cartoon techniques to make his work more accessible and satirized middle-class mores and urban misery in his *Marriage à la Mode* and *Gin Lane* series. Art would never be quite the same again. Painters had glorified kings and their wars; now Jacques-Louis David would follow the French queen Marie Antoinette to the scaffold and Goya depict the battlefield atrocities of the Napoleonic wars in Spain.

Even music, seemingly the most abstract of the arts, reflected the new terms on which the artist found himself with society. The seventeenth-century composer was dependent on church or court patronage, like Michael Delalande, whose function at Versailles is indicated by the title of one of his compositions, *Symphonies for the King's Supper.* Even Franz Josef Haydn (1732–1809), the father of classical sonata form, wore the livery of the Esterhazy family into his fifties. But in later life, Haydn was able to sign independent contracts with London and Paris publishers, and he died an international celebrity. Ludwig van Beethoven (1770–1827) supported himself by commissions and public concerts, though he was scarcely affluent, and his correspondence is full of complaints and threatened litigation against unscrupulous promoters and publishers. For better or worse, the composer had joined the painter, sculptor, and writer as an entrepreneur whose capital was his talent and whose product was his art.

Musical theater was a burgeoning art form in the eighteenth century, and from low comedy to grand opera it exhibited an often daring freedom. The lyrics of John Gay's *The Beggar's Opera* (1728) skirted a fine line between merry satire and biting social criticism:

Thro' all the employments of life
Each neighbor abuses his brother
Whore and Rogue they call Husband and Wife
All professions be-rogue one another
The Priest calls the Lawyer a cheat
The Lawyer beknaves the Divine
And the Statesman, because he's so great
Thinks his trade as honest as mine

On a more exalted plane were the operas of Wolfgang Amadeus Mozart (1756–1791), including his setting of Pierre de Beaumarchais's *The Marriage of Figaro* and his allegory of Enlightenment ideals, *The Magic Flute;* while Beethoven's opera *Fidelio* portrayed the overthrow of tyranny. Music, too, had come a long way from *Symphonies for the King's Supper.*

As the Old Regime drew toward its close, the contrast between the vitality of Europe's economy and the constriction of its social institutions was increasingly pronounced. Population, life expectancy, and literacy rates were rising generally. Though early critics of the population explosion like the English clergy-man and author Thomas Robert Malthus were concerned about the potential im-pact of such growth, the food supply kept pace with it, in part due to land clear-ance and enclosure, in part to advances in fertilizers and husbandry, the so-called Agricultural Revolution. Gold and silver bullion, the key to economic expansion during the Renaissance, had given way in large part to credit, a far more flexible and efficient instrument of growth. By any measure—capital, productivity, gross output—the European economy was larger than ever before, and for the first time it was genuinely global in scale: The two great imperial powers, Britain and France, had quadrupled the value of their foreign trade over the course of the century.

A growing alienation from the established institution of church, state, and orders was also reflected in the major cultural currents of the age, whether ex-pressed in religious populism, the demand for legal equality, or the rise of secret fellowship societies like the Freemasons, where, at least to a degree, members of different social strata could fraternize with one another. But the supreme mon-ument of the age was the great *Encyclopedia,* edited principally by the Frenchman Denis Diderot (1713–1784). Diderot, the son of a provincial artisan turned essay-ist and publicist, conceived his "classified dictionary of the sciences, arts, and trades" (to quote from the subtitle) while at work translating a British reference work. Persuading his publisher to expand the commission, and engaging a verita-ble Who's Who of the Enlightenment, including Voltaire, Rousseau, and Montes-quieu, to contribute the thousands of articles on every aspect of human knowl-edge, Diderot forged ahead with what was to become the greatest publishing venture in history. The first volume, containing controversial articles on atheism and the human soul among other subjects, appeared in 1751. It was at once at-tacked by the authorities, who first suspended and later revoked the publisher's license. The attorney general of France denounced the book as a conspiracy against public morals, the pope placed it on the Index and declared anyone buying or reading it to be excommunicated, and Diderot's coeditor, Jean d'Alembert, deserted the project. But Diderot himself worked on, issuing further volumes de-spite the ban, filling in the gaps when contributors dropped out, and often even setting up the plates. By 1765, the 17 volumes of text were complete, and seven years later the last of 11 volumes of illustration appeared.

Despite its enormous size and expense, and perhaps more because than in spite of official censorship, the *Encyclopedia* was a great commercial success, re-turning a 120 percent profit on its investment (though little more than 5 percent of this went to Diderot himself). Later editions in reduced format circulated throughout Europe, and perhaps 20,000 full sets were sold in the years before 1789, not including pirated versions and unauthorized excerpts in newspapers and periodicals. But although more than half the male population of France was at least technically literate by 1789, no more than a tenth of this number were in a position to afford it. Even the less expensive quarto editions represented more than a full year's purchase of bread for an urban laborer and his family; as Robert Darnton observes, such a person could no more buy such a book than he could a palace. Enlightenment, like most other worldly goods, was still the privilege of a few.

five

The French Revolution and Napoleon

History is a myth that men agree to believe.

Napoleon

The French Revolution was recognized throughout Europe from the moment of its inception as the supreme event of the age, even of all ages. "How much the greatest event that has happened in the world, and how much the best!" exulted the Whig politician Charles James Fox. The sense of sudden liberation and almost limitless hope inspired by the Revolution was later recalled by the English poet William Wordsworth:

> Bliss it was in that dawn to be alive
> But to be young was very heaven!

For Edmund Burke, on the other hand, the Revolution was an unparalleled calamity, a "fond election of evil" that in a single orgiastic frenzy had overturned the civilization of 1000 years.

Later historians disagreed over the meaning of the French Revolution as intensely as the original protagonists. For nineteenth-century Romantics like Thomas Carlyle and Jules Michelet, it was a cosmic upheaval, an awesome spectacle more to be wondered at than judged. To liberals before World War I, it was the foundation of bourgeois democracy, while to socialists it was the heroic precursor of the universal revolution to come. Even today, nearly 200 years after

115

the event, historians still debate the great Revolution, and still ask basic questions like, Who made the Revolution? How? and Why?

A great deal of the confusion stems from the nature of the event itself. The French Revolution was not one revolution but several. Historians now conventionally divide the Revolution into three broadly distinct phases: a "constitutional" phase (1789–1791), in which the first outburst of revolutionary energy was channeled into liberal reform; a "radical" phase (1792–1794), characterized by the abolition of the monarchy, an aggressive foreign policy, and the Terror; and a reactive "Thermidorian" phase (1795–1799), in which government returned to the moderates. For some historians, the first years of Napoleon (1799–1804) constitute a fourth phase; to others, Napoleon represents the end or even the negation of the Revolution. But even within these broad categories (in themselves not accepted by all historians), there were countercurrents. Like a river in spate, the Revolution perpetually defied all attempts to define its boundaries. Even its chief actors seemed unable to predict, let alone direct, its course. In 1791, Maximilien Robespierre said, "The Revolution is over." Yet he himself was to lead it through its most violent phase two years later.

For present purposes, we will define the Revolution as the sequence of events that took place in France between 1789 and 1799. As we shall see, most of the critical events of the Revolution were packed into a few brief, concentrated periods of violence and change. As in all revolutions, most of people's time was spent trying to cope with the results of these spasmodic outbreaks, and to guard against their recurrence.

HOW THE REVOLUTION CAME

The bulk of the eighteenth century in France was spanned by the long reign of Louis XV (1715–1774). A reaction against the autocracy of Louis XIV was inevitable, and during the regency of the Duke of Orléans (1715–1723), the provincial estates, the parlements, and the nobility in general reasserted their ancient privilege against the Crown. This happened in every royal minority, and this time the backlash was particularly severe for having been so long repressed. But Louis XV, in a sense, never emerged from his minority. Capable but indolent, he left the business of governing to others. Some of his ministers were able—Fleury, Choiseul, Maupeou—but in a system designed to function around the personal authority of the king, to delegate royal responsibility was to diminish royal power. Thus, while everywhere else the privileges of the nobility were under ideological attack from the philosophes and political pressure from enlightened despots, in France alone there was no serious effort to check them. The French nobility assumed more and more the aspect of a closed caste as access to government positions was made increasingly difficult; by the 1780s, an army commission required four generations of noble blood. Even the intendances, specifically devised by Louis XIV as a countervailing power to the nobility, had fallen mostly into their hands. In a sense France had had its enlightened despot too soon in the person of Louis XIV. There was an air of wistful decadence about the era of his successor, which is beautifully caught in the paintings of Antoine Watteau, Jean-Honoré

Fragonard, and François Boucher. The royal reign itself was measured by mistresses rather than edicts. Whether or not Louis made the famous remark attributed to him—"After me, the deluge"—it sums up his attitude and his era in a nutshell.

The most serious practical consequence of this aristocratic revival was the chronic indebtedness of the French government. Louis XIV's wars had left the state virtually bankrupt, and it never recovered. Sporadic attempts to revive Louis's taxes on the nobility, as in 1726 and 1749, met with furious resistance and had to be dropped. Taxation was, for the nobleman, the ultimate insult: Like public flogging, it was something done only to commoners. The bourgeoisie or upper merchant and professional class—a steadily expanding group in the mid-eighteenth century—also largely avoided taxation, as did the clergy. Thus, while the French nation (or at least its privileged classes) grew richer, the state became poorer, obliged as it was to rely on the poorest and most depressed sectors of the economy for support. The Crown found itself isolated, the natural target of all discontent. The nobility looked upon it with hostility and suspicion as the usurper of its privileges. The peasantry regarded it with hatred as the expropriator of its labor. The bourgeoisie, barred from state service, blamed it for exclusion from this traditional road to status and prestige. As it had been blamed for its strength under Louis XIV, it was now condemned for its weakness under his successor.

The resurgence of the aristocracy was symbolized by the revival of the parlements. The parlements, it will be recalled, were primarily law courts, but they also possessed extensive administrative and police powers. In addition, they promulgated royal edicts by formally registering them. In the past, parlements had caused constitutional crises by refusing to register edicts of which they disapproved, but under Louis XIV this practice had ceased. Now, however, it had revived, and to such an extent that the parlements had begun to act like an independent branch of government, issuing long, argumentative opinions called remonstrances and claiming broad powers of veto and judicial review. In 1763, the Parlement of Toulouse imprisoned the governor of Languedoc, and in 1766, the Parlement of Rennes jailed the military commandant of Brittany, both for attempting to execute royal orders that the local courts held illegal.

Such defiance spurred even Louis XV to act. He appointed a new chancellor, René Charles de Maupeou, who took the daring step of dissolving the old parlements outright, exiling their former judges, and creating new courts whose members no longer had hereditary tenure but were salaried officials subject to removal for defying royal edicts. The Crown rode out the immediate storm of protest. But Louis XV died suddenly in 1774, and his successor, Louis XVI, seeking to ingratiate himself with his nobility, dissolved the so-called Maupeou parlements and brought the old ones back, with all their privileges intact. It was the first of the new king's mistakes, and perhaps the one that determined all the rest.

Louis XV had had the ability to rule but not the will; Louis XVI had the will but not the ability. He was well served by a succession of able ministers: Anne Robert Turgot (1774–1776), an energetic reformer and disciple of the philosophes; Jacques Necker (1776–1781), a Swiss banker with a reputation for financial wizardry; Charles de Calonne (1783–1787), another fertile and resourceful money manager; and Étienne de Loménie de Brienne (1787–1788), the worldly old archbishop of Toulouse. All faced the same problem, the perennial bankruptcy of the Crown; all proposed the same solution, tax reform; and all fell through the same scenario of aristocratic intransigence, court intrigue, and royal weakness.

Turgot's dismissal was a pattern for the rest. Turgot was a physiocrat, one of the influential school of late eighteenth-century thinkers who argued against customs barriers and restraints on free trade and favored universal taxation. Accordingly, he moved to lift restrictions on the sale of grain; to abolish the old craft guilds, which controlled access to many trades; and to impose a general land tax on all classes for the upkeep of the royal roads. Unfortunately, a bad harvest sent the price of grain soaring, while his other measures were opposed by the guilds as well as by the aristocracy and the church. Turgot fell, and the lesson of his failure was not lost on others: Confrontation with privilege was the surest route to political suicide at the court of Louis XVI.

Necker and Calonne, more pliable men, artfully juggled the books for the next ten years, and kept the government going on credit. The situation was considerably exacerbated by French intervention in the American War of Independence (1778). The Bourbons doubtless took satisfaction at this partial revenge for the loss of their own empire, but it was purchased at the price of a greatly augmented deficit. By 1783, the annual payment on the national debt had virtually doubled, to 80 million livres. From this point, there was nothing to be done but borrow further at escalating interest until all sources of credit had run dry. That happened in the summer of 1786. Calonne published a general audit that showed a debt of 112 million livres per year. It was a declaration of bankruptcy.

Calonne now prevailed on the king to call a handpicked Assembly of Notables, to which he presented a new tax program (February, 1787). His plan was twofold: to circumvent the inevitable hostility of the parlements and to pitch his appeal to a cross section of the more liberal nobility. But the assembly, suspicious of Calonne's motives and unwilling to bypass the courts, refused to support his program. The king dismissed him, and the assembly was dissolved.

The financial crisis now became a constitutional one. The parlements predictably refused to register the new tax edicts, lecturing the king instead on the evils of despotism. Coopting the language of the Enlightenment, they argued that law was the expression of reason, the general will, and the rights of man. New taxes, they insisted, could only be granted by the representative body of the whole nation, the Estates General. This ancient feudal relic had not met since 1614, but the judges made it into a symbol of popular liberty. Throughout 1787 and 1788, the calling of the Estates General became the rallying cry of political discontent up and down the country, and observers like Thomas Jefferson felt that France was on the verge of a parliamentary revolution like that of England against the Stuarts.

By contrast, the tactics of the Crown—the arrest and exile of the dissenting magistrates and the erection of a new court system similar to the Maupeou parlements—seemed arbitrary and tyrannical. The king himself, and his frivolous Austrian queen, Marie Antoinette, symbolized the decadence of personal monarchy. The luxury of the court, an asset in the days of *gloire,* was increasingly seen as tasteless extravagance at the public expense. In August, 1788, Louis XVI capitulated. The exiled judges were recalled to heroes' welcomes, the Parlement of Paris reinstated, and the calling of the Estates General set. The revolt of the nobility had triumphed.

France was now prepared for something like constitutional government. Progressive opinion looked to the Estates General to evolve into a more or less representative modern legislature like the British Parliament or the American Congress, sharing sovereign power with the executive. But the progressives were in for a rude shock. The Parlement of Paris may have spoken in the language of Rousseau and the Declaration of Independence, but its heart was still in the Fronde. It ruled at once that the new Estates General must have the same form as the old: three separate orders representing the clergy, the nobility, and the political catchall of doctors, lawyers, civil servants, bankers, merchants, rentiers, and philosophes—in short, the professionals and the bourgeoisie—who comprised the Third Estate. Since each order voted as a separate unit, this meant that the two privileged orders could always outvote the third, leaving it merely to ratify or dissent from the decisions of its superiors.

The Third Estate discussed here was of course not the same as the Third Estate mentioned earlier, which included every Frenchman outside the nobility or the church, down to the lowliest peasant or tramp. Of that vast bulk this Third Estate was but as the tip of an iceberg. The rest of the population remained, in the political sense, submerged and invisible. When the parlements spoke of "the nation," they meant only the upper nobility and clergy. When the spokesmen of the Third Estate used the same term, they meant only to include themselves. No one in authority had any thought of giving representation to the people at large.

The situation in 1788 thus boiled down to a three-cornered struggle between the king, the privileged orders, and the politically relevant elements of the Third Estate. The nobility had launched a frontal assault on the powers of the Crown. The Third Estate, having joined the attack in hopes of picking up some of the spoil, was bitter and angry. The gates of status seemed to have closed on it for good. There was not a single commoner in the upper branches of the military or among the 135 bishops of the church. Whereas Louis XIV had deliberately raised men like Colbert to eminence, there had been only three nonnoble ministers in the past 70 years. The complaint of the Third Estate was eloquently summarized in a pamphlet circulated early in 1789 by the Abbé Sieyès, which asked:

What is the Third Estate? Everything.
What has it been thus far in the political order? Nothing.
What does it demand? To be something.

The Third Estate's discontent was the king's opportunity. If he could exploit it properly, he could outflank the opposition to tax reform and break the back of the nobles' revolt. Urged on by Necker, now restored to power, Louis ordered that the Estates General be popularly elected: nobles by nobles, clergy by clergy, and the Third Estate by all other males over 25 whose names appeared on the tax rolls. With a stroke of the pen, Louis had opened the political process for the first time to millions of Frenchmen.

In deference to the vastly greater size of the Third Estate's electorate, the king agreed to "double the Third," that is, to permit twice as many representatives to be chosen for the Third Estate as for the other two orders. But this did not affect the voting balance of the three orders. A unit rule was still in effect: one order, one vote. In terms of actual power, therefore, the Third Estate's position remained unchanged.

It is easy to see why Louis held back from this final concession. Not only had the Parlement of Paris pronounced dogmatically against any change in the voting procedure, but a second Assembly of Notables, meeting in December, 1788, proved equally opposed. The king's own family remonstrated him for going as far as he did. Louis was aware, as his nobility was not, that in the last analysis the two of them would survive or fall together. If it was impossible to imagine a king without his nobility, it was equally impossible to imagine a nobility without its king.

Meanwhile, an election fever was sweeping the country. From 40,000 electoral precincts all over France, *cahiers,* long lists of grievances compiled to be sent along with the delegates, revealed widespread dissatisfaction with the social system. There was a general demand for popular representation, legislative control of taxation, and an end to absolute monarchy. Church tithes, manorial dues, and aristocratic hunting rights were bitterly attacked. The *cahiers* of the Third Estate were virtually one in demanding full civil equality for all Frenchmen.

There was also much economic discontent in the country. After the relative boom of the mid-century years, France had entered a long cycle of depression about 1770. This had been exacerbated by a series of bad harvests, culminating in that of 1788. Starving peasants fled to the towns, swelling the urban unemployment rate to as high as 50 percent. Even those who had work found more than half their earnings consumed by the price of bread. There were food riots everywhere, and political riots, too, as bourgeois members of the provincial estates in Brittany and Provence clashed with the local nobility. Thus, the greatest political crisis in the nation's history coincided with the worst economic situation since the famines of Louis XIV's reign.

THE REVOLUTION OF 1789

The 1248 delegates to the Estates General were the focus of all hopes when they convened at Versailles on May 4, 1789. Approximately 300 members apiece sat for the first two orders, while the remainder comprised the Third Estate. Of these latter, well over half were lawyers, most of whom also held government jobs; about a quarter were merchants, businessmen, and rentiers. Despite the wide franchise, there was not a single workingman or peasant. This was partly because the final selection of delegates took place at only 200 principal district assemblies, where the influence of local notables predominated, and partly because of the traditional deference of the electorate to its superiors. The result was that the full Third Estate was represented only by its narrowest elite, albeit an angry, disillusioned elite that was less concerned to share the privileges of the nobility than to pull them down.

Had the Crown been able to assert its leadership at this point, a moderate solution might still have been found. But Louis and Necker had nothing to suggest, no program to present. Either they had misjudged the gravity of the crisis, or they despaired of mediating it. Whatever happened, the powers of the monarchy seemed certain to be diminished. Perhaps that is why Louis, fatalistically, preferred inaction instead.

Leaderless, the Estates General fell to wrangling over the question of voting by orders, with the Third Estate insisting that the three orders merge into a single body. As this would not only have given the Third Estate a numerical voting majority but abolished the principle of separate orders on which the Old Regime rested, it was stoutly resisted. On June 17, after weeks of deadlock, the Third Estate took the decisive step toward revolution: It declared itself the "National Assembly," with the right to legislate alone in the public interest. Three days later, the members of the Third found themselves locked out of their chamber. They repaired to an indoor tennis court nearby, where, in great passion and excitement, they vowed not to disband until they had given France a constitution.

At last Louis acted. He told the Estates General that he would grant it a permanent place in the state, with wide powers over the administration and budget. The king thereby accepted the principle of a limited monarchy. But he also declared the self-created National Assembly (its numbers now swollen by dissident clergy and noblemen) null and void and ordered the Estates to return to their separate chambers. They might vote together on certain issues if they wished, but on matters of fundamental fiscal and feudal privileges, no order could be stripped of its prerogatives without its consent.

The aristocracy was elated. Louis had come down for the principle of blood on which his own throne ultimately rested. But the Third Estate remained defiant. Faced with mutinous soldiers and an angry populace, Louis backed down. Four days later, on June 27, the other two orders united with the Third. The National Assembly was now a fact. The destiny of the nation was in its hands. By presenting a program that was both unacceptable and unenforceable, Louis had lost his last chance to control events.

The collapse of authority was reflected in the streets. The workers and tradesmen of Paris, fearing both rural mobs and military repression, broke into the civic arsenals and armed themselves. On July 14, they stormed the ancient fortress of the Bastille and seized its weapons, after a pitched battle in which 98 of the attackers were killed, thus giving the Revolution its baptism of blood and its famous commemoration date. In the country, there was a mass panic, the so-called Great Fear, which centered around rumors of advancing bandit armies. From town to town the cry went up, "The brigands are coming!" Since there were enough bandits in the best of times, these rumors were not entirely without foundation, but they chiefly reflected the generalized sense of disorder. In any case, they served as a pretext for looting, and by late July, a full-scale agrarian

The collapse of authority in France: seizure of the arsenal at the Garde-Meuble, July 13, 1789.

insurrection was in progress. Peasants broke into the manor houses of the nobility, systematically destroying the legal records of debts and feudal dues. It was the revenge of the illiterate, and in the high summer of 1789, the Old Regime was dying in a thousand bonfires throughout France.

The National Assembly ratified what it was powerless to prevent. On the night of August 4, two noblemen, Noailles and d'Aiguillon, coached by liberal deputies of the Third Estate, rose to denounce their own privileges. A psychological stampede ensued in which the privileges and exemptions of aristocrats, clergymen, cities, corporations, and provincial estates were all surrendered. Hoarse and exhausted, the members of the Assembly adjourned at 2 A.M. with the declaration, "Feudalism is abolished."

The Assembly's next step was to issue the Declaration of the Rights of Man and of the Citizen (August 26). Its 17 brief articles were a blueprint for the new society. All men, it declared, "are born and remain free and equal in rights." Those rights were "liberty, property, security, and resistance to oppression," which it was the fundamental duty of every state to preserve. Sovereignty was vested in the nation, and law was the expression of the general will. Freedom of speech and religion were guaranteed, and liberty—the right "to do anything that does not harm another person"—could be taken away only by due process of law. Taxation could be levied only by popular consent and was applicable to all in proportion to income. All men were equal before the law, and all equally eligible for public office.

The Declaration of the Rights of Man was an admirably succinct statement of the political principles of the Enlightenment. In a few succinct paragraphs it abolished absolutism, nobility, and the Gallican church, the basic institutions of the Old Regime, and inequality, its fundamental principle. That the members of the Assembly were able to formulate the new credo so quickly and concisely owed much to the prior examples of the English Bill of Rights and the American Declaration of Independence, but even more to the bankruptcy of the Old Regime, a system in which even its beneficiaries had largely ceased to believe. Its brevity also made it devastating propaganda, and, translated into every major European language, it shook the established order everywhere.

The events of July had made the Revolution; the events of August had established and defined it. But a serious stumbling block yet remained: the king. While not rejecting the Assembly's work, he conspicuously failed to approve it. This passive resistance was underscored by the flight of his brother, the Count of Artois, and other leading nobles into exile. It was a sensitive moment, for the Assembly was just then debating the question of a royal veto in the new constitution.

This led to the last of the revolutionary tremors of 1789. On October 5, a contingent of Parisian housewives, having previously invaded the mayor's office to protest food shortages and the continuing high price of bread, marched to Versailles and demanded that Louis return to the capital. They were soon backed up by the arrival of the newly formed Paris National Guard, 20,000 strong. Virtually undefended, the royal family was forced to accompany this motley procession back to Paris, where they took up residence in the Tuileries. The National Assembly followed a few days later, and the unhappy Louis gave his consent to the August 4 decrees and the Declaration of the Rights of Man.

Once again, spontaneous mass action had delivered the Assembly from an impasse. As the poet Chateaubriand later remarked, "The nobility began the Revolution; the people finished it." But the Revolution, having completed its chief work of demolition, had barely raised the scaffolding of a new France, and, for the time being, it was neither the nobility nor the people who led it, but a triumphant bourgeoisie.

REFORM AND REACTION (1789–1791)

All revolutions have a common mythology, that of the nation casting off unworthy leaders or outmoded institutions, and regenerating itself in brotherhood. The French Revolution summed this up in a slogan, "Liberty, Equality, Fraternity." But in reality, the people of France were far from united on the future direction of their country. On the one extreme were the 20,000 people, in large part aristocrats, who had left the country and rejected the Revolution. They were not all die-hards; there were many among them who had helped bring down the Old Regime but were irreconcilably alienated by the coercion of the king and the resort to popular violence. On the other side were those the Revolution had already satisfied in large measure, the great mass of peasants. The destruction of the manorial regime and the freeing of their land from the host of feudal imposts that remained on it was all they asked, and this they had achieved themselves, with the tardy consent of their representatives. It was true that they still owed compensation to their former lords for the loss of their privileges, but these claims were unenforceable in the climate of revolution and were finally repealed by law in 1793. Thereafter, the peasants were chiefly concerned with consolidating their gains, and they functioned as a conservative force.

Those who had not yet gained, at least materially, were the *sans-culottes** or working class of the towns, especially Paris. Artisans, laborers, jacks-of-all-trades, and apprentices, they comprised about half the capital's population of 600,000. Their number was insignificant beside 20 million peasants, but the influence of Paris was out of all proportion to its size. The municipality was nominally in bourgeois hands, but in reality the city was ruled by its neighborhoods, on an almost street-to-street basis. There were scores of local committees and clubs, and every tavern was a debating society. It was a turbulent civic democracy that looked skeptically at the national government in its midst.

The Constituent Assembly, which the National Assembly was now called as it strove to create a new government, looked back with equal suspicion on Paris. Having achieved power, it had no more use for popular rebellion. It declared martial law and press censorship; on October 21, a young laborer, Michel Adrien, was hanged for "sedition." The honeymoon of the Third Estate was over.

For the next two years, the Assembly worked to construct a modern state

---

*Literally, "without britches"; for obvious practical reasons, workingmen wore long pants instead of the silk or muslin stockings of the gentry.

out of the wreckage of the Old Regime. Its first task was to write a constitution. The product was determined by two factors: distrust of the king and fear of the people. It was inexpedient to depose Louis, the only link between the old France and the new and the only valid symbol of authority for millions of Frenchmen. On the other hand, his opposition to the new order was an established fact. The only solution was to reduce him to a figurehead. This necessarily concentrated power in the unicameral elected legislature, the Legislative Assembly, over whose actions the king had a three-year suspensive veto only. To protect the new Assembly against undue popular influence, the electoral system was made exceedingly complex and indirect. A distinction was made, contrary to Article 6 of the Declaration of the Rights of Man, between "active" and "passive" citizens. Both groups had full civil rights, but only the "actives," those meeting a minimum property qualification, had the right to vote for some 50,000 "electors," who in turn chose the 500 representatives of the Legislative Assembly. About two-thirds of the adult male population qualified for "active" citizenship, less than half for nomination as electors. This was still a far wider franchise than chose Parliament in England, and the property qualification was lower than in some states of America. But since the electors were obliged to spend several days choosing their representatives at their own expense and at perhaps a considerable distance from home, the practical (and obviously intentional) result was to limit them to men of leisure and substance, in short, men of the bourgeoisie.

The attitude of the Assembly toward the institutions of the Old Regime was well summarized by the Preamble to the Constitution of 1791:

> Nobility no longer exists, nor peerage, nor hereditary distinction of orders, nor feudal regime, nor patrimonial courts, nor titles, denominations or prerogatives deriving therefrom. . . . Property in office, and its inheritance, no longer exist. . . . Gilds and corporations for professions, arts and crafts no longer exist.

The Assembly thereupon set about to reorganize French society. All former courts and jurisdictions were abolished. A uniform code of administration was instituted for the 44,000 rural and urban municipalities of the country. The old 26 provinces, many rich with history (and memories of previous rebellions), were divided into 83 "departments," all newly named and democratically equal in size. An independent judiciary was set up, with elected judges and juries for criminal trials. In fact, despite the radical standardizing of administration, there was a good deal of local autonomy in the system. Officials were to be elected from below rather than appointed from above. In place of the old system, where royal officers met head on with impacted privilege and overlapping jurisdictions, a rational, centralized framework of administration was set up, but it was given no orders at all.

The most immediate problem of the Assembly was the unresolved financial crisis left over from the Old Regime and the crippling public debt. The Assembly had a highly expedient attitude toward property rights. It expropriated the feudal privileges of the nobility with little effective compensation, because these were not rights but "usurpations." On the other hand, since the public debt was in large part owed to members of the Assembly and others of their class, there was no question of dealing with it in the same way. The solution lay in the holdings of the church. The estimated wealth of the church was roughly equal to the national debt. By confiscating it in the name of the nation, then selling it to the public at large, the debt could be liquidated. To finance the operation, paper currency called assignats was issued. As church lands were bought up, the assignats would be returned to the government by the purchasers and, having served their function, would be destroyed. All citizens were eligible to buy this land, but of course the assignats were distributed on a preferential basis to holders of the debt. In this way, the debt was to be eliminated, and some 10 percent of the real estate of France to be redistributed to deserving—that is, bourgeois—revolutionaries.

This massive transaction made the church a ward of the state. Clergymen became salaried officials, chosen by popular election like anyone else, though parish priests had to be approved by their bishops. The bishops were reduced in number to 83, one for each department, and archbishoprics were abolished; gone forever were the great princes of the church who drew half a million livres a year. The monasteries were dissolved and the taking of religious vows prohibited. The pope was merely to be informed as a matter of courtesy when a bishop was installed, but his authority was in no other way recognized.

These changes were embodied in the Civil Constitution of the Clergy (1790). In many respects, they were not so drastic or unpalatable as might appear. The Gallican church had long been largely independent of the papacy, and bishops had been chosen by the king. Many of the lower clergy, ill paid and exploited under the Old Regime, were not unfavorably disposed toward a new employer who would nearly double their old salaries. The problem was one of ratification. The church wanted to adopt the Civil Constitution on its own authority, thus affirming its continued identity. To the Assembly, this would have been tantamount to recognizing again the existence of a First Estate, when all estates and orders had been abolished and only citizens remained. It therefore promulgated the new constitution by its own authority alone, and backed it up with an oath of allegiance that all clergy were required to swear.

This was one of the great blunders of the Revolution. Half the lower clergy refused to swear, and all but seven of the bishops. The "refractory" or "nonjuring" clergy emigrated or went underground, where, protected by loyal parishioners, they formed a natural focus of resistance to the Revolution. Far from having made the church an obedient servant of the state, the Constituent Assembly in its haste had turned it into its bitterest enemy.

The work of the Assembly had mixed results. In the long run, it laid the institutional foundations of the modern French state. But it failed to solve almost all its immediate problems. The central government, divided between an enfeebled executive and an unwieldy legislature, was not viable. Local administration, having been completely reorganized, was left to fend for itself without direction or guidance. As tax revenues fell off, assignats were recirculated instead of being destroyed, fueling inflation. The Constituent Assembly passed out of existence on September 30, 1791. The system it left behind survived it by barely ten months.

FROM MONARCHY TO REPUBLIC (1791–1793)

The first blow fell even before the Assembly had completed its work. On June 20, 1791, the royal family attempted to flee the country. Captured by peasants at the border town of Varennes, they were returned ignobly to Paris. If Louis had been at best a hostage of the Revolution, he was now clearly a prisoner.

The Assembly accepted the fiction that the king had been "kidnapped." But many who had doubted that the constitution could work were now convinced, and there was open clamor for a republic. The most influential republicans were members of the Jacobin club, the best known of the thousands of political societies that had sprung up throughout France since 1789. (By 1793, half a million Frenchmen belonged to such clubs, or nearly one of every ten adult males in the country.) The Jacobins, so called from their meeting place in an old Jacobin monastery, were bourgeois idealists with a strong commitment to the Revolution. Though often identified with radical militancy, they had in fact no common program. At moments of crisis they were divided, and as the club, like the Revolution itself, moved steadily to the left, more moderate factions periodically seceded from it. Such was the case in the summer of 1791, when a group known as the Feuillants quit the club in protest over its repudiation of the king.

The Jacobin republicans, clustered around the lawyer Jacques Brissot, became the dominant faction in the new Legislative Assembly. Knowing that Louis had conspired with the Austrians, and against the background of the Declaration of Pillnitz (August 27, 1791), in which Leopold II of Austria and Frederick William II of Prussia had threatened military intervention against France, the Brissotins clamored for "a war of peoples against kings." They patronized foreign radicals like Thomas Paine and the German Anarcharsis Cloots, the self-styled "representative of the human race." They argued that the Revolution could not be confined to France but must liberate all of Europe. If it shirked this high destiny, it would remain isolated among enemies who would never cease until they had destroyed it.

Swept on by a combination of ideological fervor and traditional anti-Hapsburg sentiment, the Assembly declared war on Austria on April 20, 1792. It was a very bad mistake. The army was in deplorable condition, two-thirds of its officers (all former nobles) having deserted or quit. The country was in the grip of soaring inflation as the unredeemed assignats fell steadily in value and peasants refused to accept them in payment for their crops. There were food riots in Paris, wild rumors of counterrevolutionary plots, and a general breakdown of order everywhere. When the war proved a fiasco, the public mood turned grim. The Revolution had been betrayed by its leaders, and by none more than Louis XVI. How could a war against kings be led by a king?

By the end of July, 47 of the 48 municipal districts of Paris had declared against the monarchy. Military recruits from the provinces mingled with the sans-culottes, who were in an almost continuous state of agitation. Brissot now backtracked to support Louis, but the Jacobin left, under Maximilien Robespierre, threw their lot in with the crowd. On August 10, Louis and his entourage were driven from the Tuileries by an armed mob, with heavy casualties on both sides. It was an event as fateful as the fall of the Bastille. A new revolutionary council, the Commune, seized control of Paris. The constitution was suspended, and a new National Convention summoned to write another.

The National Convention, elected by universal manhood suffrage, met on September 20, 1792, in an atmosphere of crisis. On that very day, the Prussian army was stopped at Valmy, only 200 miles from Paris. Earlier in the month, hysterical mobs had invaded the prisons in search of counterrevolutionaries and slaughtered between 1100 and 1400 inmates, some of them ex-aristocrats or re-fractory priests, but most of them common offenders. The authorities stood by, powerless to halt these "September massacres." The Convention had deliberately taken its name in reference to the American constitutional convention, which had written the world's first democratic constitution. But Paris in the early autumn of 1792 bore little resemblance to Philadelphia in 1787.

Nevertheless, the Convention set to work with high spirits. It not only abol-ished the monarchy but the calendar, declaring September 22 the first day of Year I of the Republic. Later, it scrapped the entire Christian calendar of months and days, commissioning a poet, Fabré d'Églantine, to rename them. Fabré decided to call his months by their seasonal characteristics; thus, July 27 was to be the ninth of Thermidor, the month of heat, November 10 to be the eighteenth of Bru-maire, the month of fog, and so forth. The year was to consist of 12 equal months of 30 days, with five leap days at the end, which were to be national holidays. Each month consisted of three weeks or "decades" of ten days each, which meant, among other things, a nine-day work week. This calendar remained officially in existence until 1804.

The Convention had reason for optimism. French armies, fired by patriotic ardor and reorganized under officers from the ranks, not only drove out the Austro-Prussian invaders but swept across the borders, occupying Frankfurt and Brussels. In two months they had accomplished more than Louis XIV had in 50 years. The Convention thereupon proceeded to offer itself to all people who wished to liberate themselves, and decreed that feudalism was abolished in all territories occupied by French forces.

The Republic was triumphant and victorious, but the problem of the king remained. Alive, he was a magnet for counterrevolution; his incriminating corre-spondence with the Austrians had been discovered. In December, 1792, he was put on trial for treason. It was a step before which many shrank; the sentence of execution passed by only a single vote, 361 to 360. Six days later, on January 21, 1793, Louis XVI was guillotined. The French Revolution had burned its last bridge to the past.

THE RADICAL PHASE (1793–1794)

The Revolution now entered its climactic phase. Into the next 18 months was crammed some of the most fevered and sometimes bizarre social experimentation in history. The most ancient values were called into question, and new ones born in the heat of events. It was a time of great passions and great excesses. The men who ruled France often worked around the clock, facing political, military, and

Louis XVI on his way to trial before the National Convention.

economic crises all at once. That they kept the country together at all was a remarkable feat. But though they were focused, of necessity, chiefly on the immediate problems before them, they knew they were also legislators for history. Out
of what they did, and what they failed to do, came much of the shape of the modern world.

The center of all this was the National Convention. Most of its members
were new; only 286 out of 750 had served in the previous two assemblies. Socially,
however, they had the same predominant makeup—lawyers, officials, merchants,
and businessmen. There were no peasants, and only two workers, a munitions
maker and a wool comber.

Politically, the Convention was divided between the two warring factions
of the Jacobin club, with the great mass of delegates in the middle. The Girondins,
so called because many of their leaders hailed from the southwest department
of the Gironde, were the party of Brissot. The Montagnards ("mountain men"),
who sat in the upper tiers of the Convention and rained down abuse on their opponents, were based mainly in Paris. They were led by the unlikely trio of Maximilien Robespierre, the prim, puritanical lawyer; Georges Danton, a huge and ge-
nially corrupt politician; and Jean-Paul Marat, a vitriolic journalist. The two
parties were separated by no great issues or principles. They both accepted the
Republic, both embraced the now successful war (Danton having discovered that
the Rhine was the "natural frontier" of France); members of both had shed the
royal blood. But in the hectic atmosphere of the moment, differences of policy
bulked as large as differences of principle, and it was easy to see one's adversary
not merely as an enemy (since so much depended on the success of the Revolution) but as a traitor in league with the counterrevolution.

There was no lack of plots. A naval conspiracy betrayed the port of Toulon
to the enemy. The French commander in chief, Dumouriez, defected to the Aus-

trians and tried to march his own army on Paris. The Convention, having declared war in a transport of enthusiasm in February, 1793, on England, the Netherlands, and Spain, found itself without a general. In March, a major peasant rebellion against conscription broke out in the western region of the Vendée, fanned by nonjuring priests and royalist agents. By midyear, there was armed resistance over three-quarters of the country. It was a war of Paris against all Europe.

And Paris was divided against itself. There were new price riots, as the assignats, now issued with no pretense at backing, fell to a quarter of their face value. This time, however, the rioters did not merely pillage the grocers but presented them with a list of prices they were willing to pay, generally about 40 to 50 percent of the current level. This assumption of power was more ominous than any looting, and the government denounced the riots as an aristocratic intrigue. But agitation continued, and, on May 2, the Convention reluctantly imposed the first *maximum* or price control on bread and flour.

This was not enough, however. Prices continued to rise, the situation in the provinces to deteriorate. The Girondins were held chiefly to blame. They were the most conspicuous figures in the Convention and wielded most of its executive power. At the same time, their base of support was mainly in the country; they were relatively unpopular in Paris. By April, there was talk in the districts about purging the Convention. Robespierre put himself "into a state of insurrection" against those who had shown "contempt" for the sans-culottes. This was the signal for mob action. On June 2, 31 Girondin leaders were forcibly expelled from the Convention.

The Montagnards were now in power, and, for the first time, the Convention was thrown open to representatives of the sans-culottes. On June 25, it was addressed by the radical street leader and ex-priest Jacques Roux:

> Liberty is nothing but a figment of the imagination when one class can deprive another of food with impunity. Liberty becomes meaningless when the rich exercise the power of life and death over their fellow creatures by means of monopolies. . . . Have you outlawed speculation? No. Have you decreed the death penalty for hoarding? No. Have you defined the limits to the freedom of trade? No. . . . Deputies of the Mountain, why have you not climbed from the third to the ninth floor of the houses of this revolutionary city? You would have been moved by the tears and sighs of an immense population without food and clothing . . . because the laws have been cruel to the poor, because they have been made only by the rich and for the rich . . . [but] the salvation of the people . . . is the supreme law.

This was the raw voice of hunger and want, a very different oratory than that to which the deputies of the Convention were accustomed. They were shocked, and well they might be. They had just finished a document of which they were very proud, the Constitution of the Year I. It confirmed the right of universal manhood suffrage, enlarged the scope of natural rights, and instituted a popular referendum. It was the most democratic constitution since that of ancient Athens, and it contained, according to Robespierre, "the essential basis of public happiness." Yet Jacques Roux told them they had accomplished nothing, that the real revolution had not even begun, that liberty without bread—political equality without economic justice—was a mere "figment." Roux was bodily removed from the Convention. He was later arrested, and, when sentenced to death, he committed suicide in his cell. But the issue he raised—what the nineteenth century called "the social question"—was to haunt the political consciousness of the West from that day forward.

The sans-culottes did wrest some concessions from the Convention, though not without further rioting. On September 29, the Convention imposed mandatory price controls, which fixed prices at one-third above the 1790 level, while raising wages by half. But even this, violating as it did the cherished bourgeois belief in free trade, fit into the larger context in which the new government was proceeding, by extraordinary and unprecedented measures, to bring the country back under control.

The first requisite was a strong executive. The Convention, like the Constituent Assembly before it, had the double responsibility not only of drafting a constitution but of governing the country ad hoc while it did so. The Executive Council exercised cabinet functions, the Revolutionary Tribunal served as a chief judiciary, and the Committee of General Security supervised the police. In April, 1793, the Convention appointed the Committee of Public Safety, whose rather vague function was to oversee the Executive Council. With the appointment of Robespierre to this committee in July, it soon became the focal point of government power.

From July on, the government took rapid steps to put down the revolt in the Vendée and elsewhere. Draconian punishment was meted out to rebels, as at Lyon, where nearly 2000 people were executed in the wake of a Girondist rising. "Representatives on mission," armed with almost unlimited authority, struck terror into the provinces.

But the Convention asked more of France than mere obedience. On August 23, it decreed the *levée en masse,* a general conscription of all able-bodied men. Of all the acts of the Convention, this was perhaps the most significant. War was no longer to be a sport of kings, but the sacred cause of the nation. Those who could not fight were to make weapons, munitions, and clothing, women to serve as nurses, old men to make patriotic speeches. It was a mass mobilization of all human and material resources in the country. Nothing like it had ever been attempted before, and the organizational problems were stupendous. But it was a logical extension of the basic principle of the Revolution, that all citizens were involved in the welfare of the nation, as the nation was involved in the welfare of all citizens. As the historian Hippolyte Taine later put it, the birthright of every citizen was henceforth a knapsack and a ballot.

There was no question of implementing the new constitution; on October 10, the provisional government was declared "revolutionary until the peace." The Constituent Assembly had sought to create a legal category of "passive citizens" in the new order, passivity itself was a crime. "You must punish," said Louis Antoine de Saint-Just, the brilliant young colleague of Robespierre, "not merely traitors but the indifferent as well; you must punish whoever is passive in the Republic." On September 17, the Law of Suspects was passed, authorizing blanket arrests. A Monsieur Blondel was promptly arrested for "thoughtlessness and in-difference," a Citizen Lachapelle because he "did not lose much sleep over the Revolution." These denunciations were made not by secret police but by zealous sans-culottes who were genuinely puzzled that anyone could lack enthusiasm for the Revolution. Who but an enemy of the Republic would not lose sleep over it?

Thus was born the Terror. It was the crystalization of a whole atmosphere of doubt, fear, and crisis in which Frenchmen had been living for the past four years, of nerves worn raw with conspiracy and intrigue. But it was also deliberate government policy, and was even elevated to the status of revolutionary philoso-phy. "Between the people and its enemies there is only the sword," said Saint-Just. The people were ruled by reason and virtue—that is, in Rousseauist terms, by their spontaneous adherence to the general will. But what of those within a commonwealth who were dedicated to its overthrow? Such people could not be educated, persuaded, or even "forced" to be free; they could only be exter-minated.

During the ten months of the Terror's duration (September, 1793–July, 1794), perhaps 300,000 people were arrested, and 40,000 executed. Of these, only 15 percent were ex-aristocrats or priests and another 15 percent bourgeois, mostly members of the Girondist resistance in the south. The overwhelming majority were ordinary workers and peasants. There were instances of mass atrocity, as at Nantes, where 2000 people were drowned in the river. In a country where indif-ference had become a potentially capital crime, the distinction between real and imaginary enemies tended to disappear.

Yet the Terror had a calculated aim: To centralize all authority in the Revo-lutionary government and to eliminate all opposition and dissent. By the law of 14 Frimaire (December 4, 1793), the Convention declared itself "the sole center of the impulse of government." All subordinate authorities were placed under the direct control of the Committee of Public Safety, which monitored them every ten days. All local officials became "national agents," subject to immediate re-moval by Paris. Committees of surveillance—that is, teams of spies—were placed over government functionaries at every level. The mere advocacy of federalism or local autonomy became a crime. The law of 14 Frimaire became the real consti-tution of France, the first blueprint of modern totalitarianism.

Having assured bureaucratic conformity, the regime now turned on politi-cal dissenters. A new group had formed on its right, the Indulgents, who wished to mitigate the Terror, while on its left were militant sans-culottes, the Enragés, whose influence in the Commune was no longer tolerable. This was a familiar phenomenon. The Montagnards had been a left opposition group in their time, just as the Girondins had before them. But the existence of dissent implied a divi-sion in the general will, which could not to be permitted. So Danton and his In-dulgents, Hébert and his Enragés, trooped to the scaffold in turn (March–April, 1794). The press was now fully censored, and all clubs suppressed save the Jaco-bins. A pall of silence fell over the country. The Convention itself walked in fear of its all-powerful Committee of Public Safety.

What finally brought down Robespierre and his colleagues was their very success. By the spring of 1794, the revolutionary army—850,000 strong—had driven the last foreign soldier out of France. The civil insurrection was under control. The objectives of the Terror had been achieved, but the Terror itself, like a mindless machine, continued. The law of 22 Prairial (June 10, 1794) greatly simplified its work. All legal forms were dispensed with, and the Revolutionary Tribunal was limited to two verdicts: acquittal or death. Among the new crimes were such offenses as spreading rumors, defaming patriots, and offending morality. It was an open death warrant for everyone in the city.

In the next six weeks, more people were guillotined in Paris than in the whole preceding year. An air of horror and unreality settled over the Revolutionary capital, even as its victorious armies streamed into the Low Countries. The members of the Committee of Public Safety even began to fear one another, and particularly Robespierre. A group of them conspired to denounce him before the Convention on 9 Thermidor (July 27). Robespierre attempted to defend himself, but was shouted down and arrested. The next day, he and Saint-Just were executed.

His enemies called Robespierre a tyrant who sought supreme power for himself. Certainly he made himself unwisely conspicuous. His participation in the Festival of the Supreme Being, an attempt to set up a Deist god of reason as a Revolutionary religion, convinced many that he aimed to be not merely the dictator of the Revolution but its high priest. In reality, Robespierre was beyond personal ambition. He never held, nor sought, any special title or distinction. When he died, he left an estate of barely 100 livres. He identified himself wholly with the general will, and considered himself merely its executant. Among the corrupt and disillusioned, he alone retained absolute faith in the ideals of the Revolution. To the end, he believed that the Terror, by purging the wicked, would create the conditions for a true democracy. In a century of utopias, he was the noblest and most deluded dreamer of all.

THE THERMIDORIAN REACTION

With the death of Robespierre, the Revolution swung sharply to the right. It was as if a fever boil had been lanced. Men were tired of terror and virtue alike. Political pragmatists, speculators, and money men came forward. The Revolution was to be transformed into a paying business. This was the Thermidorian Reaction.

The Convention scuttled the powers of the Committee of Public Safety, abolished the Commune, and closed down the Jacobin club. Aristocratic fashions and attitudes were flaunted by the *jeunesse doreé,* the "gilded youth" of the bourgeoisie. Gangs of middle-class delinquents terrorized the working quarters of Paris. Far more serious was the campaign of vengeance against ex-Robespierrists in the provinces, the White or Counter-Terror. In embittered Lyon, there was a massacre of suspected Montagnards. However, though the government winked at these incidents, it did not instigate them. The infamous law of 22 Prairial was repealed on the morrow of Robespierre's death, and the Revolutionary Tribunal suspended. The official or Red Terror had been, at least in theory, a sacramental purge in the name of virtue; the White Terror was just a settling of scores.

A similar transformation came over the prosecution of the war. The Convention discovered that, despite its magnanimous offer, the people of the Low Countries and the Rhineland had no particular desire to be liberated by French armies. The war against kings became an unvarnished war of aggression, though to the occupied territories it was a distinction without a difference. Under Jacobin or Thermidorian alike, they were looted and bilked of everything from livestock to art treasures. The unlucky Netherlands was forced to pay 100 million livres for its liberation, in return for which it received the title of the Batavian Republic, thus becoming the first official satellite of the Revolutionary wars. The Austrian Netherlands, the left bank of the Rhine, and the Mediterranean principalities of Savoy and Nice were annexed to France outright.

At home, the Thermidorian Convention (which had readmitted some 78 purged Girondins) found itself buffeted by left and right alike. Having only assented to price controls under duress, it rapidly decontrolled the economy. Severe inflation followed, compounded as usual by speculation and hoarding. By the spring of 1795, the price of bread had rocketed to an unheard-of 26 sous, and the official ration had been cut to 2 ounces per day: starvation. On May 20, the sans-culottes, backed up by four battalions of the National Guard, stormed the Convention with the cry, "Bread or death!" It was less a demand than a simple statement of fact. But the attack petered out, leaderless, and loyal guard units soon restored order. It was the last popular insurrection of the Revolution, and marked the final eclipse of the sans-culottes as a political force.

On the right, meanwhile, royalist sentiments were again being openly voiced in France. The royalists rallied around the son of Louis XVI, who had seen his father and mother led to the guillotine and was still confined in the same prison. For once it seemed that a royal minority might be a blessing to France. As the rightful heir to the throne, young Louis XVII, as he was hopefully called, might satisfy the still-powerful sentiment of legitimacy; yet, being a boy, he would be a mere figurehead who could not impede constitutional processes. But Louis died of tuberculosis in June, 1795, dashing royalist hopes. His successor was the king's brother, the Count of Provence, a figure unacceptable to anyone but the emigrés. Nonetheless, the royalists launched a desperate revolt in Paris on October 5. It was put down by a decommissioned young brigadier of artillery named Napoleon Bonaparte, who fired point-blank on the rebels—the "whiff of grapeshot" that first made his reputation.

There were roughly three political positions in France in 1795. Moderate royalists hoped for a return to the constitutional monarchy of 1791, which was indeed a plausible option until the death of their candidate. The sans-culottes and surviving Montagnards demanded implementation of the democratic Constitution of 1793, which was now a considerable embarrassment to the Convention that had drawn it. The Thermidorian majority wanted something in between. As regicides, they dared not return to the monarchy; as men of property, they wanted a government that would keep the sans-culottes in their place. Their spokesman was Boissy d'Anglas, who advocated a republic of the "best men." "The best," said Boissy, "are those who are the most educated and the most interested in maintaining the laws. With few exceptions, you will find such men only among those who, owning property, are attached to the country in which it is located, to the laws which protect it, to the peace and order which preserve it. . . . A country governed by landowners is in the social order; that which is governed by nonlandowners is in the state of nature." If we substitute the word *nobility* for *landowner,* it was a statement that would have been thoroughly acceptable anywhere in Old Regime Europe.

It was Boissy d'Anglas who introduced the new draft constitution in the Convention on June 23. It provided again for a system of electors, for whom the property qualification was so high that only 20,000 men in France met the test. The electors chose all department officials and a bicameral Legislative Assembly, which in turn chose a five-member executive, the Directory, for a term of five years. It was from this executive that the new regime was to take its name. At the end of its deliberations, the Convention decreed that at least two-thirds of the new Assembly must be made up of its own members. This crude attempt at self-perpetuation made a mockery of what remained of the electoral process. Two-thirds of Paris boycotted the ratification, and the new constitution was voted into being by barely a million Frenchmen.

THE DIRECTORY (1795–1799)

The new government was inherently unstable. It had neither the ideological appeal of Jacobinism nor the traditional appeal of monarchy. Its motives were suspect from the outset, and its political base was too narrow to generate mass support. It had no real justification except as a perpetuator of the status quo. Joseph de Maistre summed up its weaknesses trenchantly from a royalist point of view: "Whatever form one gives to governments, birth and wealth always place themselves in the first rank and nowhere do they rule more harshly than where their empire is not founded on law." In short, the Directory was a would-be aristocracy without the courage to choose its king.

The most notable challenge from the left was the movement of Gracchus Babeuf. For Babeuf, a village laborer's son turned radical journalist, the Revolution meant the achievement of total equality. At first he argued that the whole of France be literally parceled into identical lots, but this was succeeded by a "more sublime" notion: the abolition of property itself and the communization of all lands and resources. Significantly, one of Babeuf's followers was Robert Lindet, who as a member of the Committee of Public Safety had been in charge of enforcing price controls and provisioning Paris. Thus, Babeuf's program derived not only from the thinking of earlier philosophes like Rousseau and the Abbé Morelly but also from the practical experience of the Revolution itself.

As a police problem, this "conspiracy of the equals" was not serious. After Bonaparte (now commander of all forces in France) broke up Babeuf's Pantheon club, the movement went underground, only to be betrayed by an informer. A number of the conspirators were shot on the spot, and others imprisoned or deported; Babeuf was guillotined. His legacy, however, was not lost. The "conspiracy," ill-fated as it was, became the prototype of the modern political cell, and Babeuf's concept of a revolutionary vanguard that seized power on behalf of the people influenced later Marxist thought and practice. Through his colleague, Filippo Buonarroti, who escaped to pursue an underground revolutionary career for 40 years, he had a living link to the radical tradition of the nineteenth century.

The Directory was successful only at war. Napoleon's daring foray into Italy in 1796 produced a string of new satellite republics, all grandiloquently named: the Helvetic (Switzerland), the Cisalpine (Milan), the Ligurian (Genoa), the Roman (the Papal States), and the Parthenopean (Naples). Austria was compelled to recognize these conquests, as well as the annexation of its province in the Netherlands, by the Treaty of Campo Formio (October, 1797). Prussia had left the war two years before, leaving only a weary Britain of the original anti-French coalition.

As peace approached, the mood of the country turned steadily to the right. The elections of April, 1797, produced a shocking upsurge of royalist influence. Fearing a possible restoration, the Thermidorian republicans staged a preventive coup on September 4. Two of the Directors were purged, and the April elections annulled. The surviving Directors decreed that anyone advocating either the monarchy or the constitution of 1793 would be shot on sight.

With these acts, the Directory shed all pretense of legitimacy. It was henceforth merely a cabal in search of a dictator. Only a lingering repugnance for this inevitable solution propped it up two years longer. But the outbreak of general war again in 1799 made a strong government imperative. Brokered by the Abbé Sieyès, now again influential, Napoleon emerged as the man of the hour. On November 10, 1799, he dispersed the Legislative Assembly with a troop of grenadiers and seized power. It was the eighth major change of power in the Revolution. No one then realized it was to be the last.

THE UNFINISHED REVOLUTION

The Revolution of 1789 had begun like a great ship sailing into unchartered waters. At every point, there were three conflicting opinions at the rudder: of those who wanted to go back, those who wanted to go on, and those who wanted to put into the nearest port. The great majority of Frenchmen, bourgeois and peasants alike, held the last view. For them, the Revolution was accomplished in 1789 and consolidated in 1791. Their liberty was the freedom of trade, their equality was a uniform system of ownership, their fraternity stopped at the poverty line. The bourgeoisie whom Marx saw as vigorous protoindustrialists clearing the way for modern capitalism were a landed class made rich by the spoils of a deposed ruling elite. They wanted to inherit the good life of the Old Regime, not to destroy it. They lost control of the Revolution during the Jacobin Republic but regained it, though shakily, after Thermidor. In Napoleon they found at last their helmsman, or so they thought.

For the urban and rural poor, the Revolution was a cheat. They rebelled against it, but very likely their confused and inarticulate protest would have had no more effect than the peasant rebellions of the Old Regime, had they not been led by a segment of the bourgeoisie which, swayed by the ideals of the Enlightenment, thought the Revolution must mean more than a world made safe for real

estate investment. These men, of whom Robespierre was representative, were profoundly skeptical of parliamentary government. Parliaments, Robespierre felt,
tended to represent themselves, not the unitary will of the people. That will, made
known directly in the periodic outbursts of popular insurrection, took precedence
over everything else. Thus, the alliance between the Jacobins and the sans-culottes
was not merely opportunistic; it sprang from a profound belief that sovereignty
and virtue were indivisible.

Without understanding this search for the general will, and the attempt to
create the political conditions in which it could be heard, the Terror becomes
nothing but a meaningless bloodbath. In Robespierre's phrase, the Terror was
the "despotism of liberty," a purge of the private wills and vested interests that
drowned out the voice of the people. But while he attacked profiteering and speculation, Robespierre did not perceive that inequity of wealth as such must necessarily divide the social interest, that the will of a man whose stomach was empty
could not be the same as that of the man who was fed. The first concern of the
sans-culottes was bread, not virtue. This was not a new condition; what was new
was the political importance it assumed when the people were invited to make
their will known and even to overturn governments that failed to heed it. With
the Jacobin Republic, poverty became no longer merely a pious fact of life ("the
poor are always with us") but a social issue, no longer a natural phenomenon
but a social product. The Jacobins themselves were but dimly aware of the forces
they had unleashed. Perhaps Saint-Just understood it best when he remarked,
despairingly, that "the wretched are the power of the earth."

From the three basic attitudes toward the Revolution—to reverse it, to contain it, to expand it—emerged the right, center, and left of the modern political
world. The European right continued to champion the traditional social order
and at least some form of monarchy—it is often forgotten that even in France,
royalism was a real option down to the end of the nineteenth century. It was only
after World War I that the right identified itself with monarchy's spurious surro-
gate, fascism, for much the same reasons that led the French bourgeoisie to em-
brace Bonapartism in the preceding century. The center, middle-class and moderately reformist, continued to demand free trade and parliamentary democracy,
and was largely successful in achieving both before discovering it really wanted
neither. The left became the party of revolution, for whom, in the words of Babeuf's *Manifesto of the Equals,* "The French Revolution is but the forerunner
of another, far more grand, far more solemn, which will be the last. . . ."

This summary is highly schematic, and it cuts across crucial factors such
as nationalism and the Industrial Revolution, both of which matured only in the
nineteenth century. It must also be remembered that what is more or less true
for France, Italy, and Germany is not necessarily applicable to Britain, Spain,
or Russia. Nonetheless, it may still be said that the political spectrum of the modern world—the nineteenth century directly, and, under somewhat altered terms,
the twentieth as well—was generated by the great questions posed by the French
Revolution. In this sense, certainly, it is still the unfinished revolution.

Finally, and almost apart from any attitude or belief, the modern state, with
its vastly expanded power to command the lives and resources of its people, is

a product of the French Revolution. The total and arbitrary suspension of all legal rights and forms, which began with the Jacobins but was equally characteristic of the Directory, has become an increasingly casual weapon of modern regimes, just as the Terror foreshadowed the genocide of recent times. In this respect, the Revolution opened a Pandora's box by which, in the words of Dostoevski's Grand Inquisitor, "everything is permitted." But that also, as Pandora's myth reminds us, includes hope.

THE NAPOLEONIC AFTERMATH

Napoleon was barely 30 when he became master of France. He was French only by historical courtesy; the island of Corsica had been annexed to France a year before his birth there in 1769, and the Buonapartes (Napoleon dropped the "u" when he invaded Italy in 1796) were impoverished Italian nobility. Ironically, Napoleon's first youthful ambition was to free Corsica from "French tyranny," but, as a young commissioned officer caught up in the Revolution, he soon perceived, in a phrase later made famous, "a career open to talents." If he ever had any ideology, he soon shed it. By 1793, he was writing, "Since one has to take sides, it is just as well to choose the winning side, the side that loots, burns, and devastates. Given the alternative, it is better to eat than to be eaten."

In an army deserted by its senior commanders, Napoleon's rise was rapid. He first came to notice by retaking the royalist port of Toulon in 1793, and, after the stroke of luck that put him in Paris during the revolt of October, 1795, became a central figure behind most of the political upheavals of the Directory. Jealous rivals were glad to see him posted to Italy, but his campaign was so brilliant and successful that his reputation soared. Even a calamitous attack on the British in Egypt in 1798, the most enigmatic episode of his career, only added to his romantic aura. By 30, he had achieved everything but power, and that was clearly the next step. With the coup of November, 1799, he took it.

FROM REPUBLIC TO EMPIRE (1799–1804)

Napoleon, with his coconspirators Sieyès and Roger Ducos, immediately took on the new title of consul, as if to stress their distance from the discredited Directory. Within a month, they had drafted a new constitution—the fourth in eight years—in which the strong hand of Bonaparte was already evident. The legislature consisted of a Tribunate, which could debate laws but not pass them, a Legislative Body, which could pass laws but not debate them, and a Senate, which could veto but not amend. Clearly, its entire purpose was to serve as a three-stage rubber stamp for legislation prepared by the executive Council of State, whose members were nominated by Napoleon. Napoleon himself was to be First Consul, with full powers to appoint all officials and magistrates, conduct diplomacy, declare and wage war, and assure domestic tranquility—in short, monarchic sovereignty under a republican facade.

Napoleon immediately promulgated the new constitution on his own authority, and pronounced it in effect. Only then did he submit it for ratification by popular referendum. The result was predictably lopsided, especially with the government counting: 3,011,007 for, 1562 against. Napoleon was so pleased with these results that he made referendums a permanent part of his political arsenal. It was later revived by his nephew, Napoleon III, and has become a favorite technique of modern dictators.

Yet Napoleon's power did not rest on such trickery. Almost up to the very end, he retained the broad and even blind support of all classes of Frenchmen. Only die-hard royalists and republicans never accepted him, and their influence was slight. Simply stated, Napoleon gave the rich what they wanted, the poor what they would accept, and everyone a measure of glory such as Louis XIV had never dreamed. At the same time, he built an institutional foundation for his rule that brought every aspect of political, economic, and social life under the direct control of the state.

Napoleon ended the long historical debate between provincial autonomy and central control once and for all. There was only one government, the central state. All provincial officials were responsible to it up a clear chain of command, from mayors to department prefects to the Council of State and the Consul himself. The judiciary, declared independent in 1791, was brought back under executive control. All judges between the supreme Court of Cassation and local justices of the peace were appointed directly by Napoleon, and a government commissioner was assigned to each court to supervise its activities. The economy was similarly taken in hand. Napoleon applied price and export controls as he saw fit, promoted new industry, and laid down an extensive network of roads and canals. The Bank of France was chartered in 1800 to free the government from reliance on private credit, and tax collection was centralized. The French at last began to catch up with the fiscal system pioneered by the English more than a century before.

The capstone of Napoleon's reforms was the Civil Code of 1804. The culmination of efforts to produce a cogent statement of French legal and administrative principles that went back to the sixteenth century, it became the most influential code of secular law outside the Anglo-Saxon tradition since Roman times. Yet it was in many ways a backward-looking document. The main principles of the early Revolution—civil and legal equality, religious toleration, the abolition of feudalism, social orders, and hereditary aristocracy—were confirmed. But the right to subsistence guaranteed by the Constitution of 1793 was nowhere to be found. There were elaborate guarantees of property rights, detailed provisions for contracts and debts, but as for labor, it was merely "free"—free to survive or perish, as market conditions might dictate.

The society envisioned by the Code, beneath its formal impress of equality, was actually a despotic paternalism that resurrected the spirit of the Old Regime. The emphasis was always on the downflow of authority, from state to individual, employer to workman, husband to wife, parent to child. The word of an employer was automatically to prevail over that of a worker in court. Women were enjoined to obey their husbands and denied the right to administer their own property. Children might be imprisoned for up to six months on the mere word of their father and had to ask his consent to marry up to the age of 30.

The Napoleonic Code (as it was known after 1807) was not only intended for France. It also served as a basis of administration for the new French empire, through which its influence spread throughout Europe and beyond, to places as far distant as Bolivia, Egypt, and Japan. What was retrograde in France itself was often novel and progressive elsewhere, and it was by means of the Code that the Revolution was exported in its definitive form. As a solvent of old feudal structures and a model of modern government, its impact can scarcely be exaggerated.

Napoleon's greatest diplomatic achievement was reconciliation with the Catholic church. The war between the Revolution and the church had been a costly one on both sides. In the dark days of the Jacobin era, Catholic worship had actually been driven underground, and a prominent churchman resigned, declaring that Christianity was a delusion. On the other hand, nothing alienated millions of devout Frenchmen more from the Revolution than the persecution of the church. Napoleon himself had a wholly pragmatic view of religion: It would help him to govern. It was in this spirit that he negotiated the Concordat of 1801. The Vatican recognized the confiscation of its lands and tithes as permanent, so permitting its clergy to become salaried officials under the watchful eye of the prefects. It even permitted Napoleon to introduce a catechism in which disobedience to him was grounds for eternal damnation; not even divine-right monarchs had ever gone that far. In return for this, the pope was recognized as head of the church, though his bulls could not circulate without state permission, and Catholicism was declared to be the religion "of the majority of Frenchmen." By this careful formulation, Napoleon stopped short of making Catholicism the official state church, thus preserving the principle of religious equality; yet it served that role in effect. With the Concordat, his structure of authority was complete: "my gendarmes, my prefects, my priests."

In 1802, Napoleon, whose term as First Consul ran for ten years, declared himself Consul for life; in 1804, he decided to take the title of emperor and soon after created an aristocracy. The first two steps were ratified by popular referendum, but for his coronation he summoned Pope Pius VII to Paris and, in a gesture deliberately reminiscent of Charlemagne's at his coronation as Holy Roman Emperor 1000 years before, took the crown from the startled pontiff's hands and placed it on his own head. It was a strange end for a revolution against priests and kings.

NAPOLEON AT WAR (1799–1815)

From 1792 to 1815, Europe was almost continuously involved in a war that ranged all over the globe and had such ramifications as the conquest of India, the liberation of South America, and the doubling of the size of the United States. The war was instigated by the French Revolution but long outlived it, becoming in one aspect the first great war of modern nationalism, in another the last chapter of the Anglo-French competition for empire. Napoleon was its dominating figure, but even without him, it would have had the same essential character.

Revolutionary France began the war in 1792–1793, first against Austria,

Napoleon I as emperor of the French.

then virtually against the whole of Europe. The French fought, politically, to extend the Revolution, psychologically, to keep its momentum going at home, and militarily, to acquire buffer zones against the expected counterrevolutionary attack. The anti-French forces had by contrast no positive common goals and tended to desert one another in moments of crisis, as Prussia did Austria in 1795 and Austria did Russia in 1799. These powers were more concerned with each other than with France, just as Britain thought primarily in terms of its naval security rather than any political alignment on the continent. The Dutch had become a relatively minor power, the Holy Roman Empire was an empty shell, and the whole Rhine frontier no longer had the same geopolitical significance it did 100 years before (and was to reacquire 100 years later). True, there was considerable ideological fervor against France, and some people, like the Swiss journalist Mallet du Pan, called for a holy crusade. But informed military opinion, far from considering the French a menace, dismissed the Revolutionary army as a leaderless mob. It was a measure of their preoccupation with more important things, such as the division of Poland, that Austria and Prussia did not even think this defenseless France worth attacking, and confined themselves to mere diplomatic gestures.

The phenomenal success of the French took Europe wholly by surprise. No one had ever seen an army like this, which broke every rule of military practice yet kept on winning. New recruits picked up their training on the march, discipline was negligible, supplies always lacking, sanitation nil. Officers were men of any class who showed a flair for maneuvers and courage in battle. Promotions were made on merit: Napoleon's marshals included coopers, millers, masons, and stable boys. Their average age was about 30; most of Prussia's generals were over 60. It was an army of the future defeating the armies of the past.

But Austria could not long tolerate the humiliating terms of Campo Formio, nor Europe a French flank that stretched from the North Sea to the Ionian. Backed by British money and Russian troops, a second coalition drove France out of Italy in the summer of 1799. The satellite republics vanished as if blown away, and the Russians under General Suvorov ranged as far as Switzerland. At this juncture, Bonaparte seized power. "Our task," he told his troops, "is not to defend our own frontiers, but to invade enemy territory." The French counterattack was crushing. At Marengo and Hohenlinden, the Austrians sustained massive defeats, and the Treaty of Lunéville (February, 1801) set them back even worse than Campo Formio. Russia withdrew, leaving only Britain. But the 18-year ministry of William Pitt the Younger, son of the hero of the Seven Years' War, had fallen, and the British, anxious for peace, capitulated to French terms at Amiens in March, 1802.

The Peace of Amiens was merely a truce. Fourteen months later, war broke out again. By 1805, Austria and Russia were sufficiently reinvigorated to join Britain once more, with Pitt, again prime minister, subsidizing Russia with £1.25 million for every 100,000 troops deployed. At Ulm (October 15), an Austrian army of 50,000, completely outgeneraled, surrendered without firing a shot, and six weeks later (December 2), Napoleon won the greatest of all his battles over a combined Austro-Russian force at Austerlitz. Again Austria submitted to a dictated peace, which stripped it of Venice (Treaty of Pressburg, December, 1805). Only one reverse marred the French triumph: At Cape Trafalgar off the Spanish coast on October 21, an outnumbered British squadron under Admiral Horatio Nelson destroyed Napoleon's Mediterranean fleet, sinking or capturing 18 ships without the loss of a single vessel. Nelson himself was slain, but Napoleon's project of invading England was permanently foiled, as well as his hopes of challenging England's mastery of the seas.

On the continent, however, Napoleon remained invincible. Prussia, neutral since 1795, blundered into war alone in 1806 and was crushed in October in two simultaneous battles 12 miles apart, at Jena and Auerstadt. Eleven days later, Napoleon was in Berlin. The fabled Prussian army had collapsed in a single month. Only the Russians now remained, and Napoleon pursued them along the Baltic shore into East Prussia. In February, 1807, the two armies clashed indecisively in a blinding snowstorm at Eylau; five months later, Napoleon was victorious at Friedland. Tsar Alexander I, unwilling to risk himself further in a lost cause, sued for peace.

On June 25, Napoleon and Alexander met on a raft on the Niemen River near the Russian border, while King Frederick William III of Prussia paced fretfully on the bank. Well had he cause for alarm. By the Treaty of Tilsit, signed in July, Prussia was cut in half, and its army reduced to a skeletal 42,000 men. Prussian Poland became the Grand Duchy of Warsaw, a new Napoleonic satellite. In secret articles, Alexander promised aid against Britain and Napoleon support for the tsar's designs on Turkey. It is doubtful that either ruler placed much stock in the other's pledges, but if nothing else they had gained a temporary détente. To a prostrate Europe, however, they looked like two Roman emperors dividing the world.

The years after Tilsit were the high-water mark of Napoleon's fortune. From the Atlantic to the Polish steppe, from the Baltic to the Mediterranean, he ruled or dominated the whole of Europe. A swollen France stretched from the Baltic port of Lübeck to south of Rome. Spain, Switzerland, central Germany, and most of Italy were organized as satellites, mostly parceled out to Napoleon's own relatives—his brothers Joseph, Louis, and Jérôme as kings of Spain, the Netherlands, and Westphalia, respectively, and his brother-in-law Joachim Murat as king of Naples. (When Louis in the Netherlands became too independent, Napoleon deposed him and absorbed the Dutch state directly into France.) All of these territories were administered under the Napoleonic Code and were obliged to furnish conscripts for the imperial army. Prussia, Austria, Denmark, and Sweden remained nominally independent as "allies," but their freedom of action was sharply circumscribed. They were forced to sever all ties with Britain and join a French embargo—the so-called continental system—on British goods. When Austria rebelled in 1809, it was subjected to a fourth defeat. It was a crucial test of strength for Napoleon's empire, for, despite Austria's appeal to what had once been the Holy Roman Empire, not a single German prince came to its aid.

Yet the new French empire, so astonishingly built, was inherently unstable. It violated the entire balance-of-power principle on which the European state system was built. It required the subjection of the entire continent to the will of one man whose only mandate was conquest. It was not even in the interest of France, whose borders now resembled a jaw open upon all Europe. At the Erfurt conference of 1808, Napoleon's foreign minister, Talleyrand, made secret overtures to Tsar Alexander. Even at the height of the empire, Talleyrand, a man of the old school, did not believe it could last.

Napoleon himself was aware of the weakness of his position. His only hope lay in founding a dynasty. When his first wife, Josephine de Beauharnais, failed to provide him with an heir, he divorced her in favor of Princess Marie Louise of Austria. In 1811, she bore him a son, whom Napoleon grandly called the king of Rome. But nothing could obscure the fact that Napoleon, who had so often humiliated Austria, felt compelled to buy legitimacy by mixing his blood with the Hapsburgs.

There were other serious cracks in the facade. Napoleon's plans to create a purely continental economy dominated by France backfired. The British slipped his embargo at will, while their navy blockaded French ports, reducing them to economic ruin. Internal trade withered throughout Europe, producing hardship and resentment. Equally ominous was the slow awakening of national pride, particularly in Germany. By sweeping away the debris of the Holy Roman Empire

NORWAY
(To Denmark)

N O R T H
S E A

DENMARK
Copenhagen
1801
1807

Heligoland
(1807 to Br.)→

U N I T E D

K I N G D O M

London

Amsterdam

Brussels

Leipzig 1813

Waterloo
1815

Auerstädt 1806

A T L A N T I C

Aix-la-
Chapelle

Dre
Jena 1806 18

O C E A N

Amiens
1802 ⊖

1813

1806

Paris

Lunéville
1801
⊖

CONFEDERATION
OF THE RHINE
1806-1813

1805

1800

Ulm
1805

F R A N C E

SWITZERLAND

Campo Formi
1802

La Coruña
1809

Lyons

Milan

Rivoli
1796

Santander

Lodi
1796

Bayonne
1808

Marengo
1800

Valladolid
1808

Vitoria
1808

1808

Nice
1796

1815

ITALY

Salamanca

Saragossa
1809

Toulon

Marseilles

1798

PORTUGAL

Vimeiro 1808

Madrid

(To France
1808-1813)

ELBA

Torres Vedras

Barcelona

CORSICA

Lisbon

Rome

S P A I N

Na

Cordova

SARDINIA

Cadiz

Trafalgar
1805

M E D I T E R R A N E A N

EUROPE IN 1812
AT THE HEIGHT OF NAPOLEON'S POWER

French Empire ⬛   → Principal campaigns of Napoleon

     ✕ Battle site

Subject to Napoleon ⬛   ⊖ Treaty site

Temporary allies of Napoleon ⬛   ⬛ Independent states

WEDEN

BALTIC SEA

Danzig

Tilsit 1807
1812
Friedland
1807
Eylau 1807

PRUSSIA

DUCHY OF

1806

WARSAW

Warsaw

Vilna

Smolensk
1812

Borodino
1812

Moscow

R U S S I A

Austerlitz 1805

ienna   Wagram 1809

Pressburg 1805

USTRIA

Leoben

HUNGARY

BLACK   SEA

IAN PROVINCES

Constantinople

DRIATIC SEA

APLES

O T T O M A N

E M P I R E

A E G E A N   S E A

IONIAN ISLANDS
(To Venice to 1797;
to France 1797-1799
and 1807-1815; to
Russia 1799-1807)

ILY

S E A

CRETE

CYPRUS

Acre

0   500

Miles

Alexandria
1798

Cairo

(officially abolished in 1806), Napoleon catalyzed the long-dormant political consciousness of the Germans. A generation before, the proto-Romantic philosopher Johann Gottfried von Herder (1744–1803) had argued that each people had a separate and unique historical destiny shaped by its *Volksgeist,* or inner spirit. This cultural nationalism was quickly wedded to political resistance as French troops paraded through the streets of Berlin. What victory had never brought to Prussia, collapse and dismemberment did: a sense of nationhood. In 1808, the philosopher and publicist Johann Gottlieb Fichte published his *Addresses to the German Nation,* in which he asserted that the German *Volksgeist* was intrinsically superior and must preserve itself from contamination by outside cultures. The dramatist Friedrich von Schiller preached national liberation through his patriotic odes and plays, and freedom from oppression was the thinly veiled message of Beethoven's opera *Fidelio.*

This new national consciousness was a dramatic turnabout for the German intelligentsia, who had prided themselves on a lofty internationalism. Their ideal had been the tiny, idyllic dukedom of Weimar, whose ruler, Karl August (1775–1828), gathered around him the noblest spirits of the German Enlightenment, including the great Goethe. It would not be an exaggeration to say that Karl August had more poets at his court than officers in his army. But it was precisely such a luxury that Germany could no longer afford. If even militarized Prussia could not stand up to Napoleon, what could be said of a political anachronism like Weimar?

A more direct and primitive nationalism erupted in Spain when Napoleon deposed the reigning Bourbon dynasty in 1808. Spaniards of all classes rose up in spontaneous resistance and waged until 1814 a fierce guerilla war whose frightful atrocities were caught for all time by the painter Francisco Goya. Spain was the stanchless wound in Napoleon's side. He thought that 20,000 men could hold the country; ten times that many failed. A British army under Arthur Wellesley, later Duke of Wellington, linked up with the Spaniards through Portugal in what came to be known as the Peninsular War. By early 1814, southern France itself was under attack. The war ended with the British in Toulouse.

Napoleon's downfall, however, was brought about by his invasion of Russia. Relations between the tsar and the emperor had deteriorated steadily after Tilsit. Alexander had hoped to turn the Grand Duchy of Warsaw into a Russian satellite; instead it had become a French salient into Russia itself. He had looked for French support against Turkey; instead, Napoleon had done everything he could to thwart Russian ambitions in the Balkans. The Russians must never be allowed to enter Constantinople, said Napoleon, for "it is the center of world empire." Clearly, if anyone was to possess that empire, it would be Napoleon himself.

Alexander responded by breaking with the continental system, resuming trade with England, and erecting tariffs against French goods. Napoleon resolved on war. He had never regarded the tsar as an ally or peer, merely a large vassal. He would teach him a final lesson. In June, 1812, he crossed the Niemen into Russia with over 600,000 men, the largest army ever assembled for a single expedition. Characteristically, Napoleon envisaged a short, decisive campaign: His troops carried only four days' rations and the supply convoys three weeks' more. But the Russians refused to fight, retreating behind scorched earth into the inexhaustible steppe. Napoleon's army rapidly melted away. He finally caught the Russians at Borodino in September, but failed to smash them in a bloody battle; they retreated in good order beyond Moscow, which Napoleon entered unopposed on September 14. Moscow was the goal of the campaign; in conventional terms, Napoleon had won the war. But no peace delegation waited to receive him, and Alexander, in St. Petersburg, ignored his own offer of terms. Moscow itself was a ghost city, deserted by most of its 300,000 inhabitants. It was already aflame when Napoleon reached it; within a week, three-quarters of it had been burned down. Without food or shelter, Napoleon could not winter in the devastated city. On October 19, he began a retreat. Mired in snow and mud, dogged by Russian troops and Cossack irregulars, the Grand Army laid a 1000-mile track of corpses along its way. More than half a million men died, deserted, or vanished; barely 100,000 made it back to the Polish border. It was the most shattering defeat in history.

Napoleon was not with the final remnant. He raced back to Paris to avert political collapse. Miraculously raising a new army of 250,000, he faced a coalition of Russia, Prussia, Austria, and Sweden, with Britain, as usual, the paymaster. After several indecisive victories, Napoleon was defeated outside Leipzig in the great three-day Battle of the Nations (October, 1813), and thrown back upon France.

Like its predecessors, however, the coalition against Napoleon was unstable. The Austrians in particular were fearful of German nationalism and eager to have the Russians out of Europe. Their foreign minister, Count Klemens von Metternich, offered Napoleon the French borders of 1792, including Belgium and the west bank of the Rhine. Though the alternative was an invasion against hopeless odds, Napoleon refused. For the emperor of the French, the only stakes were all or nothing.

Napoleon's intransigence cast the die. Russia, Prussia, Austria, and Britain entered the Quadruple Alliance, a 20-year mutual security agreement against France. Meanwhile, their armies swept into France from Belgium, the middle Rhine, and Switzerland, with Wellington attacking from the south. Napoleon's defense was the most brilliant campaign of his career, a military classic of rapid deployment against a vastly superior foe. But the result was foregone, and even his political support had vanished. On April 4, 1814, the emperor abdicated in favor of his 3-year-old son, a day after his Senate had deposed him.

THE RESTORATION AND THE HUNDRED DAYS

The victorious allies wanted none of the king of Rome, as Napoleon called his son, nor any other claimant spawned by the terrible Revolution. Aided by Talleyrand, they restored the Bourbon dynasty. The Count of Provence became Louis XVIII, and it was he who signed the Treaty of Paris on May 30, 1814, officially ending Europe's 22-year war with France. The terms were exceedingly moderate. France would simply return to its prewar boundaries. No indemnities or reparations were imposed. Even Napoleon was treated leniently. He was exiled to an 86-square-mile rock called Elba off the west coast of Italy, but was permitted to retain the title of emperor and granted a pension of 2 million francs a year. The allies were making every effort to stabilize the new Bourbon regime.

At home, Louis XVIII issued a Constitutional Charter that paid lip service to the principles of legal and social equality and confirmed the Revolutionary land settlement and the Napoleonic Code. Louis remained in theory an absolute king, but he agreed to govern with a two-chamber assembly chosen by a restricted suffrage of large landowners. The same moderation, however, was not evident in the king's followers. Thousands of vengeful emigrés returned in his train, eager to settle old scores. These Ultraroyalists, or "Ultras," as they were called, would be satisfied by nothing less than a total restoration of the Old Regime. Their activities, together with the inevitable letdown from the excitement of Napoleon's conquests, cost the Bourbon regime whatever credit it had.

It was Napoleon himself who reaped the benefit. On March 1, 1815, he landed with 1000 troops on the southern coast of France. His swift journey to Paris was a triumphal progress. Louis XVIII, deserted by his army, fled to Belgium. While Napoleon declared himself restored "by the unanimous wish of a great nation," the allies in Vienna branded him a public outlaw.

To gain breathing space for his new regime, Napoleon made vaguely conciliatory gestures to both the right and the left. But the real test, as he knew, would be trial by battle. Raising yet another army, he crossed the Belgian frontier in mid-June. On June 18, he met a combined force under the Duke of Wellington and the Prussian general Gerhard von Blücher at Waterloo on the road to Brussels, and was defeated in day-long combat. It was Napoleon's last throw. Hastening to Paris to rally support in the Chamber of Deputies, he was met with a stony demand for abdication. The second reign of Napoleon had lasted exactly 100 days.

After an abortive attempt to flee to America, Napoleon surrendered to the British. They exiled him to St. Helena, a bleak speck in the south Atlantic 4000 miles from Europe. There he died in 1821, of stomach cancer. But the death of Napoleon the man was the birth of Napoleon the legend. A veritable cult grew up around him, climaxed by the return and reentombment of his body in France in 1840. To this day he remains the subject of passionate controversy. He has been the symbol of a glorious past to the French in moments of nationalistic fervor, of egocentric despotism in periods of liberal democracy.

Talleyrand wrote of Napoleon that he squandered a golden opportunity to create a lasting political equilibrium in Europe. Napoleon himself said that the man of genius is a meteor who illumines his time but does not transform it. Yet Napoleon did leave a permanent legacy. His Code became the matrix of modern French society. His conquests stimulated both anti-French nationalism and aspirations for a liberal society on the French model. His suppression of the Holy Roman Empire was the first step toward German unification. If the ideas he spread were those of the Revolution rather than his own, they might never have traveled so far without him. Napoleon failed to make Europe a province of France, but he did make the French Revolution European.

THE CONGRESS OF VIENNA

The victorious allies met in Vienna in September, 1814, to try to untangle 20 years of war and revolution. It was the first general congress of European powers since the Peace of Westphalia in 1648. Every state on the continent sent representatives, including defunct ones seeking reinstatement. But only five parties really counted—Austria, Britain, Prussia, Russia, and France, represented, respectively, by Prince Metternich, Viscount Castlereagh, Baron Hardenburg, Tsar Alexander I (the only sovereign taking direct part in the proceedings), and the ubiquitous Talleyrand.

The allies at Vienna knew broadly what they wanted: to restore the old order as far as possible, to prevent any single-state domination of Europe (what they called "universal monarchy"), and to contain the virus of revolution, that root of all evil. To implement this, they created a structure of collective security that was essentially a classic balance-of-power system tinctured by the agreement to suppress radical political activity wherever it occurred. The framework for this system already existed in the Quadruple Alliance, to which France, after a suitable period of probation, was admitted in 1818. This in turn evolved into the so-called Concert of Europe, the informal great-power consensus that kept the peace of Europe, or at least took credit for doing so, until 1914.

The basic novelty of the system was the recognition that war, because it unleashed revolution, had become too dangerous a luxury for Europe to afford. Not everyone, however, was equally sanguine about collective security as a means of avoiding it. Alexander I, for whom it represented not merely a political instrument but a spiritual compact, actually bullied his fellow sovereigns (except for the pope, the Turkish sultan, and the regent of England) into signing a "holy alliance" against war and for Christian concord. On a more realistic plane, Metternich conceived collective security as a sanction to intervene in the affairs of any state threatened by revolution, a principle he later applied in the cases of Spain and Naples. The British, however, reverting to a lone hand after years of marshaling coalitions, refused to commit themselves to any joint command. Prussia, always the most isolationist power on the continent, was skeptical of anything Austria and Russia could agree on—and, indeed, the dispute between these three over the so-called Polish-Saxon question nearly torpedoed the congress.

The heart of the problem was Poland. Napoleon had taken away almost all the territory gained by Austria and Prussia in the partitions to flesh out his Grand Duchy of Warsaw. When this state collapsed along with the empire, a vacuum of power was again created in eastern Europe. Alexander I insisted on reconstituting the original prepartition Poland, with himself as king. To gain Prussia's support, he offered to cede it Saxony, which had become vulnerable as the last German state to desert Napoleon. Metternich, appalled, sought out Castlereagh and Talleyrand, who agreed with him to resist the Russian plan, if necessary by force. Thus, in the very first months of the peace conference, the allies were already divided against each other and treating secretly with the defeated enemy, France.

The Polish-Saxon question was finally settled by compromise. Alexander received a reduced "Congress" Poland that was roughly equivalent to Napoleon's Grand Duchy, and Prussia two-fifths of Saxony. But the whole episode pointed up the inherent contradiction of the congress system, or for that matter any political order based on individually sovereign states: It presupposed cooperation between parties whose interests were fundamentally separate and frequently antagonistic.

The Congress of Vienna did, however, decide a wide range of issues, which set the diplomatic framework for the nineteenth century. Uppermost in the minds of the allies was the creation of buffer zones, primarily against France but more subtly against Russia as well, which had now encroached farther westward than ever before. A new Belgo-Dutch Kingdom of the Netherlands was erected as a barrier to the Low Countries, and Prussia was given a solid bloc of territory on the Rhine as reinforcement. With the acquisition of the Rhineland—which, with the Saxon strip, made it the largest territorial gainer at the congress—Prussia now overarched northern Germany, facing France to the west and Russia to the east. Austria was reinstalled in northern Italy and expanded along the Dalmatian coast, where, from a southern vantage, it could serve as a check against Russian designs on Turkey and French ones on Italy. The British, as usual, sought no territorial acquisitions on the continent, but they added several key islands and stations in the West Indies and the Far East to their unrivaled sea empire. They now controlled the Mediterranean through Gibraltar, Malta, and the Ionian Islands, the south Atlantic through the West Indies and the Cape of Good Hope, the Indian Ocean and the South China Sea through Ceylon, Mauritius, and Singapore. Uniquely situated on the major ocean arteries of the entire globe, Britain was on the verge of a century of world leadership.

On the question of Germany as a whole, the congress satisfied neither nationalist aspirations for a united Fatherland nor the claimants of liquidated states who wanted a return to the benign chaos of the Holy Roman Empire. Germany remained with the 39 states (including Prussia and Austria) to which Napoleon had reduced it, loosely linked in a confederation whose main function was to keep the small states from gravitating toward France. France itself, after the Hundred Days, was treated rather more severely. Some snippets of territory were taken away, an indemnity of 700 million francs imposed, and an army of occupation posted for three years.

The diplomats at Vienna were all men formed under the Old Regime. Their conception of society was still patriarchal; in the words of the Holy Alliance, the sovereigns of Europe were "as fathers of families towards their subjects and armies." In redrawing the map of the continent, they acted in the high-handed manner of old, parceling out peoples and territories solely according to the abstract scales of power. It would never have occurred to them to ask the Belgians whether they wanted to be under the Dutch, or the Venetians under Austria, or the Poles under Russia. None of them did, in fact, and ultimately, all of them rebelled. But that was no business of the men in Vienna, whose job, as they saw it, was to reward the victors and punish the losers of a great war (but always in moderation), and to restore an order in which the established powers could play the comfortable old game of politics.

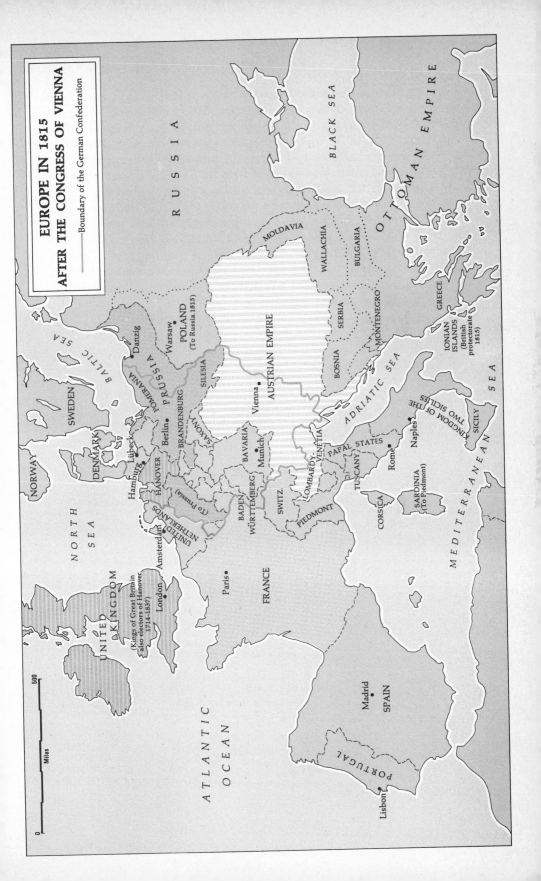

EUROPE IN 1815
AFTER THE CONGRESS OF VIENNA

———— Boundary of the German Confederation

But the forces of change had irreparably undermined the old dynastic order. Nationalism, the sentiment that a land belonged to its people and not to its ruler, domestic or foreign, was to conquer Europe and the Americas in the nineteenth century and the rest of the world in the twentieth. The Industrial Revolution, well established only in Britain by 1815, was to transform the very nature of economic and political power, transferring it from land and those who owned it to machines and those who controlled them. In this context, the Old Regime may be seen not only as the last chapter of a particular segment of European history but of the history of mankind itself. We are still only at the beginning of this great transformation, which has brought both the age-old dream of abundance and the nightmare of final destruction from the realm of fantasy to that of factual possibility. In that sense, the apocalyptic expectations of the prophets and millenarians of the seventeenth century were perhaps only premature. The world has ended, at least as the men and women of that age knew it, and the new one that is replacing it is, after two centuries, still in its birth throes.

select bibliography

The following bibliography represents a selection of major titles dealing with the period covered by this book. The emphasis, wherever possible, has been on the most recent scholarship, but a sample of classic texts has also been included.

INTRODUCTION

Aston, Trevor, ed. *Crisis in Europe: 1560–1660.* Garden City, N.Y., 1967.

Braudel, Fernand. *Civilization and Capitalism, 15th–18th Century.* Vol. I. *The Structures of Everyday Life.* New York, 1981. Vol. II. *The Wheels of Commerce.* New York, 1982.

————. *The Mediterranean and the Mediterranean World in the Age of Philip II,* 2 vols. New York, 1976.

Dunn, Richard S. *The Age of Religious Wars 1559–1715.* New York, 1979.

Kamen, Henry. *The Iron Century: Social Change in Europe 1550–1650.* New York, 1971.

Parry, J. H. *The Age of Reconnaissance.* Cleveland, Ohio, 1963.

Skinner, Quentin. *A History of Modern Political Thought,* 2 vols. New York, 1978.

Stone, Lawrence. *The Causes of the English Revolution 1529–1642.* London, 1972.

Wallerstein, Immanuel. *The Modern World System.* Vol. I. *Capitalist Agriculture and the Origins of the European Economy in the Sixteenth Century.* New York, 1976.

Wedgwood, C. V. *The Thirty Years War.* New York, 1961.

Zagorin, Perez. *Rebels and Rulers, 1500–1650,* 2 vols. New York, 1982.

PART ONE

Ariès, Philippe. *Centuries of Childhood: A Social History of Family Life.* New York, 1965.

Bitton, Davis. *The French Nobility in Crisis, 1560–1640.* Stanford, Calif., 1969.

Burke, Peter. *Popular Culture in Early Modern Europe.* New York, 1979.

Callaghan, William J., and Higgs, David, eds. *Church and Society in the Catholic Europe of the Eighteenth Century.* New York, 1979.

Corfield, P. J. *The Impact of English Towns 1700–1800.* New York, 1982.

Corvisier, André. *Armies and Societies in Europe, 1494–1789.* Bloomington, Ind., 1979.

Cragg, Gerald R. *The Church and the Age of Reason, 1648–1789.* London, 1966.

de Vries, Jan. *The Economy of Europe in an Age of Crisis, 1600–1750.* New York, 1976.

Drummond, A. L. *German Protestantism since Luther.* London, 1951.

Ford, Franklin L. *Robe and Sword: The Regrouping of the French Aristocracy after Louis XIV.* Cambridge, Mass., 1953.

————. *Strasbourg in Transition, 1648–1789.* Cambridge, Mass., 1958.

Furet, François. *Reading and Writing: Literacy in France from Calvin to Jules Ferry.* New York, 1982.

George, M. Dorothy. *London Life in the Eighteenth Century.* New York, 1925.

Goodwin, Albert, ed. *The European Nobility in the Eighteenth Century.* London, 1953.

Goubert, Pierre. *The Ancien Regime, 1600–1750.* New York, 1973.

————. *Louis XIV and Twenty Million Frenchmen.* New York, 1972.

Hufton, Olwen. *The Poor of Eighteenth Century France.* New York, 1974.

Kaplow, Jeffry. *The Names of Kings: The Parisian Laboring Poor in the Eighteenth Century.* New York, 1972.

Laslett, Peter. *The World We Have Lost.* London, 1965.

McKeown, Thomas. *The Modern Rise of Population.* New York, 1976.

Martz, Linda. *Poverty and Welfare in Habsburg Spain: The Example of Toledo.* New York, 1983.

Mousnier, Roland E. *The Institutions of France under the Absolute Monarchy, 1598–1789.* Chicago, 1979.

The New Cambridge Modern History, 14 vols. New York, 1957–1979. (Vols. V–IX pertain to our period.)

Rudé, George. *Paris and London in the Eighteenth Century.* New York, 1972.

Stone, Lawrence. *The Crisis of the Aristocracy 1558–1641.* New York, 1965.

————. *The Family, Sex and Marriage in England, 1500–1800.* New York, 1977.

Thompson, E. P. *Whigs and Hunters: The Origin of the Black Act.* New York, 1978.

Walker, Mack. *German Home Towns: Community, State, and General Estate, 1648–1871.* Ithaca, N.Y., 1971.

Wallerstein, Immanuel. *The Modern World System.* Vol. II: *Mercantilism and the Consolidation of the European World Economy,* 1600–1750. New York, 1980.

Wilson, Charles, and Parker, Geoffrey, eds. *An Introduction to the Sources of European Economic History, 1500–1800.* Ithaca, N.Y., 1977.

Woloch, Isser, comp. *The Peasantry in the Old Regime: Conditions and Protests.* Huntington, N.Y., 1977.

Wrigley, E. A., and Schofield, R. S. *The Population History of England, 1541–1871: A Reconstruction.* New York, 1982.

Yelling, J. A. *Common Field and Enclosure in England, 1450–1850.* Hamden, Conn., 1977.

PART TWO

Baxter, Stephen B. *William III and the Defense of European Liberty, 1650–1702.* New York, 1966.

Bernard, Leon. *The Emerging City: Paris in the Age of Louis XIV.* Durham, N.C., 1970.

Bonney, Richard. *Political Change in France under Richelieu and Mazarin, 1624–1661.* New York, 1978.

Bots, J. A. H. *The Peace of Nijmegen.* Amsterdam, 1980.

Boxer, C. R. *The Dutch Seaborne Empire, 1600–1800.* New York, 1965.

Clark, G. N. *The Later Stuarts, 1660–1714.* New York, 1955.

———. *War and Society in the Seventeenth Century.* New York, 1958.

Ekberg, Carl J. *The Failure of Louis XIV's Dutch War.* Chapel Hill, N.C., 1979.

Evans, R. J. W. *The Making of the Habsburg Monarchy, 1550–1700.* New York, 1979.

Gardner, Brian. *The East India Company: A History.* New York, 1972.

Geyl, Pieter. *The Netherlands in the Seventeenth Century,* 2 vols. New York, 1961–1964.

Hatton, Ragnhild M., ed. *Louis XIV and Absolutism.* Columbus, Ohio, 1977.

Hatton, Ragnhild M., and Bromley, John S., eds. *William III and Louis XIV.* Liverpool, 1967.

Heckscher, Eli. *Mercantilism,* 2 vols. New York, 1955.

Holborn, Hajo. *A History of Modern Germany.* Volume II: 1648–1840. Princeton, N.J., 1982.

Ingrao, Charles W. *In Quest and Crisis: Emperor Joseph I and the Habsburg Monarchy.* West Lafayette, Ind., 1979.

Kamen, Henry. *Spain in the Later Seventeenth Century.* London, 1971.

Lynch, John. *Spain under the Habsburgs,* 2 vols. New York, 1981.

McKay, Derek. *Prince Eugene of Savoy.* London, 1977.

Ranum, Orest. *Paris in the Age of Absolutism.* New York, 1968.

Rowen, Herbert H. *John de Witt, Grand Pensionary of Holland, 1625–1672.* Princeton, N.J., 1978.

———. *The King's State: Proprietary Dynasticism in Early Modern France.* New Brunswick, N.J., 1980.

Rule, John, ed. *Louis XIV and the Craft of Kingship.* Columbus, Ohio, 1970.

Spielman, John P. *Leopold I of Austria.* Brunswick, N.J., 1977.

Stradling, R. A. *Europe and the Decline of Spain: A Study of the Spanish System, 1580–1720.* London, 1981.

Wolf, John B. *Louis XIV.* New York, 1968.

PART THREE

Blum, Jerome. *Lord and Peasant in Russia from the Ninth to the Nineteenth Century.* Princeton, N.J., 1961.

Brown, Peter Douglas. *William Pitt, Earl of Chatham: The Great Commoner.* Winchester, Mass., 1979.

Butler, Rohan. *Choiseul.* Vol. I: *Father and Son, 1719–1754.* New York, 1980.

Carsten, F. L. *The Origins of Prussia.* Westport, Conn., 1981.

Curtin, Philip. *The Atlantic Slave Trade: A Census.* Madison, Wis., 1969.

Davies, Norman. *God's Playground. A History of Poland.* 2 vols. New York, 1982.

Davis, David Brion. *The Problem of Slavery in the Age of Revolution.* Ithaca, N.Y., 1966.

Davis, Ralph. *The Rise of the Atlantic Economies.* Ithaca, N.Y., 1973.

Dickinson, H. T. *Liberty and Property: Political Ideology in Eighteenth-Century Britain.* New York, 1978.

Dickson, P. G. M. *The Financial Revolution in England: A Study in the Development of Public Credit, 1688–1756.* London, 1967.

Ergang, Robert. *The Potsdam Fuhrer: Frederick William I, Father of Prussian Militarism.* New York, 1941.

Fox-Genovese, Elizabeth, and Genovese, Eugene D. *Fruits of Merchant Capital: Slavery and Bourgeois Property in the Rise and Expansion of Capitalism.* New York, 1983.

Gulick, Edward V. *Europe's Classical Balance of Power.* New York, 1967.

Hatton, Ragnhild M., and Anderson, M. S. *Studies in Eighteenth-Century Diplomacy.* Hamden, Conn., 1970.

Hellie, Richard. *Slavery in Russia, 1450–1725.* Chicago, 1982.

Holmes, Geoffrey. *Augustan England.* Winchester, Mass., 1983.

Klyuchevsky, V. O. *Peter the Great.* New York, 1958.

Parry, J. H. *Trade and Dominion: European Overseas Empires in the Eighteenth Century.* London, 1971.

Plumb, J. H. *The Growth of Political Stability in England, 1675–1725.* Boston, 1967.

———. *Sir Robert Walpole,* 2 vols. Boston, 1956–1960.

Rawley, James A. *The Transatlantic Slave Trade.* New York, 1981.

Roberts, Michael, ed. *Essays in Swedish History.* Minneapolis, Minn., 1968.

Rosenberg, Hans. *Bureaucracy, Aristocracy, and Autocracy: the Prussian Experience, 1660–1815.* Boston, 1958.

Speck, W. A. *Stability and Strife: England, 1714–1760.* Cambridge, Mass., 1977.

Stone, Daniel. *Polish Politics and National Reform 1775–1788.* New York, 1976.

Sumner, B. H. *Peter the Great and the Emergence of Russia.* New York, 1951.

Wilson, Arthur. *French Foreign Policy during the Administration of Cardinal Fleury, 1726–1743.* New York, 1936.

Wolpert, Stanley. *A New History of India.* New York, 1977.

PART FOUR

Anchor, Robert. *The Enlightenment Tradition.* Berkeley, Calif., 1979.

Bernard, Paul P. *Jesuits and Jacobins: Enlightenment and Enlightened Despotism in Austria.* Urbana, Ill., 1971.

———. *Joseph II.* New York, 1968.

Besterman, Theodore. *Voltaire.* New York, 1969.

Blanning, T. C. W. *Joseph II and Enlightened Despotism.* London, 1970.

Butterfield, Herbert. *The Origins of Modern Science.* New York, 1957.

Cassirer, Ernst. *The Philosophy of the Enlightenment.* Princeton, N.J., 1951.

Cobban, Alfred. *History of Modern France,* 2 vols. Baltimore, Md., 1966.

Crocker, Lester. *An Age of Crisis: Man and World in Eighteenth Century Thought.* Baltimore, Md. 1959.

Darnton, Robert. *The Business of Enlightenment: A Publishing History of the Encyclopedia, 1775–1800.* Cambridge, Mass., 1979.

———. *The Literary Underground of the Old Regime.* Cambridge, Mass., 1982.

de Madariaga, Isabel. *Russia in the Age of Catherine the Great.* New Haven, Conn., 1981.

Friedenthal, Richard. *Goethe: His Life and Times.* Cleveland, Ohio, 1965.

Gagliardo, John. *Enlightened Despotism.* New York, 1967.

Gay, Peter. *The Enlightenment: An Interpretation,* 2 vols. New York, 1966–1969.

———. *Voltaire's Politics: The Poet as Realist.* Princeton, N.J., 1959.

Gillespie, C. C. *The Edge of Objectivity.* Princeton, N.J., 1966.

Gough, J. W. *The Social Contract.* Westport, Conn., 1978.

Hahn, Roger. *The Anatomy of a Scientific Revolution: The Paris Academy of Sciences, 1666–1803.* Berkeley, Calif., 1971.

Hall, A. R. *From Galileo to Newton, 1630–1720.* New York, 1963.

———. *The Scientific Revolution, 1500–1800.* Boston, 1966.

Hazard, Paul. *The European Mind, 1680–1715.* New Haven, Conn., 1935.

Herr, Richard. *The Eighteenth Century Revolution in Spain.* Princeton, N.J., 1958.

Jacob, Margaret. *The Radical Enlightenment: Pantheists, Freemasons and Republicans.* Winchester, Mass., 1980.

Johnson, Hubert C. *Frederick the Great and His Officials.* New Haven, Conn., 1975.

Jones, Robert E. *The Emancipation of the Russian Nobility, 1762–1785.* Princeton, N.J., 1973.

Király, Béla. *Hungary in the Late Eighteenth Century.* New York, 1969.

Korshin, Paul J., ed. *The Widening Circle: Essays on the Circulation of Literature in Eighteenth-Century Europe.* Philadelphia, Pa., 1976.

Koyré, Alexander. *From the Closed World to the Infinite Universe.* Baltimore, Md., 1957.

Krieger, Leonard. *An Essay on the Theory of Enlightened Despotism.* Chicago, 1975.

Kuhn, Thomas S. *The Structure of Scientific Revolutions.* Chicago, 1970.

Labrousse, Elisabeth. *Bayle.* New York, 1983.

Levy, Darline Gay. *The Ideas and Careers of Simon-Nicolas-Henri-Linguet.* Urbana, Ill., 1980.

Lough, John. *The Encyclopédie.* New York, 1971.

MacPherson, C. B. *The Politics of Possessive Individualism: Hobbes to Locke.* New York, 1962.

Mandrou, Robert. *From Humanism to Science: 1480–1700.* New York, 1979.

Manuel, Frank E. *The Eighteenth Century Confronts the Gods.* Cambridge, Mass., 1959.

Ornstein, Martha. *The Role of Scientific Societies in the Seventeenth Century.* Hamden, Conn., 1963.

Popkin, Richard. *History of Scepticism from Erasmus to Spinoza.* Berkeley, Calif., 1979.

Ritter, Gerhard. *Frederick the Great: A Historical Profile.* Berkeley, Calif., 1968.

Roider, Karl A., Jr. *Austria's Eastern Question, 1700–1790.* Princeton, N.J., 1982.

Shklar, Judith. *Men and Citizens: A Study of Rousseau's Social Theory.* London, 1969.

Thomas, Keith. *Religion and the Decline of Magic.* New York, 1971.

Tucker, Robert W., and Hendrickson, David C. *The Fall of the First British Empire.* Baltimore, Md., 1982.

Wade, Ira O. *The Intellectual Origins of the French Enlightenment.* Princeton, N.J., 1957.

Wangermann, Ernst. *The Austrian Achievement, 1700–1800.* London, 1973.

Westfall, Richard S. *Never at Rest: A Biography of Isaac Newton.* New York, 1981.

Wilson, Arthur. *Diderot,* 2 vols. New York, 1957–1972.

PART FIVE

Bergeron, Louis. *France under Napoleon.* New York, 1981.

Bosher, John. *French Finances 1770–1795: From Business to Bureaucracy.* Cambridge, Mass., 1971.

Censer, Jack Richard. *Prelude to Power: The Parisian Radical Press, 1789–1791.* Baltimore, Md., 1977.

Chandler, D. G. *The Campaigns of Napoleon.* New York, 1966.

de Tocqueville, Alexis. *The Old Regime and the French Revolution.* New York, 1955.

Doyle, William. *Origins of the French Revolution.* New York, 1981.

Egret, Jean. *The French Pre-Revolution, 1787–1788.* Chicago, 1978.

Forrest, Alan. *The French Revolution and the Poor.* New York, 1981.

Furet, François. *Interpreting the French Revolution.* New York, 1981.

Geyl, Pieter. *Napoleon: For and Against.* New Haven, Conn., 1949.

Godechot, Jacques. *The Counter-Revolution: Doctrine and Action 1789–1804.* New York, 1971.

Harris, Robert. *Necker, Reform Statesman of the Ancien Regime.* Berkeley, Calif., 1979.

Higonnet, Patrice. *Class, Ideology, and the Rights of Nobles during the French Revolution.* New York, 1981.

Hyslop, Beatrice. *A Guide to the General Cahiers of 1789, with the Texts of Unedited Cahiers.* New York, 1936.

Jordan, David P. *The King's Trial: The French Revolution vs. Louis XVI.* Berkeley, Calif., 1979.

Kennedy, Michael L. *The Jacobin Clubs in the French Revolution.* Vol. I: *The Early Years.* Princeton, N.J., 1982.

Lefebvre, Georges. *The Coming of the French Revolution.* Princeton, N.J., 1967.

———. *The French Revolution,* 2 vols. New York, 1962–1964.

———. *The Great Fear of 1789.* New York, 1973.

———. *Napoleon,* 2 vols. New York, 1969.

Lewis, Gwynne, and Lucas, Colin. *Beyond the Terror: Essays in French Regional and Social History, 1794–1815.* New York, 1983.

Palmer, R. R. *The Age of the Democratic Revolutions: A History of Europe and America, 1760–1800,* 2 vols. Princeton, N. J., 1959, 1964.

———. *Twelve Who Ruled: The Committee of Public Safety during the Terror.* Princeton, N.J., 1958.

Patrick, Alison. *The Men of the First French Convention: Political Alignments in the National Convention of 1792.* Baltimore, Md., 1972.

Roberts, J. M. *The French Revolution.* New York, 1978.

Rose, R. B. *Gracchus Babeuf: The First Revolutionary Communist.* Stanford, Calif., 1978.

Rudé, George. *The Crowd in the French Revolution.* New York, 1967.

Schama, Simon. *Patriots and Liberators: Revolution in the Netherlands, 1780–1813.* New York, 1977.

Soboul, Albert. *The Parisian Sans-Culottes and the French Revolution, 1793–4.* Westport, Conn., 1979.

———. *A Short History of the French Revolution.* Berkeley, Calif., 1977.

Talmon, J. L. *The Origins of Totalitarian Democracy.* New York, 1960.

Thompson, J. M. *Napoleon Bonaparte.* New York, 1952.

Webster, C. K. *The Congress of Vienna, 1814–1815.* New York, 1919.

Woloch, Isser. *Jacobin Legacy: The Democratic Movement under the Directory.* Princeton, N.J., 1979.

index

Adrien, Michel, 124
Africa
  exploration of, 87
  and the slave trade, 61–64
Agricultural Revolution, 114
Aiguillon, Armand de Vigneron du Plessis
    de Richelieu, Duke d', 123
Aix-la-Chapelle, Treaty of (1668), 41
Aix-la-Chapelle, Treaty of (1748), 82
Alberoni, Giulio Cardinal, 84
Alembert, Jean Le Rond d', 91, 114
Alexander I, tsar, 142–143, 146–147,
    149–150
America. *See also* Colonization; Slave trade
  British expansion in, 61
  colonization of, 55–56, 60–61
  discovery of, 87
  effects of Napoleonic wars on, 140
  French expansion in, 64–65
  and the Great Awakening, 109
  and image of the noble savage, 100
  influence of Locke on development of, 99
  and King William's war, 47
  as new society, 97
  in Seven Years' War, 83
  and Spanish empire, 49
  war of independence, 118
  and War of the Spanish Succession, 51
Amiens, Peace of, 142
Ancients and the Moderns, The, 94
Anglas, Boissy d', 134–135
Anne, queen of England, 51, 58
Aristocracy. *See also* Nobility of the Robe;
    Nobility of the Sword
  abolished in England, 3
  description of, 14–19
  and Enlightened Despots, 103, 104
  and fine arts, 112
  and Louis XIV, 38
  as natural elite, 11, 12
  in Poland, 75–76
  in Prussia, 106
  reacts against Joseph II, 109
  re-created by Napoleon, 140
  relations with the peasantry, 24–25
  resurgence of in France, 116–119
  in Russia, 71–75 *passim.*
  and sale of office, 36–37
  and towns, 30–31
  wider definition of, 21
Artois, Charles Phillipe, Count d' (later
    Charles X, king of France), 123
Atheism, 92–93
Auerstadt, Battle of, 142
Augsburg, League of, 47
Augsburg, War of the League of, 45–49
Austerlitz, Battle of, 142
Austria. *See also* Hapsburg, House of

alliance with England, 47, 50
conflict with France, 1–2
and Congress of Vienna, 149–151
in European concert of power, 78
opposes France, 127
under Joseph II, 106–109
and partition of Poland, 76
and Peace of Utrecht, 51–53
population of, 8
Seven Years' War, 81–84
in War of the Austrian Succession, 81–82
wars with France, 140–143 *passim.*, 147
war with the Ottoman Empire, 46
Austrian Netherlands (Flanders, Belgium),
    51, 82, 108, 133, 134, 147, 148, 150
Austrian Succession, War of, 81–82

Babeuf, Francois-Nöel (Gracchus), 135–136,
    137
Bach, Johann Sebastian, 110
Bacon, Sir Francis, 89
Balance of power
  concept of, 78–79, 83
  at the Congress of Vienna, 149
Bank of England, 54, 59–60, 62
Bayle, Pierre, 92, 95
Beachy Head, Battle of, 47
Beauharnais, Josephine de, empress of the
    French, 143
Beaumarchais, Pierre de, 112
Beccaria, Cesare, 97
Beethoven, Ludwig van, 113, 146
Bellers, John, 84
Bentham, Jeremy, 83
Berkeley, George, Bishop, 90
Bill of Rights (England), 56, 123
Blenheim, Battle of, 51
Blücher, Gebhard von, 148
Böhme, Jakob, 109
Bologna, Concordat of, 37
Bonaparte, Jérôme, 143
Bonaparte, Joseph, 143
Bonaparte, Louis, 143
Bonaparte, Napoleon I, 51, 149, 150
  abdication and return, 147–148
  consolidation of power and reforms of,
      138–140
  exile and death, 148
  and the French Revolution, 116, 134–136
  quoted, 115
  wars of, 140–147
Bonaparte, Napoleon II (king of Rome, duke
    of Reichstadt), 143, 147
Book of Common Prayer, quoted, 11
Borodino, Battle of, 147
Bossuet, Jacques Bénigne, Bishop, 19–20, 92,
    98
Boucher, François, 117

Bourbon dynasty, 1, 6, 49, 78, 82, 146, 147
Bourgeoisie, 3, 31, 33, 119, 124, 136, 137
Boyle, Robert, 91, 92
Brandenburg, Mark of, 8, 79. *See also*
    Prussia
Braudel, Fernand, 1
Brazil, 64
Brienne, Étienne Charles Loménie de,
    Archbishop, 118
Brienne, Henri-Auguste de Loménie de,
    Count, 35
Brissot, Jacques, 127, 129
Brissot de Warville, Jacques Pierre, 103
British East India Company, 66–67
Brouwer, Adrien, 113
Brueghel, Pieter, 113
Bruno, Giordano, 86, 87, 91
Buonarotti, Filippo Michele, 136
Burke, Edmund, 12, 22, 67, 115
Butler, Joseph, 109

Calonne, Charles de, 118
Campo Formio, Treaty of, 136, 142
Cantillon, Richard, quoted, 31
Carlyle, Thomas, 115
Casanova, Giovanni, 108
Castiglione, Baldassare, 18
Castlereagh, Robert, Viscount, 149, 150
Catherine, infanta of Portugal, wife of
    Charles II of England, 44
Catherine II (the Great), empress of Russia,
    74–76, 82
Catholic church. *See also* Jesuits; Papacy
    attacked by Pombal, 104
    concordat with Napoleon, 140
    decline of, 19
    and Jansenism, 110
    and Joseph II, 108
    noble monopoly of, 119
    property in France, 20–21
    in revolutionary France, 125–126
Censorship, 12, 92, 97, 108, 112, 114, 124,
    132
Centralization, 2
    through enlightened despotism, 103–104,
    108
    example of the Bourbons, 5
    during the French Revolution, 125–126,
    132
    limits of in prerevolutionary France,
    117–118
    under Louis XIV, 35–40, 53–54
    under Napoleon, 139–140
    as a result of the French Revolution,
    137–138
    in Russia, 71–75, *passim.*
Charles, archduke of Austria, later Charles
    VI, emperor of Austria, 49, 51, 81
Charles I, king of England, 3
Charles II, king of England, 5, 43–44, 56, 57
Charles II, king of Spain, 13, 41, 49
Charles III, king of Spain, 104
Charles XII, king of Sweden, 72–73

Charles Albert, elector of Bavaria, 81
Charter of the Nobility, 75
Chateaubriand, François René, Viscount de,
    quoted, 124
Choiseul, Étienne-François, Duke de, 116
Christian VII, king of Denmark, 104
Christina, queen of Sweden, 88
Civil Constitution of the Clergy (1790), 126
Clarendon, Edward Hyde, first Earl of, 43,
    44
Clarke, Samuel, 109
Clarkson, Thomas, 64
Clement XI, pope, 110
Clergy, estate of, 19–21, 109–110, 120, 123
Clive, Robert, 66
Cloots, Anarcharsis, 127
Colbert, Jean-Baptiste, 38–39, 41, 42, 65, 93,
    119
Coleridge, Samuel Taylor, quoted, 29
Colonization, 5
    in the Far East, 65–67
    of the New World, 55–56, 60–61
Committee of Public Safety, 131–133, 135
Condé, Prince Louis de Bourbon, 18
Condorcet, Marie Jean de Caritat, Marquis
    de, 94, 103
Constituent Assembly, the, 124–127. *See also*
    National Assembly
Continental system, 143, 146
Copenhagen, Treaty of, 5
Copernicus, Nicholas, 86–88
Corneille, Pierre, 40
Corsica, 101, 138
Craig, John, 91
Cromwell, Oliver, 3

Dante Alighieri, 85–86
Danton, Georges, 129
Darnton, Robert, 114
David, Jacques-Louis, 113
Declaration of Independence, 119, 123
Declaration of Pillnitz, 127
Declaration of the Rights of Man and of the
    Citizen, 123, 124, 125
Defoe, Daniel, 112
Deism, 92, 93
Delalande, Michel, 113
Demography
    declining levels of in seventeenth century
    Europe, 2
    distribution of, 8, 23
    and famine of 1694, 27–28
    growth of population in Russia, 76
    in the latter part of the Old Regime,
    113–114
    mortality rates, 29, 32
    urban decline, 34
Denmark
    aspirations of, 1
    enlightened despotism in, 104
    under Napoleonic domination, 143
    population of, 8
    and wars of Louis XIV, 42

war with Russia, 72, 73
war with Sweden, 2
Descartes, René, 87, 89–92 *passim.*
Devolution, War of, 41–42
Diderot, Denis, 93, 114
Directory, The, 135–136, 138
Disraeli, Benjamin, 67
Divine Right, theory of, 11, 12–14, 57, 70, 98, 106
Donne, John, 86–87
Dostoevski, Fyodor, 138
Dover, Treaty of, 42, 44, 45
Ducos, Roger, 139
Dumouriez, Charles François, admiral, 129
Dupleix, Joseph, 65–66

Education, 11–12, 94–95. *See also* Literacy
Eglantine, Fabre d', 128
Embrun, Archbishop of, quoted, 16
Encyclopedia (Diderot), 93, 112, 114
England (after 1707, Great Britain)
    alliance with Austria, 47, 50
    and Anglican church, 20
    colonization and slave plantation by, 61–64
    commercial growth of, 9
    and Congress of Vienna, 149–151
    continental policies of, 55
    fleet in the Baltic, 73
    and the Glorious Revolution, 43–45
    history of, 1689–c. 1725, 56–60
    indoctrination of the young in, 11
    and Industrial Revolution, 152
    institutions of, 54
    and Methodism, 109–110
    and Peace of Utrecht, 51–53
    poll tax in, 21
    population of, 8
    and the Puritan Revolution, 3, 93
    rise of, 78
    ruling elite of, 15
    warlike character of, 40
    in War of the Austrian Succession and Seven Years' War, 81–83
    and wars of Louis XIV, 41ff.
    wars with France, 140, 142, 143, 146, 148
Enlightened Despots, 103–109
Enlightenment, the, 93–97, 102. *See also* Enlightened Despots; Philosophes
    effect on radical bourgeoisie, 136
    and *Encyclopedia,* 114
    in Germany, 146
    reaction against, 109–111
Estates (orders)
    abolished in France, 123, 125, 139
    concept of attacked, 120
    defined, 10–11
Estates General, 118–121. *See also* National Assembly
Eugene, prince of Savoy, 50–51
Eylau, Battle of, 142

Famine of 1694, 27–28
Fénelon, François de la Mothe, Abbé, 27–28

Feudalism. *See also* Serfdom
    declared abolished, 123
    in Eastern Europe, 28–29
    residual elements in Western Europe, 24–25
Fichte, Johann Gottlieb, 146
Fielding, Henry, 30, 32
Fleurus, Battle of, 47
Fleury, André Hercule, Cardinal de, 65, 82, 116
Fontenelle, Bernard de, 90, 91, 94
Fox, Charles James, 115
Fragonard, Jean-Honoré, 117
France. *See also* Bourbon dynasty
    aristocracy of, 15–17
    commercial expansion of, 114
    and Congress of Vienna, 149, 150
    empire of, 64–66
    and the French Revolution, 9, 120–138 *passim.*
    hegemony of, 55–56
    literacy rates in, 111, 114
    and Louis XIV, 5, 6, 35–40
    under Louis XV and Louis XVI, 116–120
    military supremacy of, 43
    mortality rates in, 29
    and Napoleon, 138ff.
    and Peace of Utrecht, 51–53
    peasantry of, 24–28
    population of, 8
    rebellion in, 3
    revolutionary wars of, 127, 128, 130, 134, 136, 140–142
    rivalry with Spain and Austria, 1
    in War of the Austrian Succession and Seven Years' War, 81–83
    wars of, 142–147
Francis I, emperor of Austria, 108
Frederick I, king of Prussia (Frederick III, elector of Brandenburg-Prussia), 79
Frederick II (the Great), king of Prussia, 14, 34, 35, 81–82, 96, 105–106, 107
Frederick William, elector of Brandenburg, 79
Frederick William I, king of Prussia, 79–81, 106
Frederick William II, king of Prussia, 127
Frederick William III, king of Prussia, 142
Freemasons, 114
French Revolution, 9, 10, 33, 94, 103, 108. *See also* Directory; Terror; Thermidorian Reaction
    background of, 116–120
    and Napoleon, 140
    nature and significance of, 116, 136–138
    phases of, 120–136
    seen by contemporaries, 115–116
    wars of. *See* France, revolutionary wars of
Friedland, Battle of, 142
Frimaire, Law of 14, 132
Fronde, 37

Gabelle, 25
Galilei, Galileo, 87, 88, 89, 97

Gallican church, 37, 123, 126
Gay, John, 113
Gee, Joshua, quoted, 62
General will, concept of, 101, 132, 133, 137
Genoa, 8, 46
Gentz, Friedrich von, 78
George I, king of England, elector of
  Hanover, 58, 60
George II, king of England, 58
Germany. *See also* Holy Roman Empire
  and Congress of Vienna, 150
  economic decline of, 6
  effects of Thirty Years' War on, 2
  Lutheranism in, 20
  under Napoleonic domination, 143
  national revival of, 146, 148
  and Pietism, 109–110
  population of, 8
  religious geography of, 1
  towns of, 33–34
  and wars of Louis XIV, 42–43, 45, 47, 50
Gilbert, William, 89
Gilds, 32, 107, 118
Gin Act (1751), 32
Gloire, concept of, 41
Glorious Revolution, 43–45, 56–57
  and thought of John Locke, 99
Godolphin, Sidney, 51
Goethe, Johann Wolfgang von, 110–111,
  112, 146
Goya, Francisco, 113, 146
Grand Alliance, 49–50
Great Chain of Being, 11
Great Northern War, 73
Grotius, Hugo, 83
Guardi, Francesco, 34
Gustavus III, king of Sweden, 104

Haiti, rebellion in, 64
Hanseatic League, 6, 34
Hapsburg, House of, 1, 2, 6, 13, 34, 46, 49,
  78, 81, 82, 143
Hardenburg, Prince Karl August von, 149
Harrison, William, 21
Harvey, William, 87
Hastings, Francis Rawdon, first Lord,
  quoted, 67
Haydn, Franz Josef, 113
Hébert, Jacques René, 132
Helvétius, Claude Adrien, 95, 102
Henry IV, king of France, 39
Herder, Johann Gottfried von, 20, 111, 146
Hoadly, Benjamin, 20
Hobbes, Thomas, 6, 40, 97–99, 101
Hohenlinden, Battle of, 142
Hohenzollern dynasty, 79–81
Holbach, Paul Henri Dietrich, Baron d',92,
  93
Holy Alliance, 149, 150
Holy Roman Empire
  abolished, 143, 148
  desuetude of, 141

free cities of, 33–34
mentioned, 150
and states of Germany, 8
Hooke, Robert, 89
Hubertusberg, Treaty of, 82
Huguenots, 35, 95
Hume, David, 90, 93, 111
Hundred Days, the, 148
Hungary
  reacts against Joseph II, 108
  rebellions of, 46, 50
  and War of the Austrian Succession, 81
Huygens, Christian, 89

India, colonization and conquest of, 65–67,
  83, 140
Industrial Revolution, 10, 137, 152
Intendants, 39, 116
Ireland
  James II's invasion of, 47
  rebellion of, 6
  tariffs levied against, 43
Italy
  ceded to Austria, 51
  decline of, 6
  description of, 8
  invaded by Napoleon, 136
Ivan IV, tsar, 28, 70

Jacobins, 127, 129, 132, 133, 137, 138
Jamaica, 61, 62, 64, 83
James I, king of England, 40
James II, king of England, 44–45, 47, 51, 56,
  57, 58, 99
James Edward, prince of England, 58
Jansen, Cornelius, 110
Jefferson, Thomas, 118
Jena, Battle of, 142
Jenkins' Ear, War of, 40
Jesuit order (Society of Jesus), 65, 104, 106
Jews
  given civil equality by Joseph II, 108
  hostility of Methodists toward, 110
  millenarianism of, 3
Johnson, Samuel, 64
Jonson, Ben, 111
Joseph II, emperor of Austria, 105, 106–109,
  110
Joseph Ferdinand, prince of Bavaria, 49
Justi, Johann Heinrich Gottlob von, 79

Kant, Immanuel, 83, 111
Karl August, Duke of Weimar, 146
Karlowitz, Treaty of, 49
Kaunitz, Count Wenzel Anton von, 82, 83,
  107
Kepler, Johannes, 87, 88, 89
King, Gregory, 91

Labrousse, C. A., 33
Lagos, Battle of, 83
Lahontan, Baron de, 92
La Mettrie, Julien Offroy de, 92, 93, 106

Land ownership, patterns of. *See also*
  Property
  and aristocracy, 17–18
  under Catherine the Great, 75
  feudal restraint on abolished in France, 124
  under Frederick the Great, 106
  and peasantry, 24–25, 26
Law, John, 60
Law of Suspects, 131–132
Leeuwenhoek, Anton von, 87
Legislative Assembly (1791), 125, 127
Legislative Assembly (1795), 135, 136
Legitimacy, principle of, 12–13
Leibniz, Gottfried Wilhelm von, 83, 90, 92,
  95, 109
Leopold I, emperor of Austria, 41, 43, 46,
  47, 49, 50
Leopold II, emperor of Austria, 108, 127
Levée en masse, 131
Liberum veto, 75
Lindet, Robert, 135
Linguet, Simon-Henri, 103
Literacy, 22–23, 111–112, 114. *See also*
  Education
Locke, John, 91, 93, 95, 98, 99–100, 101
London, 29–32
Louis XIII, king of France, 12
Louis XIV, king of France
  accession of, 5, 6, 12
  attitude toward kingship, 14
  and Bishop Bossuet, 19–20
  centralizing policies of, 33, 35–40
  death of, 53–54
  and divine right, 11, 13
  and England, 44–45
  and famine of 1694, 27–28
  legacy of, 116–117
  and letter from Vauban, 55
  mentioned, 70, 78, 83, 94, 95, 103, 105,
    110, 112, 119, 128, 139
  tax policies of, 25
  and Versailles, 16–17
  wars of, 41–43, 45–51
  wars with the Netherlands, 9
Louis XV, king of France, 12, 110, 116–117
Louis XVI, king of France
  flight of, 127
  and the French Revolution, 121–125 *pas-*
    sim.
  mentioned, 134
  prerevolutionary reign of, 117–120
  trial and execution of, 128, 129
Louis XVII (uncrowned), 134
Louis XVIII, king of France, previously
  count of Provence, 134, 147–148
L'Ouverture, François Dominique Toussaint,
  64
Louvois, François Michel de Tellier, Marquis
  de, 47
Lunéville, Treaty of, 142
Lutheranism, 20, 106
Luynes, Charles Philippe d'Albert, Duke de,
  17

Mably, Gabriel Bonnot de, 103
Machiavelli, Niccolò, 34
Macmillan, Harold, 58
Maintenon, Madame de, 28, 53
Maistre, Joseph de, 95, 135
Malebranche, Nicolas, 91
Mallet du Pan, Jacques, 141
Malplaquet, Battle of, 51
Malthus, Thomas Robert, 114
Mandeville, Bernard de, 100
Marat, Jean-Paul, 129
Marengo, Battle of, 142
Maria Theresa, empress of Austria, queen of
  Hungary, 19, 81, 107, 110
Maria Theresa, infanta of Spain, wife of
  Louis XIV, 5, 41
Marie Antoinette, queen of France, 113,
  119
Marie Louise, princess of Austria, empress
  of the French, 143
Marivaux, Pierre de, 110
Marlborough, John Churchill, first Duke of,
  51, 54
Marx, Karl, 103, 109, 136
Mary II, queen of England, 45
Maupeou, René Nicolas de, 116, 117
Mazarin, Jules, Cardinal de, 38
Mediterranean, economic decline of, 5, 6
Mercantilism, 3
Mersenne, Marin, 88
Methodism, 20, 109–110
Metternich, Count Klemens von, 147, 149,
  150
Michelet, Jules, 115
Middle passage. *See* Slave trade
Molière, Jean-Baptiste, 15, 73, 112
Molinos, Miguel de, 20
Monarchy, institution of
  abolished in France, 128
  and aristocracy, 16–17, 117
  in England, 3, 56–57
  and enlightened despotism, 103–109
  general description of, 12–14
  and Hobbes, 98–99
  and Louis XIV, 16–17, 35–40, 53–54
  and Louis XVI, 118–119
  restoration in France, 147–148
  and royalism, 134, 136, 137
Montaigne, Michel de, 30
Montesquieu, Charles de Secondat, Baron de
  La Brède et de, 95, 102, 114
More, Hannah, quoted, 111
More, Henry, 92
Morelly (or Morellet), André, Abbé de, 102,
  135
Mozart, Wolfgang Amadeus, 113
Murat, Joachim, 143
Muscovy, princedom of, 70. *See also* Russia.

Nantes, Edict of, 37, 95
Napoleon. *See* Bonaparte, Napoleon I
Napoleonic Code, 139–140, 143, 148
Narva, Battle of, 72, 76

National Assembly, 121–124. *See also*
    Estates General
National Convention, 128–133
Nationalism, 137, 140, 146, 147, 148, 152
Nations, Battle of the, 147
Necker, Jacques, 117–118, 119, 121
Nelson, Horatio Lord, 142
Netherlands, The (United Provinces, Dutch
    Republic)
  absorbed by France, 143
  and Colbert, 38
  empire of, 61, 65
  in the European concert of power, 78
  general description of, 8–9
  invaded by France, 133, 134
  mentioned, 141
  and Peace of Utrecht, 51–53
  reconstituted at the Congress of Vienna,
    150
  relations with England, 44–45, 50
  and the Seven Years' War, 82
  and the Thirty Years' War, 3
  visit of Peter the Great to, 72
  war of independence, 1
  wars with France, 41–43
Newton, Sir Isaac, 89–91, 92, 96
Nijmegen, Treaty of, 42, 45
Noailles, Louis Viscount de, 123
Nobility of the Robe, 15–17, 25, 36–37, 102
Nobility of the Sword, 15–17
Nystadt, Treaty of, 73

Oates, Titus, 44
Ogilvie, William, 103
Old Regime, concept of, 9–11
Oliva, Treaty of, 5
Orléans, Philippe, Duke d', regency of, 116
Ottoman Empire (Turkey)
  defeat of, 47, 49
  expansion of, 5
  during the Napoleonic period, 143, 146,
    150
  peasants of, 29
  and siege of Vienna, 46
  wars with Russia, 75, 76
Oudenarde, Battle of, 51

Paine, Thomas, 64, 127
Papacy. *See also* Catholic church
  concordat with Napoleon, 140
  decline of, 14, 19
  and the *Encyclopedia,* 114
  and Jansenism, 110
Papal States, 8, 136
Paris, 29, 30, 32, 39, 95
  and the French Revolution, 121–135 *pas-
    sim.*
Paris, Treaty of (1763), 83
Paris, Treaty of (1814), 147
Parlements (French), 37, 39, 117, 118, 119
Parliament (English)
  and the Bank of England, 54
  Convention and Cavalier, 43, 44

under Cromwell, 3, 93
evolution of, 119
after the Glorious Revolution, 56–59
and India, 66–67
representation in, 57, 125
and urban unrest, 32
and the War of Jenkins' Ear, 40
Pascal, Blaise, 89, 93, 110, 111
Peasantry. *See also* Feudalism; Serfdom
  and the aristocracy, 18, 24–25, 26, 28
  and the French monarchy, 117
  and the French Revolution, 124, 130,
    136
  general description of, 23–29
  rebellion of in France, 121, 123
  and reforms of Joseph II, 108
  in Russia, 71, 74, 75
Peninsular War, 146
Penn, William, 84
Pestalozzi, Johann, 95
Peter I (the Great), tsar, 14, 19, 71–74
Peter III, tsar, 74, 82
Petty, Sir William, 91
Pezzl, Johann, quoted, 101
Philip IV, king of Spain, 14, 41
Philip V (Philip of Anjou), king of Spain,
    49, 51
Philosophes, 93, 95–96, 103
Physiocrats, 118
Pietism, 20, 109–110
Pitt, William, the Elder, 83
Pitt, William, the Younger, 142
Pius VII, pope, 140
Plassey, Battle of, 66
Poland
  at Congress of Vienna, 149–151
  constitution devised by Rousseau, 101
  general description of, 8
  as Napoleonic satellite, 143
  partitions of, 76, 78
  relations with Russia, 70, 72, 75–76
Police, 30, 39
Poltava, Battle of, 73
Pombal, Sebastião José de Carvalho e Mello,
    Marquis de, 104
Poniatowski, Stanislas, king of Poland, 76
Pope, Alexander, quoted, 90, 96
Popular rebellion
  in France, 25–26
  during the French Revolution, 120,
    121–124, 127–128, 130, 131, 134
  and the mid-seventeenth century crisis, 3,
    5, 6
  in Russia, 71, 73, 75
  significance of, 137
Popular representation
  in England, 57
  and the French constitution of 1791, 125
  and the National Convention, 128, 129,
    130, 135
Portugal
  alliance with Louis XIV, 49
  empire of, 61, 65

enlightened despotism in, 104
rebellion of, 3, 6
Pragmatic Sanction, 81
Prairial, Law of 22, 133
Pressburg, Treaty of, 142
Progress, doctrine of, 94–95
Property. See also Land ownership, patterns of
  attacked in principle, 100, 102, 103, 135
  as basis of aristocratic power, 17–18
  defended as the basis of government, 135
  expropriation of during the French Revolution, 125–126
  guaranteed by the Napoleonic Code, 139
  as natural right, 99–100
  in office, 36–37, 125
  as voting qualification, 125
Provence, count of. See Louis XVIII, king of France
Prussia. See also Brandenburg, Mark of
  attains great power status, 78
  and Congress of Vienna, 149–151
  development of, 79–81
  effects of Thirty Years' War on, 3
  under Frederick the Great, 105–106
  mentioned, 6
  militarism of, 2
  under Napoleonic domination, 143
  opposes France, 127, 147
  and partition of Poland, 76
  relations with Russia, 72
  revival of, 146
  in War of the Austrian Succession and Seven Years' War, 81–84
  wars with France, 128, 141
Ptolemy, system of, 86, 87
Pufendorf, Samuel von, 99, 105
Pugachev, Emilian Ivanovich, rebellion of, 75
Pyrenees, Peace of the, 5

Quadruple Alliance, 147, 149
Quiberon Bay, Battle of, 83
Quietism, 20

Ramillies, Battle of, 51
Rastadt, Treaty of, 51
Rationalism, 93–95
  reaction to, 109–111
Ratisbon, Treaty of, 46
Razin, Stenka (Stepan), rebellion of, 71, 75
Reformation, political significance of, 1, 95
Religion. See also Clergy, estate of
  aristocratic careers in, 18
  and the Counter-Enlightenment, 109–111
  decline of organized churches, 19–20
  and enlightened despotism, 103, 106
  festivals and popular violence, 29
  popular revival of, 20
  religious minorities, 32, 35, 36, 43, 44
  and science, 91–93
  and tsarism, 70–71
  wars of, 1–2, 46

Restif de la Bretonne, Nicolas Edmé, 103
Richardson, Samuel, 110
Richelieu, Armand du Plessis, Cardinal de, 38, 39
Robespierre, Maximilien, 116, 127, 129, 130, 131, 133, 137
Rohan-Chabot, Gui Auguste, Chevalier de, 96
Rousseau, Jean-Jacques, 78, 94–95, 100–102, 103, 111, 114, 135
Roux, Jacques, 130–131
Russia
  and Congress of Vienna, 149–151
  expansion of, 56, 67–78
  and the French Revolution, 10
  Napoleonic invasion of, 146–147
  population of, 8
  in the Seven Years' War, 82
  wars with France, 141, 142–143
Ryswick, Treaty of, 47–49

Saint-Just, Louis Antoine de, 131–133, 137
St. Petersburg, building of, 73, 74
Saint-Pierre, Charles Iréné Castel, Abbé de, 83
Saint-Simon, Louis de Rouvroy, Duke de, 17
Sale of office, 17, 36–37
Sanchez, François, 89
Sans-culottes, 124, 130, 131, 132, 135, 137
Savoy
  annexed, 134
  general description of, 8
  joins anti-French alliance, 47
Schiller, Friedrich von, 146
Scientific Revolution
  diffusion of, 91–93, 96
  early development of, 85–91
  and scientism, 91
  scientific societies in, 88–89
Scotland
  rebellion of, 58, 93
  tariffs levied against, 43
  united with England, 60
Secularism, 92–94, 100, 106
Selden, John, 40
Serfdom
  in Austria, 107, 108
  in Hungary, 19
  in Prussia, 106
  rise of, in eastern Europe, 28–29
  and Rousseau, 102
  in Russia, 71, 74, 75
Settlement, Act of, 56, 58
Seven Years' War, 75, 82–83, 106
Sieyès, Emmanuel Joseph, Abbé de, 119, 136
Simon, Richard, 92
Skepticism, 86–87, 89–93 passim., 106, 114
Slave trade, 61–64
Smith, Adam, 64, 100
Smith, Thomas, 23
Sobieski, John, king of Poland, 46
Social contract, theories of, 97–101
South Sea Company, 59–60
Spain
  aristocracy of, 15, 17, 19

Spain (continued)
  colonization by, 5
  decline of, 6, 8
  effects of Thirty Years' War on, 3
  empire of, 61
  enlightened despotism in, 104
  and House of Hapsburg, 1, 13, 49
  joins anti-French alliance, 47
  as Napoleonic satellite, 143
  rebellion of, 146
  and War of the Spanish Succession, 13,
    49–53 passim.
  war with England, 40
  war with France, 46
Spanish Netherlands (Flanders), 41, 46, 51
Spanish Succession, War of the, 13, 45,
  49–53, 55
Spence, Thomas, 103
Spener, Philipp Jakob, 20, 109
Spinoza, Baruch (Benedict), 91, 92
Standing armies, 2, 56, 76, 79, 81
Steele, Richard, quoted, 11–12
Strassburg, 34, 46, 49, 51
Struensee, Johann Friedrich von, 104
Suvorov, Count Alexander Vasilievich,
  Marshal, 142
Sweden
  alliance against France, 147
  effects of Thirty Years' War on, 3
  enlightened despotism in, 104
  under Napoleonic domination, 143
  population of, 8
  and wars of Louis XIV, 41, 42, 47
  war with Denmark, 2
  war with Russia, 72–73

Taine, Hippolyte, 131
Talleyrand-Périgord, Charles Maurice de, 19,
  143, 147, 148, 149
Taxation, patterns of
  aristocratic exemption from, 16
  avoidance in France, 117
  English and French compared, 54
  and peasantry, 18, 24–25
  rates of in England, 21, 44
  reforms called for, 118, 120
  royal control of curbed in England, 56
  sale of offices as indirect taxation, 36
  subjected to popular consent, 133
  urban rates, 33
Terror, The, 132–133, 137
Thermidorian Reaction, 133–135
Third Estate, concept of, 23, 119–121
Thirty Years' War, The, 1–2, 5, 6, 46, 47, 49
Tilsit, Treaty of, 142–143
Tocqueville, Alexis de, 9
Toleration, 37, 44, 56, 95, 108, 139
Toleration Act, 56
Town life, 29–34
Trafalgar, Battle of, 142
Triennial Act, 56
Triple Alliance, 41–42

Turgot, Anne Robert Jacques, Baron de,
  117, 118
Tuscany, 8, 88

Ulm, Battle of, 142
Union, Act of, 60
Urban VIII, Pope, 19
Urban workers, condition of. See also
  Sans-culottes.
  general description of, 31–33, 38
  results of Revolution for, 136
  in revolutionary Paris, 124, 127–128, 130,
    131, 132, 134
  under the Napoleonic Code, 139
Utrecht, Peace of, 51–53, 78

Valmy, Battle of, 128
Vauban, Sebastian Le Prestre, Marquis de,
  42, 47, 55
Venice
  decline of, 34
  status of, 8
  taken from Austria, 142
Versailles, Court of, 16–17
Vesalius, Andreas, 87
Vienna, Congress of, 149–152
Villars, Claude Louis, Duke de, 51
Violence, levels of, 25, 29, 30
  in Gordon riots, 32
  in Russia, 71
Voltaire (François Marie Arouet), 74, 92, 95,
  96–97, 103, 105, 114

Wallenstein, Count Albrecht Wenzel von, 2
Walpole, Horace, 110
Walpole, Sir Robert, 57–60, 82
War. See also Standing armies
  effects of, 2, 3, 27–28
  changing attitudes toward, 113
  as value, 15–16, 40–41
Warsaw, Grand Duchy of, 143, 146, 149.
  See also Poland
Waterloo, Battle of, 148
Watteau, Antoine, 116
Wellington, Arthur Wellesley, first Duke of,
  146, 147, 148
Wesley, Charles, 109
Wesley, John, 20, 109–110
Westphalia, Treaty of, 2, 6, 42, 79, 149
Whigs and Tories, in British politics, 56–60
Whitehead, George, 109
Wilberforce, William, 64
William III, king of England, Stadhouder of
  the Netherlands, 14, 42–50 passim., 56,
  57, 59, 72
Wilson, Harold, 58
Witt, Jan de, 42
Wordsworth, William, 115

Zenta, Battle of, 49
Zinzendorf, Count Nikolaus Ludwig von, 20,
  109
Zosima, Metropolitan, 70

84 85 86 87 9 8 7 6 5 4 3 2 1